The Invention of
Permanent Poverty

Norman Dennis

IEA Health and
London,

D0892602

First published January 1997
Reprinted May 1998

The IEA Health and Welfare Unit
2 Lord North St
London SW1P 3LB

© The IEA Health and Welfare Unit 1997

ISBN 0-255 36392-3
ISSN 1362-9565

Typeset by the IEA Health and Welfare Unit
in Bookman 10 point
Printed in Great Britain by
St Edmundsbury Press Ltd
Blenheim Industrial Park, Newmarket Road
Bury St Edmunds, Suffolk

Contents

Foreword

This book is a criticism of what might be called the 'no-fault' theory of human conduct, a doctrine that has become the favourite explanation for some of the disturbing developments of our time, such as family breakdown and rising crime.

Criminals, it is said, are not bad people but victims of circumstance. They are poor or unemployed and, because of their poverty, commit crimes. Why has there been an increase in crime? According to no-fault theory, it is because there has been an increase in poverty.

Norman Dennis takes issue with this doctrine on two fronts. First, using the very same statistical sources as the poverty lobbies, he demolishes the claim that there has been an increase in poverty. In doing so, he reveals the statistical manoeuvres they typically deploy to substantiate their false claims.

Secondly, he takes apart the theory that crime is caused by poverty and unemployment.

Writing as a member of the Labour party, he seeks to renew understanding of the earlier Labour tradition that placed the personal responsibility of the individual at the centre of its ideal. According to this tradition of 'ethical socialism', even in unfortunate circumstances not of our own making, we have a continuing responsibility to consider others, and at the minimum we should not take our resentments out on our neighbours by stealing from them or making their lives a misery through violence or intimidation. And we all, especially those who can command the attention of audiences wider than their face-to-face circle, have a duty to uphold by personal example the institutions and habits of conduct that promote mutual respect.

In attacking the no-fault theory favoured by social-affairs intellectuals, he takes the *Joseph Rowntree Foundation Inquiry into Income and Wealth* of 1995 as his chief target, not because it is the only organisation propagating the erroneous no-fault theory, but because the Joseph Rowntree Foundation has been, as Dennis puts it, 'at the forefront of those receiving the most media attention and respect' and because the membership of its Inquiry comprised the very cream of the great and good. The willingness of both the General Secretary of the TUC and the

Director-General of the CBI to sign the same report gave the impression that the truth of no-fault theory was the taken-for-granted assumption of those in the know.

In this outstanding book Norman Dennis reveals the exaggerations of the poverty lobby exemplified by the Rowntree Inquiry and exposes the flaws in the no-fault theory of crime prevalent among the social-affairs intelligentsia.

David G. Green

Dedicated to

Sarah Jane Hodkinson
Born 8 February 1996

Acknowledgements

My first thanks must go to David Green. He asked me to write this book. The subject it tries to tackle is of the utmost importance. As A.N. Whitehead said in his Preface to *Science and the Modern World*, the mentality of each epoch springs from the view of the world that dominates the educated sections of the community, and a key issue must be the quality of contemporary cultural leadership. My friends at the University of Newcastle upon Tyne have been unstinting in their generosity and enthusiasm in our Thursday seminars. I have always been conscious that I have been given the opportunity of a university education at its best from the social psychology of George Erdos, the sociology of Peter Collison and Jon Davies, the anthropology of Ahmed al Shahi and Harry Powell, the statistics of John Kennedy and Betty Gittus, and the broad general knowledge, the good humour and the wisdom of them all. Julia Jane Hodkinson, of Holyport, Berkshire, and Robert Whelan, of the IEA, greatly improved the text in substance and in detail. I am extremely grateful to them both. My life-long debt to my oldest friend, Chelly Halsey, is immeasurable, but perhaps especially stemming from the collaboration in 1987-88 on our *English Ethical Socialism*. I am conscious of it as I write every line, even though the responsibility for what I have said here is strictly my own.

Norman Dennis
Sunderland
2 November 1996

The Author

Norman Dennis is Guest Fellow in the Department of Religious Studies, at the University of Newcastle upon Tyne. With Professor A.H. Halsey he is author of *English Ethical Socialism*, Clarendon Press, 1988. The IEA Health and Welfare Unit is the publisher of his *Families Without Fatherhood* (co-author George Erdos), 1993 (second edition) and *Rising Crime and the Dismembered Family*, 1993. He is also well-known for his study of a Yorkshire coal-mining town, *Coal Is Our Life* (with Cliff Slaughter and Fernando Henriques), and his two studies of national and local bureaucracy and politics as they affected a working-class district of Sunderland, *People and Planning*, 1970, and *Public Participation and Planners' Blight*, 1972.

As Leverhulme Fellow he is currently studying the struggle between the bureaucratic, political and media advocates of drug, educational and family permissiveness in the European Union and Switzerland, and one of their most important opponents, a Zürich citizens' organization called the VPM.

1

Introduction

T he topic of this book is not poverty as such or unemployment as such. The book is about the *relationship between*, on the one hand, relative and absolute poverty and unemployment, and on the other, theft, vandalism, arson, hooliganism, riot, political violence and drug abuse in Britain.

It is an anomaly that a life-long Labour supporter should find an outlet for his work in the publications of the Institute of Economic Affairs. So far as I could tell, my concerns from the mid-1980s about crime and the family were heard with respect in Colliery ward, Sunderland; at the meetings of the Sunderland Fabian Society; and in my ordinary conversations in the working-class circles of my relatives. Indeed, to them, the only query was why my contributions were limited to the statement of the obvious. The wonder was that anyone could be in a well-paid job just for saying things that were the plainest common sense. But as recently as three of four years ago they were anathema to the academic and metropolitan Labour intelligentsia.

Things have changed markedly for the better in the intervening period. The 'moral-panic' theory—that crime had not increased dramatically in the forty years from the mid-1950s, and that 'crime' was an illusion whipped up by the popular press—is heard now only from those sections of the population that catch up with intellectual fashions just as they are disappearing from the scene—bishops, radical millionaires, senior officials in the Magistrates Association and so on. The 'moral-panic' theory of the family—that it is not deteriorating, only changing—has also lost most of its credibility. In a speech to the Commonwealth Press Union in October 1996 Tony Blair, the Leader of the Labour party, stressed the need for parents (in the plural) to understand

1

their duties to their children. He was calling, he said, for a 'return to the basic decent values I grew up with and which have been eroded'.[1] Yet it was only in 1990 that Neil Kinnock, at that time the Leader of the Labour party, addressed the Association of Directors of Social Services to say that births outside marriage and lone parenthood meant only that the family was adapting, not collapsing, and that those who disagreed with this view had 'no intentions that could be described as good'.[2] That Panglossianism now seems an age away.

The favourable local and the hostile metropolitan reception of my ideas is explained by the fact that neither the weak local control of criminals nor opposition to the family are 'old Labour' traits at all. Neighbourhood criminality as 'legitimate rage' in the face of material deprivation was largely a spin-off from the student movements of the 1960s—the theory that the working-class had become too affluent to fulfil its allotted revolutionary role, and revolution would come only from society's outsiders. Ordinary people on housing estates objected more and more to bearing the brunt of the rage, legitimate or not, and were not convinced by the serious media, clergymen and social experts from the universities that they were only imagining that something very unpleasant was happening to them in their communities. Before the 1960s the Labour party supported parenthood by the permanently married couple as the stringent norm. Support for life-long monogamy had nothing whatsoever to do with support for women's subordination and restriction to the home, or with any particular division of labour between the sexes beyond the biologically given ones of pregnancy and childbirth. At the centre of old Labour's ideology, furthermore, was the aspiration that the values of the virtuous working-class family (solidarity, self-sacrifice, fidelity, the primacy of the family's common good) should be spread to all areas of society.

'Progressive' and 'enlightened' ideas shifted the focus from children as the reason for having a lifelong spouse, to sex as the point of having a partner. Labour's ideal had been to soften commercial relationships with the values of the family. Now family relationships were to be modelled, not even on functioning market relationships as we actually find them, but on the crudest caricature of the wholly self-servicing transaction. These ideas were not the product of anyone with a background in working-class Labour thinking. The shift of focus was the product of (to use an old-fashioned word) the academic establishment, the artistic establishment, the religious establishment, and to an extent by their recent examples the royal establishment.

As for the legal establishment: one senior lawyer, whose much publicized personal view was that 'logically' we have already reached the point at which we should be considering whether 'the legal institution of marriage continues to serve any useful purpose',[3] was appointed as one of the country's five Law Commissioners. The provisions of the Family Law Act 1996 broadly followed the Commissioners' proposals, with the support of those for whom marriage and its morals were merely a nuisance to their sexual life and a growing irrelevance, without even the publicity value any more of 'scandal'.

As for the royal establishment: in the early twentieth century the pre-marital and extra-marital sexual exploits of a king or a male aristocrat, permitted in his own circles, were concealed as much as possible. It was assumed that if such conduct were to be generalized, the effects would be disruptive of the whole social order. Once in the public domain they were not regarded as 'peccadillos', as little sins, to use the favoured term of the mid-1990s. If their irregular marital activities became public knowledge, they had to be universally condemned as disgraceful. That was still the cultural position at the time of the abdication crisis in the 1930s. King Edward VIII's affair with a divorced woman was kept secret for as long as possible. But when it became known, it was a 'scandal'—the only 'scandalous' element being the simple fact that she was *divorced*, that she had failed in the undertaking of life-long monogamy. For the king, the supreme governor of the Church of England, to violate the Church of England's rule against a divorced person marrying during the lifetime of the former spouse, was an option rejected by vocal public opinion at that time, with very few exceptions, from the top of British society to the bottom.

But by the 1990s 'a senior source' (presumably a senior palace source) could be quoted as saying that, yes, the newly-divorced Prince of Wales had been cohabiting with a mistress, and 'yes, they sleep together, but they are discreet and would certainly not flaunt their relationship in front of his children'. The 'senior source' said that the heir to the throne would 'always put his *duty* first'.[4] By 1996 what was his duty? The Church of England's marriage ceremony nowhere hints that a husband's duty is discharged, and his solemn vows are fulfilled, so long as he does not flaunt his adultery in front of his children. How could his duty be fulfilled now by his being 'discreet', on the old regal and aristocratic model, in the full glare of world-wide publicity? Was it his duty to become a divorced king and marry his divorced mistress? Was it to become king and retain his mistress but not marry her? Was it to be a celibate king? Was it to give up the throne for the sake of the woman he loved? The essence of duty is that its demands supersede one's own personal wishes and personal interests. In John Keats's words, its only pleasure lies in 'trying the resources of the spirit'.[5]

The senior spokesman gave no indication of where duty did lie. No consensus remained in what had been the cultural establishment on what duty would demand. These two facts were sufficient indication that the decay of a viable culture of the family was not of 'underclass' origin. On the contrary, the troubles of the underclass were the natural consequence, under modern conditions of media exposure and commercially profitable mass prurience, of the reckless sexual self-indulgence of the supposed guarantors of cultural stability.

For thirty years or forty years, from the mid-1950s to the mid-1990s, it was supposed to be Left to be anti-family. In Labour terms this was an aberration. The newly dominant idea was that anybody who had, or through a sexual relationship might beget or bear, children should be able to please himself or herself about it, and it was none of the public's business. Until the 1960s that had been at least as abhorrent to Labour as the idea that anybody who wanted to employ children should please himself or herself about that.

When we started the sexual revolution in the late 1950s and in the 1960s, with the divorce revolution hard on its heels, no one was to know that it would fail so comprehensively to fulfil its promises; still less that by the mid-1990s it would have finally proved itself beyond any further doubt to be a catastrophe for children and, in terms of crime rates, for citizens.

The divorce revolution and the revolution of unwed-parenthood may or may not have delivered substantially on its promise of an increase, on balance, in self-centred adult happiness of the partners. But while benefiting perhaps most adults, it has inflicted hardships on children who have seen their homes broken by divorce, and on children who were neither conceived nor brought up by two married parents. Nobody (except people employed in the security and repair industries) has gained from the social costs that have been incurred by all of us in terms of the rise in criminal violence, burglary and theft.

In June 1996 a university professor, closely associated with the Joseph Rowntree Foundation in its work on both the family and poverty, asserted in a broadcast that a person or household was in poverty if in receipt of less than half of average earnings. The professor said that the vast majority of social scientists throughout the world accepted that was poverty, and not an income below subsistence level. On that basis, he said, the proportion in poverty has gone up in 1979-96 from seven per cent of the population to 25 per cent. Poverty, that is, was the condition in which millions of people found themselves in Britain in 1996. Furthermore, the problem was nearly four times worse than it had been in 1979. For him, it was the role of the state to eliminate the poverty of having to live in Britain in 1996 on less than half of average earnings. In particular, he said, the state should combat the developments in the global economy that during the 1980s had lowered the earnings of the unskilled and unqualified.[6]

No doubt in some disciplines and in some universities 'professor' had lost much of its former connotation of academic excellence, and had become a title accorded increasingly for managerial responsibilities and research-fund entrepreneurship. But the general public still widely regarded 'professor' as the designation of outstanding expertise in scholarship or science. According to Rowntree's Information Officer, one publication that supported the professor's claims had drawn on research costing no less than £1.5 million, and about £1 million worth of careful research had gone into another single book.[7] How many listeners would imagine that their own opinion would be a match, not just for these millions of pounds worth of careful research and the knowledge and authority of this particular professor, but for 'the vast majority of social scientists in the world' who (he said) agreed with him?

The two volumes of *The Joseph Rowntree Foundation Inquiry into Income and Wealth* were published in 1995. The first volume names no single author, but lists the members of the 'Income and Wealth Inquiry Group'.[8] The second volume was written by an LSE academic, John Hills.[9] The Joseph Rowntree Inquiry Group was convened to do two things. First, to consider evidence relating to living standards. It was to inquire specifically into personal income and wealth. Secondly, it was asked to make recommendations for changes in policy and practice. 'The facts and views expressed in the report are those of the authors and not necessarily those of the Joseph Rowntree Foundation.' That being understood, for the sake of brevity I shall refer to the contents of these two volumes as 'Rowntree'.

Rowntree makes much of an analogy. If income were proportional to a person's height, then twenty per cent of the British population in the 1990s would be under 2ft 10ins, twenty per cent of the population would be over 7ft 8ins, the average person would be 4ft 10ins, and the richest person would be 4 miles high.[10] The analogy is curious, because it implies that cash goes to the heart of what it is to be a person. He is a physical giant if he is rich, and a physical dwarf if he is poor. This is in direct opposition to older Left-wing imagery that, judged by his conduct and not by his income, a man can be ten feet tall.

Rowntree also reported that income inequality had decreased for several centuries, i.e. the relative income of the poor had been steadily improving, and the gap between the rich and the poor was at its narrowest in the 1970s. From the late 1970s, however, the gap widened.[11] The rise in inequality from 1978 to the early 1990s was more than large enough to offset all the decline in inequality between 1949 and 1978, and was almost large enough to take inequality back to the levels of 1938.[12] The growth of inequality may have halted at the start of the 1990s, Rowntree said, but is was too early to identify a new trend.[13]

The real standard of living for the whole population rose by about one-third in the period 1961-79, and it rose by another third in the period 1979-92. According to Rowntree's figures, during the 1961-79 period all income groups shared roughly proportionately in this improvement in the standard of living, with the exception of the poorest tenth of the population, who did much better than the average. The income of the poorest tenth went up by over 50 per cent.[14] But in the 1979-92 period all income groups did not share proportionately in the one-third rise in the standard of living. Only the top three-tenths of the income distribution increased their standard of living by the average or by more than the average. On Rowntree's calculations, the households in the poorest tenth of the population did not increase their standard of living at all. If the income of these poorest households is counted as what is left to them to spend after their housing has been paid for, then in 1992 they were actually about 16 per cent worse off in real terms than their equivalents in 1979.[15]

In bold type Rowntree then draws the causal implications of these facts. 'As the gap between rich and poor grows, the problems of the marginalized groups which are left behind rebound on the more comfortable majority.' It is in the interests of all to remove 'the factors that are fostering the social diseases of drugs, crime, political extremism and social unrest'. In the rioting of recent years, for example, the cause has always been the same: groups of young men with 'no stake in society'.[16]

Though the incentive to write *The Invention of Permanent Poverty* was the appearance of those two Rowntree volumes, it is not solely about the work of the Rowntree Foundation. It is concerned with a set of ideas about the relationship between what money can buy and conduct. These ideas about money and morality are embedded in a comprehensive way of looking at the world in empirical and judgemental terms—in this case mainly non-judgemental terms—and they became the conventional wisdom of British social-affairs intellectuals from the 1960s to the 1990s.[17]

This book is not about high or low incomes in themselves. That everyone should end up with more money legally is, in the abstract, a matter that is settled in modern societies. It is true that Christianity—along with nearly all the other world's great religions—once valued voluntary poverty very highly. It deemed it virtuous of the poor man to accept his lot gracefully. The Sermon on the Mount which, if anything can, can be regarded as the Christian Manifesto, is very weak on consumption values.[18] The only material request in Christianity's principal prayer is for a minimum subsistence standard. It is a long time, however, since bishops whose speciality is social comment have suggested that any sensible Christian should take any of that quite literally.

Wariness about voracious consumerism was strongly represented in the Labour party in the 1920s and 1930s (and remnants even into the late 1950s), both in its still explicit Christian form and in a secularized one.[19] What C. Wright Mills said about his own country in 1956 became increasingly true of this:

> Of all the possible values of human society, one and only one is the truly sovereign, truly universal, truly sound, truly and completely acceptable goal ... That goal is money, and let there be no sour grapes about it from the losers.[20]

This remark was well-timed for Britain, for Crosland's influential *The Future of Socialism*, advocating that Labour adopt the objective of a limitlessly higher standard of living and 'the good life', was published in the same year.[21]

I am not discussing inequality or unemployment as such. Attitudes to activities that contribute to the well-being of other people have probably not changed very much over recent years—perhaps not for millennia. People approve of such activities. Socially-useful activities, paid or unpaid, are generally thought, too, to contribute substantially to the well-being, development and self-fulfilment—even the happiness—of the person engaging in them.

But attitudes to paid work under the discipline of management have changed wildly even within the same group over relatively short periods of time. Unemployment was very low after the Second World War. In the earlier years low unemployment was universally welcomed. But in the 1960s and 1970s considerable propaganda stemmed from the new radical movements to the effect that (a) employee-work was no longer necessary for most people for most of their time, because 'the economy' was rich enough to supply everything in abundance, (b) the paid and controlled work in the workplace that most people had to do was 'alienated labour', and (c) restriction on personal autonomy was the most intolerable of all the obnoxious features of modern employment. The phrase they often used in the days of full employment was 'shit work'. Most of these radical movements claimed to be in one sense or another Marxist (however remote their own views were from what Marx or Engels had ever written or advocated).[22]

But when unemployment, especially youth unemployment, rose sharply in the 1970s little more was heard of the horrors of alienated work. Not worthwhile activity, but paid work under subordination, outside the home, in a disciplined workplace (capitalist as much as in any other), suddenly became the one thing necessary. The absence of such activity was suddenly the origin of school-children's and youths' 'anger' and the justification of all the ways in which they expressed it.

Rowntree paints a picture of 'a dramatic social and economic change in Britain over the 1980s'. It says there are no simple explanations for the change. They range, the Report says, from 'international competitiveness' to 'high unemployment council estates'.[23] That is, for Rowntree, they 'range' from one *economic* explanation to another *economic* explanation. The possibility and importance of individually creative and responsible reactions to circumstances, culturally inculcated and sanctioned, have no place in the Group's frame of reference. Social evaluations and cultural mechanisms, requiring that the individual takes personal responsibility to make the most of his given circumstances, have first been dismantled. Then their previous effectiveness (or even their very historical existence) has been denied.

In general, explanations for an association between crime and riot on the one hand and unemployment and poverty on the other stretch across a wide range. At one extreme are those who deny that there is any significant connection, and who stress genetic endowment. ('A fellow by the hand of nature marked/ Quoted and signed to do a deed of shame'.)[24] These theories were quite popular in the late nineteenth century and into the 1930s. In those years Lombroso in Italy and Kretschmer in the United States used the differential distribution of physiological types to explain social-class differences in crime rates.[25] Consonant with a stronger women's movement, today's version emphasizes rather the genetic inheritance of the male to explain bad behaviour.

At the other extreme are those who see unemployment and poverty not only as the main cause of crime, but who see the crimes of the poor and unemployed as a service to the community. Here, the criminal is extraordinary only in being more heroic than his peers. He is a 'prefigurative revolutionary'. The bandit is a 'primitive rebel'. The rioter is a public benefactor. That this doctrine of the *criminal* as political actor should be favoured by self-styled 'left-wingers' was 'quite baffling' to the philosopher Hannah Arendt. How could any explanation of crime possibly be called left-wing (much less Marxist), she asks, that has put its faith in 'classless idlers', and believes that 'in the lumpenproletariat the revolution will find its urban spearhead', and trusts that 'gangsters will light the way for the people'?[26]

Rowntree implicitly denies that there has been any change in the *propensity* to commit crime, riot and use illicit drugs. For Rowntree, there were simply more people in the categories that produced criminals, rioters and drug addicts. The explanation for more crime, riot and the use of illicit drugs given by Rowntree (or simply insinuated, as what everyone takes for granted as being true) is that more young men are becoming more impoverished, and more young men are joining the long-term unemployed. Rowntree's materialistic no-fault theory looks plausible as a crude overall account of parts of 1979-92. But it is valid only if what happened in the period 1979-92 was simply a manifestation of an established theoretical connection between disorder and economic hardship. If poverty and unemployment were the main causes of the rise in crime and social disorder in the 1980s and 1990s, as Rowntree claims, then at all times similar levels of poverty and unemployment would have caused corresponding levels of crime, riotous conduct, drug use, random destructiveness, and so forth.

Even within the period 1979-92, on Rowntree's materialistic no-fault theory, when unemployment rose, more people would have been 'forced to commit more crimes', and when unemployment fell, crime would have fallen correspondingly. But that did not happen. When the unemployment rate fell from time to time in the period 1979-92, the crime rate did not revert to its lower figure. When the unemployment rate rose again, the crime rate was far ahead of what it had been previously at that higher level of unemployment.

The materialistic no-fault theory, if it were valid, would have to apply to periods other than 1979-92. It would have to apply to the other main period Rowntree deals with, 1961-79. Unemployment for most of that period was extremely low. According to Rowntree's own claims, both absolute and relative poverty fell. On Rowntree's theory, therefore, between 1961 and 1979 crime and disorder would also have been falling. Yet all the data we have show that crime and disorder were rising steeply.

On the materialistic no-fault theory, far more people must have been 'forced' into crime and disorder when their material standard of living was far lower, and unemployment was much worse, during the post-war troubles of the 1920s and the great depression of the 1930s than during the 1990s. Yet by the standards of the 1990s, crime and disorder between the wars stood at very low levels. On the materialistic no-fault theory, crime and disorder would have been far higher under the employment, housing and household-income conditions of the industrial cities of the late nineteenth century than in the 1990s. Yet not only was there less crime and disorder in the late nineteenth century than in the late twentieth century: the levels of crime and disorder consistently fell in the late nineteenth century.

The growth and decline in absolute poverty, relative poverty and unemployment can be used to explain *variations around* trends in crime and childhood neglect and abuse. But they cannot be used at all to explain the *enormous growth in the past thirty or forty years* or so in the burden put upon children by parents who divorce or never marry, and the burden put upon people in general by levels of crime which are unprecedented.

William James wrote somewhere of 'the murder of a beautiful theory by a gang of brutal facts'. The argument of *The Invention of Permanent Poverty* is not only that Rowntree's theory is contradicted by James's 'irreducible and stubborn facts', but that its theory is actually destroyed by the facts that Rowntree itself prominently produces. The murder of its beautiful theory, if it had lifted its head for a moment from the axe it was grinding, would have clearly revealed itself even to Rowntree as an inside job.

Rowntree publications have been only one outlet for these no-fault ideas, but in recent years they have been at the forefront of those receiving the most media attention and respect. Anyone knowing the membership of the Rowntree Foundation Inquiry Group 1995 might think that this point, about the dominance of the view of the world of 'the social-affairs intelligentsia' in giving precedence to what money can buy in any explanation of conduct is seriously weakened when the Group's composition is revealed. For the Inquiry Group, the joint author of the first volume of the Rowntree Report 1995, was the very cream of the United Kingdom's great and the good. But far from detracting from my case, the Group and its authorship of the first volume is a striking illustration of it. The message to the public, that Rowntree's underlying assumptions as well as its findings and recommendation are uncontroversial, is decisively symbolized by its composition.

It may well be that some or all of the authors of the first volume were passive rather than active in their authorship, approving rather than creating. If and in so far as they were creative, then they were active propagators of the consensus. If and in so far as they were merely supervisory, they show in their endorsement of its blatantly flawed arguments that they lacked any clear world-view of their own that gave them an alternative to the world-view of materialism. That is what a *Weltanshauung* does. It stops its adherents recognizing nonsense when it is as large as life and shouting and waving its arms in front of their faces.

The social-affairs intelligentsia is not homogeneous. In all of the great institutions where the social-affairs intellectuals ply their trade there are mavericks who have resisted the blandishments of the conventional wisdom on 'social deprivation', its causes, its extent and its consequences. Compared with many of their seniors in the national serious press, local journalists, for example, have been slower to follow and propagate the latest intellectual fashion in the field of social disorder and the identification of inequality with 'poverty'. Common sense and modesty about their own right to mould public opinion have controlled its reporters and editors more closely. But the local press as much as any other element in society cannot but succumb to the gradually changed 'common sense' eventually created by the greater reach of more powerful media. Lenin long ago stressed the importance of the distinction between the activist and 'the termite and useful idiot', or what Finkielkraut later called the terrible and ridiculous symbiosis of the fanatic and the zombie.[27]

The thing that changed fundamentally from the 1950s to the early and mid-1990s, always in the same direction and always in step with rising crime and childhood distress, were sexual and childrearing practices, and the crumbling to the point of extinction of the *culture* of life-long monogamy as a matter of *public* concern. A change in public opinion was crucial in bringing about the revolution of men's sexual liberation. Only a change in public opinion, not higher cash benefits or job training programmes (however desirable such improvements are in themselves), will put limits to the psychological and social consequences it has wrought on children and on civic life.

The academic who is not wasting his time necessarily deals with something that is relevant to what Bacon called 'the relief of man's estate'. But if he is to be useful he must also be committed to the view that the empirical truth stands a better chance of advancing human welfare than do empirical errors or falsehoods; that it is better to be right in the long run than to be merely comfortable and convincing in the short; and, that a society has been sent on a fool's errand if it has been persuaded that it can solve its cultural and spiritual problems by monetary and material means.

2

The End of Denial
Crime and Social Disorder in the Nineteen-Nineties

U p to the early 1990s the problems of crime and other forms of social disorder in Britain had not been faced because it had been systematically and successfully denied for thirty years that there were any such problems. The growth of crime and disorder had been dismissed as the creation of ill-informed people in the throes of 'moral panic'. Every generation that ever existed had believed that crime and disorder were increasing. 'Since the dawn of time, the old have decried the young as degenerate and summoned a crusade to lift them from moral squalor. It is the hoariest cliché in the book'[1]—therefore (runs the *non sequitur*) the old have never been justified in any of their concerns in any generation. Specifically, the old in this country were not justified in their concerns since the 1960s that burglary, robbery, vandalism, riot and drug-taking had been increasing. The reiteration of the 'moral-panic' argument, where it did not fully persuade, at least silenced social-affairs intellectuals in key positions of responsibility. Still in 1994 a Bishop who had served for five years in the key position of Chairman of the Church of England Board of Education could take for granted the truth of the 'moral-panic' school's—quite erroneous—contention that every generation has feared that society was travelling downhill. The fact that there was 'persistent debate' about whether there was—this is the example he gives—more *vandalism* than there had been in the past, released him from coming to his own conclusion—if he doubted the decisive figures—on the evidence of his own eyes. 'Perhaps we shall have to wait longer for history to make a reliable decision.'[2]

By the mid-1990s, however, there were many signs that the pernicious consensus of social-affairs intellectuals was crumbling under the sheer weight of the facts that contradicted it.[3] By the mid-1990s the notion of 'moral panic' had almost disappeared from *The Sunday Times* (which indeed had taken an early lead in attacking the 'moral-panic' consensus) and, as might be expected, from the explicitly conservative broadsheets. With a diminishing number of exceptions, the official criminal statistics came to be accepted across the political spectrum as showing the *broad drift* downwards in British civility in the period 1979-92 considered by Rowntree. The number of serious offences recorded by the police rose from 2.5 million in 1979 to 5.4 million in 1992. The number of offences per 100,000 of the population rose from 5,100 in 1980 to 10,500 in 1992.[4] At the beginning of that thirteen year period there were 1.6 million reported cases of theft and handling stolen goods a year. At the end of the period there were 2.6 million. At the beginning there were 720,000 burglaries reported. At the end, 1.3 million. At the beginning, 390,000 cases of criminal damage. At the end, 930,000. At the beginning, 100,000 reported cases of violence against the person. At the end 220,000.[5]

In the mid-1990s crime rates briefly responded to the increased utilization of technological innovations (such as television surveillance, entry phones and car-security devices) and changes in police practices (such as targeting particular crimes and criminals, and 'zero tolerance' campaigns). But the year 1995-96 again saw a rise in annual numbers that would have been unthinkable even twenty years before. Crimes of violence, including robbery and assaults, rose in almost all the 29 police-force areas surveyed. From July 1995 to June 1996 robberies rose by nine per cent. In the Humberside police area they rose by 40 per cent in this twelve-month period, in Merseyside by 35 per cent and in South Yorkshire by 25 per cent. Violent assaults increased by 20 per cent in Cleveland and 20 per cent in Lancashire, and by 16 per cent in both Nottinghamshire and Staffordshire.[6] The British Crime Survey (BCS) figures, which depend upon the offences that victims had experienced in the previous twelve months, whether they reported them or not, show an increase in BCS offences from 11 million in 1981, to 15 million in 1991, and to 19 million in 1995.[7] The BCS figures on all so-called acquisitive crimes rose from three million in 1981 to six million in 1991. Crimes of violence rose from 670,000 in 1981 to 809,000 in 1991.

Obviously, these more or less unremitting rises in the crime figures year by year could no longer be explained with any shadow of plausibility in terms of 'more people having phones', 'changes in the law', 'the desire of the police to obtain more repressive powers by exaggerating the figures', 'greater public sensitivity to anti-social behaviour', 'more things to steal', 'insurance policies requiring a theft to be reported to the police'. Whatever slight value there might have been in throwing doubt on the comparability of figures from *widely separated points of time*, they could not explain the more or less uninterrupted, inexorable and large increases *one year after the next* since 1955, when the figures started to rise steeply.

The data which helped more than any other to undermine the previously successful assertions by the 'moral-panic' school, that crime and disorder had not increased, were those contained in the BCS reports in the 1990s. The BCS 'victim' surveys confirmed the steep upward trends of the conventional crime statistics in the 1980s. They threw doubt on the validity of the decline in the figures of reported crime 1993-95. They showed a slackening of the pace of growth of crime since the figures were first collected in 1981, but there was still a two per cent rise, not a fall.[8] But crucially they gave information also on trends in the proportion of crimes that were reported to the police. In the 1980s crime reported to the police did increase more quickly than crime reported to the BCS by victims. As common sense had indicated, and contrary to the 'moral-panic' case that said that there was more reporting of the unchanged level of crime, in the 1990s a *decreasing* not an increasing proportion of certain crimes were reported to the police, because people thought that nothing would be done about them.[9]

For those to whom the date '1979' was crucial for propaganda purposes, however, the beauty of the Home Office 'victim' surveys was that there had been none before 1979—the first BCS report appeared in 1981. BCS figures could not therefore be used to refute the new version of the 'moral-panic' argument, which was that crime had *not* risen *before* 1979.

The weight of the facts, then, was not the only consideration in the tactical retreat from the full 'moral-panic' position. It seemed to dawn on the people who had propagated the doctrine of 'moral panic' that if crime and disorder *had* risen, blame could now be placed exclusively on Tory governments. That is the importance of the date 1979 that figures so prominently in the new history of crime.

In the mid-1990s 'moral panic' was a term that was to be heard and read from people who had picked it up as what they erroneously believed was still a phrase in vogue, or who were taught social sciences in the 1970s and 1980s. (Someone no less eminent and influential as a social-affairs intellectual than an ex-editor of *The Times*, Simon Jenkins, was particularly tenacious in holding on to his 'moral-panic' view of our present and past discontents.)[10] But it was no longer standard doctrine among those who had taught it. The new conformist doctrine was now that crime and disorder had risen—*but only since 1979.*

> It is in the interests of all to remove the factors which are fostering the social diseases of drugs, crime, political extremism, and social unrest. For instance, in recent years many parts of the country have seen outbreaks of riots ... the inflammable material has been the same: groups of disaffected young men with no role in and no stake in society or in an economy for which they have no skills that are valued.[11]

The nature and seriousness of disorder to which the Rowntree refers can be sketched by using a few from countless examples of crime, riot, vandalism and drug abuse.

In Cardiff in 1993 a 45-year-old man, a father with three children, reprimanded nine young men on his housing estate who were doing something to a traffic bollard. *The Times* reported they were wrecking it. The *Guardian* said they were kicking around an already broken bollard. The man and his friend were overwhelmed by this gang. According to *The Times* they had been watching, according to the *Guardian* they were planning to watch, the video 'Juice' (a slang American expression for respect), in which a family man is killed trying to enforce law and order. After drinking cans of cider and lager they were roaming the area. The two men were so severely beaten, the prosecuting counsel said, that one of them died from the 55 separate wounds on his body—it was as if he had been in a serious car crash. According to the *Guardian*, 'They laughed as they repeatedly kicked and stamped on Mr Reed's head'. One kick had stretched the victim's spinal cord.

A 20-year-old and two seventeen-year-olds were convicted of murder, and a twenty-year-old of manslaughter. One of the two seventeen-year-olds had told a friend, said the prosecution, that 'when you have a fight you don't stop stamping until they are dead'. According to the prosecution, when the seventeen-year-old was told by another member of the gang that the man had been killed, he had said, 'I hope so'. Two of the suspects were soon contacted by the police, as they had sprayed their names in aerosol paint at the scene of the murder. After the fatal attack one of the gang was alleged to have said: 'I've got the juice'.[12]

A week previously ten men and youths whose ages ranged from 15 to 24 were found guilty on various charges relating to a brick attack on a police car on the estate where they lived, Pennywell, Sunderland. At one stage the trial had been halted after a witness had been threatened outside the courtroom. Another witness, a security guard, chose to suffer a 21-month jail sentence rather than give evidence. He said that he had already suffered enough after making a statement to the police. He had been beaten up and there had been attacks on his mother's and partner's homes. The policeman's life was saved, but he left the force due to brain damage. One local newspaper carried photographs of four of the youths on the bus as they left the court to begin their sentences, laughing and giving the one-finger sign of defiance at the guilty verdicts, to the cheers of their supporters.[13] These scenes were also transmitted by the local television news programme.

The edition of another paper that carried the report of the guilty verdicts also carried a report that at 8.50 a.m. on the previous day a brick was hurled through the windscreen of a bus at Pennywell. On a neighbouring estate that evening windows were smashed on another bus which 'had to run the gauntlet between gangs of youths on both sides of the road'. Other 'brickings', as they are called, occurred that day in a former industrial village adjacent to Pennywell.[14]

In central Newcastle upon Tyne, a few hundred yards from the central police station on the one side and City Hall on the other, doors of steel and wood costing £700 each, with multiple bolts, were fitted in the mid-1990s to all the flats in the housing association block. Council tenants were fitting their own security doors to prevent them being broken down by vandals and burglars. An arsonist sprayed petrol through the letter box of a couple who had done that in Grantham Road, Stockwell, South London. A 14-year-old girl who lived next door said she had heard the couple trying to escape. 'There was a very loud thumping as though someone was desperate to get out. I heard it four or five times—then suddenly it stopped.' Firemen reached the dead couple after having to saw through the metal bolts that held the steel security door.[15]

The first words of a discussion of city housing estates in a later Rowntree Report in 1996 lead the reader straight into the mind-set that housing-estate vandalism, crime and drugs are the creation of Tory policies since 1979: 'With the sale of the over one million council houses ...'[16] There is also the liberal use of the slack term 'inner city'. But there was no attempt in the 1996 Report to deny that vandalism, crime and drugs were rife.

> The police are constantly being called out because of fights, drinking and drugs.

> You see them ... all at the back of the garages at night. They're sniffing like ... and other stuff. They don't even hide it ...

> I can't sleep, me. Just keep thinking, every little noise, they're going to break in. ... It makes you sick after a while ... worrying and no sleep and the bairns and all that.

> I don't go out any more. I only go to the paper shop and come back, about as far as I dare to go ... I just walk in here and bolt and chain the door every time and lock it.

> I've been broke into twice. First time they pinched my pension books, mobility books; the next time they broke in they pinched my remote control television ... my wireless and my watch. I was out one day, 20 minutes ... when I came back, no windows, they broke the lot. ... Smoking drugs next door, shouting and bawling, four o'clock in the morning taxis come up, shouting and bawling ...[17]

Meadow Well is a suburban estate. Nevertheless, it is conveniently only fifteen minutes walk from the centre of North Shields. The semi-detached two-storey houses are built in blocks of short terraces, all with their own gardens, along tree-lined streets. The Metro station is right in the middle of the estate, giving Meadow Well's residents cheap and swift access to the whole labour market on both sides of the Tyne.

On 9 September 1991 rioting broke out on the estate, and then spread to an inner-city area of Newcastle upon Tyne. The riot at

Meadow Well took place on the post-war section of the estate. Two youths had been killed when they crashed a car they had stolen for a ram-raiding burglary. They were being pursued by a police car at the time. Their peers at Meadow Well set alight Meadow Well shops, community buildings and houses. Fifty looters broke into the newsagent's shop while she slept. She, her husband and their two children escaped only with the clothes they were able to put on. The business and home of the owner of the fish-and-chip shop were attacked. Graffiti on the wall beside the burned-out community centre after the riot were threats against the police—perhaps threats to the lives of named policemen:

Pc Coombes you are next Ha Ha

ramraids revenge

police are murders

Dale Colin we no the score we haven't started yet

Tyson you coul'l'dnt catch a cold never mind a ram raider

Dr Hobbs, a sociology and criminology lecturer from an élite university was interviewed by one of the newspapers in the area. He was—as the reporter said—'a man well-placed to provide an answer', to define authoritatively the factual and moral situation.[18]

The man well-placed to do these things said that the rioters had 'declared war on society'. He was surprised, he said, that it had taken so long. The reason for the riots was that there had been many changes *since 1979*. One of the main changes, Dr Hobbs said, was that the rioters had been brought up in a political climate which said 'if they wanted something they should take it.'

Absolute poverty had played its role. The rioters were either poorer than any of their predecessors had ever been in the past (or possibly than they themselves have ever been in their life before—he did not make his point clearly). 'These people possess less than *ever before* because of benefit cuts.'[19] The *only* way they can get what they wanted, the criminologist said, was through *crime*.

Relative poverty was 'far greater' than 'in the 1930s'. (Rowntree claims only that the growth in inequality 1979-92 had returned the relative position of the poor *almost* to the levels of 1938.) The reason Dr Hobbs adduced for making his statement was that the poor in the 1990s were more likely to be living cheek by jowl with far more affluent people than they were formerly. Yet that statement was clearly quite untrue of the Meadow Well area. It was not 'cheek-by-jowl' with a richer area at all. It is a distinct estate to the west of the working-class west end of North Shields.

Applying his theory to the inner-city area of Newcastle upon Tyne to which the rioting spread he said: 'In Benwell you have these very impoverished areas ... and a couple of streets away there are solid Georgian houses costing £200,000.' According to him, then, previous generations of Benwell residents had not lived 'cheek-by-jowl' with these same solid Georgian houses—and at a time when the contrast between their richer former occupants and the worst streets of Tyneside flats (many now demolished) was much starker than in the 1990s. Unlike their amazingly dim and unobservant predecessors (that is the implication of Dr Hobbs' theory) only after 1979 were 'the kids' able to get 'an inkling of a lifestyle they know they will never share'.

Dr Hobbs continues: The boys and young men have a grievance against the people who created such an estate as Meadow Well, and against unspecified people who had committed unspecified 'economic crimes' against them.

> No one should condone what happened, but what about moral judgements on the people who created these estates and carried out the economic crimes which created a breeding ground for crime?

Dr Hobbs had just said that the boys and young men had declared war on society. He then changes his description entirely. Rioting was no longer a war, but a leisure pursuit, 'like joyriding'. Indeed, the public ought to recognize the riots as a rather good natured couple of nights out for the boys. 'The rioters can run around with their friends and the police can't catch them.'

> It is worth noting that here, no one was hurt. In some ways the mood was quite playful. I know it is difficult to say that to a fireman who is being stoned, but there simply hasn't been the ferocity there has been elsewhere.

He said that there were huge differences between the disturbances at Meadow Well and Benwell and those which had 'torn apart' London, Birmingham, Liverpool, and Bristol in the *early* 1980s.

Though hatred of the police had played a role in sparking the Tyneside riots there was nothing like the intensity of hatred there was in Brixton, St. Paul's, Toxteth or Handsworth. There the rioters, he said, were trying to kill the police, using knives and guns.

Like the writers of the Rowntree Report 1995 who depend upon the argument that crime and riot only emerged with increased relative and absolute poverty of the bottom tenth of the population after 1979 (though they themselves do not put it), Dr Hobbs is apparently unconscious of the damage his statement, that the worst rioting look place in 1981, does to his theory that the cause of the rioting was the twelve years of Thatcherism 1979-92 and the cuts in benefit of 1988.

On the Ely estate, Cardiff, Abdul Waheed had locked in his shop a local youth he believed was shoplifting. The youth escaped by smashing the glass door. The youth then returned with his friends to attack the shop. The *Socialist Worker's* report says, 'The fact that people felt they could attack Waheed's shop and threaten to burn him out if he returns to the estate is based on racist ideas. ... Waheed is now in hiding, unable to return to the estate'.

Up to 200 police were drafted to the estate to control the situation. 'Many more young people then joined in fighting back against the police. As many as 600 people were involved at the height of the rioting.'[20] When asked by the *Socialist Worker* about the cause of the rioting, people talked about the poverty and youth unemployment that existed in Ely.

In 1995 Rowntree said that the 'spark' for different riots had taken different forms. The two sparks it mentioned were 'police action' and 'antagonism between (sic) shopkeepers'. The underlying reason Rowntree gave for riots was that young men had 'no stake' in society; a substantial proportion of the population was becoming 'excluded from the mainstream of society'.[21] In 1991 the *Socialist Worker's* report on the rioting on the Ely estate had said that one 'spark' had been an 'explosion of anger against the police'. Another 'spark' had been 'a fight between two neighbouring shops'. As to the fundamental reason, a social worker is quoted as saying that people do not riot until they feel that they are 'no longer a part of mainstream society'.

Marsh Farm is a largely pedestrianized Luton housing estate of pleasant houses, bungalows and some flats. Wednesday, 5 July 1995 saw the start of several nights of rioting there.[22] The rioting began when a 13-year-old boy who had absconded from a detention centre was arrested. A false 999 call lured police onto the estate, where they were attacked. Police hoped that it had been an isolated night of trouble involving a group of excitable youths. The next night mixed groups of white, black and Asian youths started gathering. The police, now in riot gear, tried to disperse them, but were attacked with petrol bombs and bricks raining from rooftops and the windows of flats. A television cameraman filmed his own Volvo being set alight; he had parked it next to police vans for safety. Youths wearing balaclavas were seen running away with film equipment worth £30,000 from the Volvo's boot.

The schools were set on fire, three cars were stolen and set alight, and there was looting in a shopping centre during four hours of sustained rioting by gangs of youths armed with petrol bombs and bricks.

A policeman was stabbed in the abdomen. He survived only because he was wearing a protective vest. Six other police officers were injured.

Somabhai Patel, aged 80, was hit by a brick as he and his son tried to defend their grocery shop against looters. His son, Barry, 30, had been warned at 3 a.m. that a gang, which had looted a shop on the other side of the estate, were heading towards his store. He went outside to hold off 40 or 50 youths with his Alsatian dog.

> The next thing they did was to start pelting us with bricks. My dad came out to help me and he got hit in the face. They calmed down after that because a lot of my customers came around and pleaded with them to stop breaking their own schools and shops.

The TV cameraman who had lost his Volvo and equipment said, 'It was very frightening. I have covered a lot of riots, but this one was different. The police seemed to have no control'. The Chief Constable of Bedfordshire said that it had been a warm night and the youths had had a few beers. But the disorder was the worst he had seen in 41 years of policing, and somebody could have been killed. A police sergeant said, 'It's just about 200 yobs who have nothing better to do than to pop the police'.

Sixteen people, mainly locals in their late teens or early twenties, were arrested on suspicion of burglary, arson, possession of offensive weapons, and assault. A charge of attempted murder was under consideration.

Ordsall estate, Salford, July 1992:

Wednesday, 1 July: The latest violence began when a council neighbourhood office was set on fire. Vehicles were burned close by, and in Broughton, two miles away, five cars were set on fire in what the police say was a related incident.

Thursday, 2 July: A carpet warehouse was burned in a suspected arson attack. A security guard at a block of flats was beaten up and a petrol bomb thrown into an office at Salford University. More cars were damaged or burned at Ordsall.

Friday, 3 July: A housing office was set on fire, there were skirmishes with youths, and for the first time in the current violence police received reports, so far unconfirmed, of gunfire in the area.

Saturday, 4 July: A quieter day, with only one car burned out and a day centre set on fire.

Sunday, 5 July: A McDonald's restaurant was set on fire and a fire bomb thrown at a police station. A careers office and a recreation centre were also set on fire.

Monday, 6 July: Shots were fired at two police vans and a fire engine. The first police vehicle attacked was struck by two bullets. Two officers in the van were slightly grazed, both believed to be from ricochets.

'In the surrounding streets there were glimpses of the £15 million Salford council has spent since 1990 trying to restore dignity to its 1970s' estate.'

'There's loads of jobs round here', sulked a shaven head. 'It's all scousers and Burnley bastards.'

Mainly, however, the men blamed the police. The bad feeling had boiled over, the *Guardian* reporter said, after the riot squad had impounded cars that might have been stolen. A young man elaborated:

There's people who can't pay their electricity. And they're at home in bed, in the dark, and the door's kicked in and all they can see is big torches coming up the stairs and the Bill is saying, 'Stay where you are or you'll get your heads blown off'.

Another man said, 'The police don't relate to the kids'. A man in his mid-twenties, according to the *Guardian* reporter, said that there were lots of guns in Salford. He said that everyone, not just a minority, was outraged at being treated like scum.

There's lots of guns in Salford. There's lots of lads not a million miles from where you are standing who will say 'Do it!' and we'll do it.

'None of the males milling around Kwiksave would put their name to anything'. Around them, 'most of the centre's entrepreneurs seemed to have rattled down the shutters and thrown away the key'.[23]

On 4 May 1996 good-natured crowds of drunken football fans celebrated Newcastle United's successful football season after the last game at St James' Park. But hundreds of them also attacked police with bottles and beer glasses.[24] Fighting broke out at Newcastle Central Station when a crowd of about 100 football supporters who were being escorted from the station suddenly turned on the police, pelting them with bottles. Officers wearing riot gear were also attacked in the Bigg Market. Two police officers were hurt and another man was knocked unconscious by the missiles. Taxi drivers said a police van was overturned outside the central police station and another police vehicle attacked. The windows of some big stores around Grey's Monument were smashed, and there were thefts from shop displays. On the monument are these words, inscribed in 1932:

> After a century of civil peace, the People renew their gratitude to the author of the Great Reform Bill.

The front page of the *Sunderland Echo*, 10 June 1996—an everyday story of North Country folk:

> Families on Houghton's Villa Estate fear someone will be killed after a spate of arson attacks near their homes. They took to the streets last night to deter young thugs from setting fire to cars and property.
>
> Stolen cars have been dumped and torched outside houses in the past few days, while fences, sheds and dustbins have been set on fire...
>
> One mother, who asked not to be named for fear of reprisals, said she was horrified by what was going on and was particularly fearful for pensioners in old people's bungalows in Burn Park Road ...
>
> 'We organized a patrol last night. There is no way in which we are vigilantes but it is the only way we are going to get any sleep.'
>
> Superintendent Dick Spring of Houghton and Washington Police said fine weather and light nights usually led to a rise in problems.
>
> 'We will step up our presence and hopefully quell the situation.'

On the same front page on the same day:

> A Sunderland man is recovering in hospital today after being viciously attacked while he slept. Ronald Fenwick, 53, was in bed at his home in Chester Road when the attack took place early on Saturday. His attacker burst into his bedroom and started making demands for money ... Then without warning he suddenly started to repeatedly hit Mr Fenwick with a rolling pin around the arms, knees and body ... Mr

Fenwick was taken to Sunderland General Hospital suffering from multiple injuries, and was detained. A hospital spokesman said today that Mr Fenwick was in a stable and comfortable condition and his injuries were not believed to be life-threatening. A 16-year-old was arrested by detectives and questioned in connection with the attack. He is expected to appear before Sunderland juvenile court today, charged with attempted murder.

Tucked away on page 63 of the same daily newspaper a few days later is the report of another run-of-the-mill incident on a local housing estate:

Two police officers were injured in Sunderland last night while dealing with an alleged hammer attack ... 'They found a man with a head injury who would not give any details to them. They requested an ambulance and while they were waiting for it to arrive a large crowd gathered.' A police inspector and a constable were then allegedly attacked. About 12 police vehicles arrived on the scene and CS gas was used to subdue some members of the crowd.[25]

Experiences of riotous youths on their own housing estates (not 'The Gorbals' or 'Seven Dials', but 'Farms' and 'Wells') became commonplace by the end of the 1979-92 period. But disturbances, destructive unruliness, drugs, arson, and crime had already by the early 1980s become the fabric of everyday life.

Downhill estate in Sunderland was built in the 1960s. In July 1983 the Downhill Action Group presented a petition to the local council demanding that 14 blocks of flats on the estate be demolished, and the remaining tenants be rehoused. The petition stated that the half-empty flats were dangerous to the residents because they had become 'meeting places for glue-sniffing vandals'.

Mother of a 22-month-old boy, Miss Margaret Strong, said: 'I am terrified there will be another fire. There are no fire escapes in these buildings so you are trapped and all the windows are stuck so there is no way out. The fire was just the last straw. These flats have been getting worse during the last few years and something has got to be done. They are just not fit to live in any more.'[26]

When the North Peckham estate in Liddle ward, Southwark, was opened in 1972, it had already won an architectural design award. It was part of a larger design which would have allowed people to go from the Elephant and Castle to Peckham on raised walkways. The last of its dwellings was not completed until 1977.

This is a report on this and a neighbouring estate ten years later, in 1987:

Milkmen have not set foot on the North Peckham estate in south London for three years. The Express Dairy was the last to withdraw after a series of incidents in which roundsmen were threatened, beaten up and robbed ... The postman still calls to the 1,500 homes, though he once needed a police escort ... 'The average milk bottle lasts 20 journeys, but we never got them back from these estates. The devils throw them off the balconies. We had a milk float stolen. We even had a milkman kidnapped. In the end we pulled out. We are not a social service.'

Doris Nourse, 65, ... and her husband Henry, 66, have lived on the Camden estate in Southwark for 12 years. Thieves have broken into their maisonette 10 times in the past two years. Eighteen months ago Mrs. Nourse was mugged and robbed of her purse. At Christmas, a man was stabbed to death on the stairs leading to her home; another was murdered on a footbridge 100 yards away.[27]

According to spokesman for Southwark Borough Council, although 50 per cent of North Peckham's 1,400 households were in receipt of housing benefit, rent arrears for the estate totalled £1.5 million. In 1987 the proportion of children living with a lone parent was high by previous standards, 10 per cent, even though it was low by the standards of only a few years later.

A local doctor, who asked not to be named, said,

Most doctors will not even go there unless they are accompanied by the police. Too many of them have been attacked, beaten, and stabbed.[28]

Inviting comparison with the noise problem in the Braydon Road area in the early 1950s,[29] the doctor said that one of the commonest problems she had to deal with was lack of consideration of neighbours for one another.

People suffer terribly from non-stop noise from all sides. Many of them say they will go mad because of it.

She continued:

Young people who are obviously bright write themselves off at 15 or so, and put all their energy into playing the system to their advantage.

When the tenants were consulted about the estate's future, their first suggestion was to demolish the whole of it. The spokesman for Southwark Borough Council was quoted as saying that this would have been too expensive. Another 1,400 new dwellings would have had to be supplied to rehouse them, while the local authority would still be paying off the loan on the demolished houses for decades to come. 'It was a dream in the 1960s', the spokesman said, 'a reality in the 1970s, and a nightmare in the 1980s'.

The Government did, however, approve the first phase of a £37 million plan which would eventually divide the estate into five smaller 'villages'.

The doctor said that the young people 'believe that no one really gives a damn about them'. Because they believe that, she said, they 'just try to make their lives as easy and as comfortable as possible'. But her assessment? 'And who can blame them?' The doctor *shares the young people's definition of the situation*, the definition of the situation of the young people on the estate who exclude doctors from making home visits because 'too many of them have been attacked, beaten and stabbed', and who 'make their lives as easy and comfortable as possible' by 'playing the system'.

The acting head of the primary school also blames the physical environment. He 'knows that many of the problems of the estate are rooted in the way the estate is built'.

The reporters themselves report beatings and stabbings, and people driven to distraction by neighbours' noise, and lone parenthood, and young people giving up hope and playing the system to their advantage, and £1.5 million of rent arrears. But when they explain the problems of the estate I doubt whether they have the concrete things they have described in mind at all. They have forgotten the problems of the estate and explain only something woolly and abstract they think of as the problems of 'the inner city'. Thus one explanation they offer is 'the economic crash of the 1970s'. The other is the fact that on this prize-winning estate completed in 1977 there was bad behaviour by 1987 because its physical fabric was 'crumbling'.

These were the conventional, materialistic, explanations provided by doctors, head teachers and journalists by the mid-1980s, because these were the explanations that had been provided to them by the universities and the churches. (The Church of England's *Faith in the City* had been published in 1985.)

But how could the differences between the housing estates of the 1970s, 1980s and 1990s on the one hand and those of the

1930s, 1940s and 1950s on the other be explained by material and economic factors which were incomparably more severe at the earlier than at the later time?

One explanation put forward in mid-1980s that did at least take account of the fact that civility had already steeply declined from, at the latest, the early 1970s, and not just from 1979, was the 'improvement' in housing itself. The best known version of this idea in Britain came from Alice Coleman, professor of geography at King's College, London University. In 1985 she traced the already obvious and ever-mounting problems of bad behaviour to a forty-year reign of expert planners and architects. She was interested in the increasing incidence of such 'lapses in civilized behaviour' as family breakdown leading to children being placed in care; litter dropping; graffiti scrawling; vandalism; and excrement pollution in lifts and other common areas of housing estates.

> It is a tragic thought that Utopian designers with their idealistic ambitions have tipped the balance sufficiently to make criminals out of potentially law-abiding citizens and victims out of potentially secure and happy people.[30]

Her ideas were certainly useful within a relatively narrow range of post-war housing types. They were beneficial where they were applicable and were applied. They had an immediate effect on the serious press. They felt intuitively right and their applicability could be vividly demonstrated from obvious examples.

> Being neither an architect nor a sociologist, she applies only the robust common sense of the schoolmistress she once was. She looks at the buildings and at the evidence: litter, graffiti, vandalism and urine pollution. She does not even inquire, on her tours, who the architects were. 'It probably got some design award', she will say, and pass on. ... Earlier this year I went with her to Robin Hood Gardens estate in London's Tower Hamlets, and we stared gloomily down the windswept, stinking second-floor concrete walkway to the deserted, litter-strewn alley between the burnt-out garages below. 'A perfect place', mused Coleman, 'for gangs to get together'.[31]

It appealed to local housing authorities because it gave them a glimmer of hope that things could be 'dramatically improved by a few simple adjustments', and Professor Coleman was a welcome speaker at, for example, the Design Against Crime conference at Tynemouth in July 1987.[32]

But there were two great defects of this excellent limited theory. One was that the collapse of civility had commenced before the great housing clearances of the 1960s and the replacement of nineteenth-century dwellings with (for the first time in this country) concrete walkways-in-the-air and system-built high-rise blocks of flats on a large scale. (I do not doubt, however, that these developments did have an accelerating effect.)[33] The second was that the collapse in civility was by no means confined to blocks of flats built in the 1960s. It was worst there. But it happened to almost the same extent, at the same speed and over the same time period on inter-war and post-war housing estates on the garden-city model of 12 houses to the acre with their own gardens back and front.

Rowntree did not deny that crime and social disorder had risen and were a serious matter. But, in conformity with the new doctrine, it concentrated all the rise into the period 1979-92. Whether it was justified in doing so is the topic of chapters 3, 4 and 5.

3

Low Unemployment, Declining Poverty and Rising Crime 1961-1979

T he Rowntree Report's lack of interest in work published before 1992 is remarkable, and the paucity of historical analysis is very striking. The first volume lists 68 references. Fifty-six of them were published 1992-94 or were 'forthcoming'. The earliest date of the other references is 1986, as if no work on poverty, unemployment and social disorder worthy of consideration had ever been done on the subject until this generation began to receive its Rowntree grants. In the second volume, 87 references date from 1992. None of the other 19 references stems from the 1960s or earlier. Four of the six listed from the earliest dates, in the 1970s, are from works written or edited by the same author who, when the Rowntree Report was published in 1995, was himself director of a centre supported by the Joseph Rowntree Foundation, and of which the author of the second volume of the Rowntree Report 1995 was also a director.[1]

The strongest impression left not just by the text, but by such evidence as this, is of a large body of people reinforcing one another's set opinions of what data are relevant and can be counted as true, and how they may be properly interpreted to one another and to the public.

But if the Rowntree Report's assumptions about the relationship between anti-social activities and poverty were to have any pretensions to validity, they could not be limited to the period 1979-95. They would have to be true for other periods as well.

At the very least, they would have to apply to the earlier period dealt with in the Rowntree Report, 1961-79. The Report itself shows that 1961-79 was a period of *rising* incomes and *declining* absolute *and* relative poverty.[2] It was a period of uniquely *low* unemployment for most of the time (to the best of my knowledge no one has ever contested this).

But it was also a period of rapidly rising recorded crime, riot, political extremism and drug abuse.

If the facts of 1961-79 can be reconciled with its theory, it would have been necessary for the Rowntree Report to explain how it accomplished that reconciliation. Astonishingly, the Rowntree Foundation's Report 1995 is silent on this crucial matter.

There are only three explanations I can think of.

One is that nobody noticed this fatal contradiction in the report. If that is the explanation, then the Chairman did not notice. It was not noticed by the Chair of Barnardos, or by the Deputy Chairman of British Telecom, or by the representative of the NCH Action for Children. It was not even noticed by Mr Howard Davies, the Director General of the Confederation of British Industry. I can scarcely believe it was not noticed by the careful Kathleen Kiernan, Senior Research Fellow in Population Studies; or by the Secretary of the Inquiry Group, her colleague at the London School of Economics, Pamela Meadows, the Director of the Policy Studies Institute; John Willman, The Features Editor of the *Financial Times*; John Monks, the General Secretary of the Trades Union Congress; Robin Wendt, the Chief Executive of the Association of County Councils—these were all members of the Inquiry Group. Did none of them notice?

The second possibility is that the authors are followers of the doctrine of a Reith Lecturer, who said it was the duty of the intellectual to be on the side of the poor. The intellectual's role model, he said, must be Robin Hood.[3] Clearly that could be taken as a hint that one must not be too pernickety about mere data. Be certain only that your the heart is in the right place.

Melanie Phillips records a vivid example of this mind-set from a conversation she had with a professor closely connected with the work of the Rowntree Foundation. (The topic of the conversation was in this case not poverty, but the family.)

> Telephoned to discover upon what research he based his criticism, this academic proved reluctant to answer the question. Instead he released a stream of invective ... Pressed to identify the research that

would prove Dennis and Halsey wrong, he eventually said, in summary, this: *of course they were correct as far as the research went,* but where did that get anyone?[4]

In robbing the rich to feed the poor (or in favouring any other weak section of the population) what right-minded person would jib at a little subterfuge; what person of good will would be critical of any hero who has used guile to outwit the enemy? If in its pragmatic effects an argument consistently serves the cause, why worry overmuch about its mere truth-value?

That was a central tenet of the social philosophy of the writers to whom the leaders of the student generation of the late 1960s and 1970s were drawn ('the sixty-eighters' as the Germans call them)—the so-called 'anti-positivist' philosophy of the Frankfurt School. No one but the permanent critic of our unequal society can be a genuine social-affairs intellectual. Affirmation of hierarchy is *ipso facto* falsehood.[5] Whoever is not an unremitting critic of existing institutional arrangements and patterns of income distribution and employment opportunities is a 'mere means at the disposal of the existing order'. As so many data, mere facts, unfortunately do affirm the social order (they recognize that) a primary task must be to overcome 'the present triumph of the factual mentality'. The 'tyranny' of 'facticity' has to be broken.[6]

This much can be said in favour of the sixty-eighters' adherence to this doctrine. Some of them had at least read about it, thought about it and argued about it. They considered that they had a case that had to be defended, but that they were capable of defending it. They were familiar with both its philosophical justification, such as it was, and the Jewish experience in Nazi Europe which was its main engine.

I shall deal more fully with the third possible explanation. It is that, in the early 1990s in social policy and social science circles, the 'moral-panic' theory of crime, riot and drug statistics was still more or less taken for granted as the correct one. Restricting the discussion to crime, then according to this theory crime did not increase rapidly in the period 1961-79. Only the crime figures did.

According to the 'moral-panic' school of thought the crime figures rose for quite other reasons. They were inflated by the powers-that-be in order to increase the scope and extent of state repression. They were exaggerated by the police, who were seeking more resources. The popular newspapers were whipping up public anxieties by sensationalizing crime stories because of their commercial interest in circulation. The public was becoming more sensitive to violent conduct. This meant, according to the 'moral-panic' school, that in 1961 they had stoically ignored news that an old lady down the street had been knocked to the ground by a boy or a youth. By the 1970s the volume of criminal conduct was the same. All that had changed was that victims and their friends were letting their 'respectable fears' run away with them when they heard of the same thing in the 1970s. A break-in, and the disappearance of the husband's pocket watch, or the family's hard-won Sunday crockery and the mother's purse with the week's wages in it, would have passed unnoticed once upon a time. Nobody had anything worth stealing, so nobody missed these unimportant items when they were stolen. But in the 1960s people began to acquire telephones. According to the 'moral-panic' school of thought, they could report crimes easily to the police—something they had not been able to do, apparently, from a public phone-box or by telling the policeman at the police box or on the beat. Items were now insured against theft (why were they not before?) and thefts for that reason had to appear in the police records. And so on and so forth. The rise in crime was a fiction of the imagination of the 'moronic right'.

Until the mid-1990s, the thesis that crime did not really rise from the 1960s to the 1990s was more or less consensual in academic and social-affairs research foundation circles.[7] The case that growing relative poverty caused growing 'moral panic', but *not* growing crime, was clearly put by Professor Stuart Hall:

> Society's self-appointed moral guardians who desire greater social controls, more authority, discipline and restraint and who *because of the progressive polarization of society* feel that things are slipping from bad to worse ... may have their worst fears daily and nightly confirmed by the relatively independent processes of the media, who find it convenient to classify problematic or threatening events into and through these widening circles of disturbance.

An interesting aspect of that quotation is that it stems from the period 1961-79 when the Rowntree Report 1995 says polarization was *diminishing*.[8] It would be difficult to find, indeed, comments written in the 1961-79 period from any social-affairs intellectual who endorsed the Rowntree Report's findings in 1995 which suggest that relative poverty was being alleviated 1961-79. The Rowntree Report's claim that polarization had diminished 1961-79 (actually 1961-77) became acceptable only when it could be contrasted with its claim that relative poverty increased during the period of Tory governments 1979-92.

A representative example of the thesis that the only rise that took place was in 'moral panic', and not real crime, is *Hooligan: The History of Respectable Fears*. It is a well-known university and Open University book, frequently reissued.

This book is about street crime and violence. But it is also about ... the myth of the 'British way of life' according to which after centuries of domestic peace, the streets of Britain have been suddenly plunged into an unnatural state of disorder that betrays the stable traditions of the past. ... What I hope to show, by contrast, is that the real traditions are quite different.[9]

Pearson makes two claims. First, crime has not increased or indeed significantly fluctuated in this country over past centuries. Secondly, in the public mind (but only in the public mind) 'generation by generation, crime and disorder increase by leaps and bounds'.[10]

He quotes two sets of headlines from the 1930s. One reads: 'Daring Raids by Bag Snatchers. Widow Badly Injured and Robbed.' The other reads: 'Woman injured by Violent Bag-Snatcher'. She had been 'thrown to the ground and bruised'.

He finds these headlines in a *national* mass-circulation Sunday newspaper. An old woman had been '*thrown to the ground* and *bruised*'! The two sets of headlines are separated by a period of five years. Would a woman being 'bruised' be a national headline in 1979, when the rise in crime is supposed to have begun?

To show that there was as much crime in the inter-war period as there was when Pearson was writing (and when his book was being solemnly reissued and recommended to generations of Open University students), Pearson takes street robbery as a key test. The case of street robbery is particularly important for his thesis, he says, 'because this is commonly the most sensitive area for registering public concern about crime and violence'.

There was 'ample evidence', he writes, of 'sharp increases' in street violence in the inter-war period, for between 1925 and 1929 there was a 90 per cent increase in 'bag snatches' in London.[11]

Delicately, Pearson does not give the numbers, only the percentages. But how many bag snatches were there in the entire Metropolitan Police District in the entire year 1925? There were 66. At the end of Pearson's 1920s crime wave in 1929 there were 127.[12] This is presented as evidence that there was as much crime in the inter-war period as in the 1960s and 1970s, and the apparent rise in the 1960s and the 1970s was the result of more recording and 'moral panic'—that in the 1920s there had been an 'insubstantial reaction' to the 'upsurge' in bag-snatchings—what are today called 'muggings'. Pearson also makes much of the fact that 'shop raids' increased by 70 per cent in the Metropolitan Police District between 1925 and 1929. In numbers the increase was from 135 to 230.

In 1933 reference was made in Parliament to 'pulling down the shutters of an empty kiosk and stealing cigarettes and sweets'. This example was used by the MP to distinguish between 'trivial acts' and 'real crime' in 1933. Pearson uses it as evidence that crimes that would not have been recorded in the 1930s but would have been recorded in the 1960s and 1970s, for 'it is evident' from this example 'that certain kinds of common theft, damage and injury were regarded as wholly commonplace in pre-war years and hardly worth a moment's thought'. Pulling down the shutters of an empty shop or kiosk would have been regarded as 'looting', he says, 'in the aftermath of Brixton and Toxteth'.

On this evidence, Pearson asserts, street robbery, burglary and looting were 'viewed leniently' in the interwar period, and did not appear in the criminal statistics. In the 'moral panic' of the period after 1961-79 they were no longer viewed leniently, and were recorded.

'Bag snatching' is not a figure that is consistently given. The figures for *felonious woundings and other acts endangering life* are given in the annual criminal statistics. In 1900 the national recorded figure was only 260. In 1927 it was lower still, 122. In stark contrast, between 1969 and 1978 the figure *rose* by 1,800, i.e. by seven times the *total* for 1900, and by *fifteen times* the *total* for 1927.

The thesis that crime and violence had not increased, and that society was simply amplifying an unchanging volume of crime and violence, seeped into every nook and cranny of sociological 'analysis' from the late 1960s onwards. Ian R. Taylor, for example, argued that soccer had been characterized by violence 'throughout its lengthy history as a sub-culture within the working class' and that its 'association with social conflicts was nothing new'.[13] So-called 'thugs' in contemporary soccer were simply the 'most active members of the soccer sub-culture'. They differed from their predecessors if not only, then principally in the way that their conduct was described and condemned. Their conduct was a response to 'the lack of control felt by the sub-culture over their club', but they had been unable to resist the new attribution of the label of 'thug' to them by 'soccer's power-ful'.[14] They were not working-class hooligans, they were working-class heroes.

The third explanation for the Rowntree Report's extraordinary insouciance about a possible fatal flaw in its theory of poverty and social disorder is, then, closely linked to the 'moral-panic' consensus that crime, social disorder and drug abuse had not really increased at all. This third explanation is thus that the Rowntree theory went off 'half-cock'. Long-time adherents of the 'moral-panic' theory in the poverty lobby came to see in crime a stick with which to beat the government on behalf of the poor. But they did not take the trouble to reconcile their new stance with their previous one. They crudely applied their new stance to the 1979-92 period it dealt with, but retained their old stance with regard to the 1961-79 period that it also dealt with.[15]

All of the rise 1961-92 was now concentrated in the period 1979-92. The awkward data of the rise in crime 1961-79 were unconsciously disposed of by continuing to apply the 'moral-panic' theory to all periods prior to 1979. Crime had not risen 1961-79. But it had risen 1979-92, and over that period all the responsibility could be laid at the door of Thatcherite govern-ments.

The Rowntree Report's argument fails disastrously if crime *did* rise significantly towards 1990s levels in a more-or-less unbro-ken trend during the period of *narrowing* relativities of income and *low* unemployment in the 1961-79 period.

For if Rowntree's theory of crime, unemployment and poverty growth is correct, and if Rowntree is correct in its claim that crime was at about the same *real* levels in 1961 as were *recorded* in 1979, then crime rates must have been as high prior to 1960 as they were in 1979. For, according to the implicit assumption of the Rowntree Report, they began their real rise only from 1979.

The period 1979-92 was not so exceptional as was lightly assumed in the 1990s in its insecurity of employment. It was not therefore so exceptional as assumed as a breeding-ground for crime, even on the Rowntree Report's own hypothesis that unemployment is a principal cause of such disorders. The idea that in any period up to the 1950s a working-class man or woman ordinarily enjoyed, or expected to enjoy, a life-time in his or her job is sheer fantasy. The period of low unemployment 1939-79 and, in the latter part of that period, the idea of a person's 'ownership of his job', was brief. Before the 1990s few left-oriented intellectuals would have dreamed of claiming that working-class jobs were safe. In a book he published in 1958, Richard Titmuss, at that time the doyen of social policy academics, typically stressed in his analysis of the life of the manual worker the fact of the pervasive insecurity of employment. In the factory, he wrote, stability is an important attribute neither in theory nor in practice. The employment situation of manual workers generally is one of uncertainty about tomorrow. This is what provokes his preference for 'immediacy of living', and hinders long-range planning from being a feature of his home and community life.[16] Coal is our Life, a 1950s study of a mining town in West Yorkshire, found that, contrary to what sponsors of the research had expected, the pitmen were not adopting middle-class lifestyles at that time. The book's thesis was that the whole culture of the community was geared to cope with employment insecurity, which was still severe for a miner, even in a time of full employment. In the twentieth century up to the 1950s, crime, riot, and hooliganism had not been part of that cultural adjustment.[17]

No reports before 1961 and going back to at least 1875 give a picture that is in the slightest degree consistent with the theory that crime, riot, hooliganism, self-centred drug consumption, and vandalism were as rife then as in the 1980s and 1990s. And no reports give the slightest support to any suggestion that, if crime and other manifestations of social disorder were lower, this must have been due to lower or falling levels of poverty, lower or falling levels of unemployment, or a sense of lower or falling levels of inequality.

My father-in-law (who was unemployed for six months in the year my wife was born) was a miner at Monkwearmouth colliery, Sunderland. My grandfather had once worked there. I lived with a miner and his family in the village of Leasingthorne, County Durham, for more than a year in 1939 and 1940, and kept contact with him until he died in the 1960s. All three of them believed (this is true) that it was a fact (I do not know whether that is true) that Lady Londonderry spent more on flowers for a single reception at her mansion in London than the total weekly wage bill of the Londonderry colliery of Vane Tempest.

None of them, nor any of their friends, and extremely few of their workmates and their families, ever stole anything from their neighbours, or anybody else, on that or any other account.

There are those who contend that in these circumstances of poverty, insecurity, and inequality there ought to have been more riot, crime, political extremism and dropping out of alienating and degrading work into drug-induced euphoria. That brings us full circle, of course, to the theory of the criminal, the rioter and the user of legal or illicit drugs as working-class hero. But the question is not whether, in conditions of unemployment and poverty, young people in Britain *ought* to have been criminals, rioters and drop-outs from the educational and industrial system. The question is whether as many of them *were*. In the mid-1950s the excise returns showed that the *per capita* consumption of liquid beer had fallen continuously since the First World War, and in terms of alcohol intake from beer the *per capita* consumption had fallen more steeply still. The same was true of spirits. Wine consumption had risen somewhat, but from small beginnings and was still at a very low level. In 1955, as the annual Home Office reports show, narcotic addicts numbered a few hundred people in special groups such as musicians and doctors. By the prosperous, low-unemployment mid-1960s the system of treatment suited to the small scale of the phenomenon in 1950s, allowing doctors to prescribe heroin to addicts, had broken down as it became the prey of widespread abuse. Addicts in the 1990s were counted in their tens of thousands. In the small Northumberland town of Blyth alone, eleven drug-related fatalities were reported in three years in the early to mid-1990s.[18]

Rowntree assumes that poverty and unemployment are the *principal* causes of crime and other disorders. They are not just contributory to them at any given level of the propensity to engage in crime and disorder in the face of frustration, whatever the source of the frustration. Rowntree does not raise the possibility that both crime and unemployment have their roots in anti-social and self-destructive attitudes created or not coped with by families, schools, churches, the entertainment industry, the news media and so on.

Rowntree's assumption is plausible only if crime and disorder began their main rise in its period 1979-92, and not in its other period 1961-79. On the poverty side of its argument, Rowntree is at least able to provide some carefully selected figures. Those on *income* that *was reported*, give some colour to its case that the real income of the poorest did not increase 1979-92. The figures on what remained of reported income after the rent or mortgage payments had been made give some colour to its case that the real income of the poorest available for expenditures other than housing *fell* 1979-92. In the period 1979-92, too, unemployment rose to a post-war high of over 13 per cent. That that peak was reached as early as 1984 is an embarrassment to the Rowntree theory. There are various ways, however, of making a reasonable case that unemployment did remain high, and did hit men, young men, and unskilled young men particularly hard.

When we turn to most of the period 1961-79, Rowntree does not present even weak and tendentious evidence of worsening poverty and high and rising unemployment. It presents no evidence to that effect at all. The annual growth rate of the economy of the United Kingdom had been 2.5 per cent compound since the Second World War, and this growth rate continued through the 1960s and 1970s. In real purchasing power, for every £1.00 the average Briton had to spend in 1992, he had had under 50p in 1961, but 80p by 1979.[19] From 1961 to 1979 both absolute and relative poverty diminished dramatically. *The Rowntree Report 1995 emphasizes this fact.* The proportion of the total population with below half of average income was 11 per cent in 1961. By 1977 it had reached its lowest point of seven per cent.[20] Unemployment was extraordinarily low for most of the period. If crime and disorder nevertheless rose between 1961-79, the Report's theory that poverty and unemployment are their principal cause would be totally destroyed.

In the course of 1961-79 recorded crime did indeed rise steeply. The number of serious offences recorded by the police was 871,000 in 1961. It was 2,377,000 in 1979. The number of offences per 100,000 of the population rose from 1,900 to 4,800.

Figure 1
Number of Serious Offences recorded by the Police:
England and Wales (Millions)

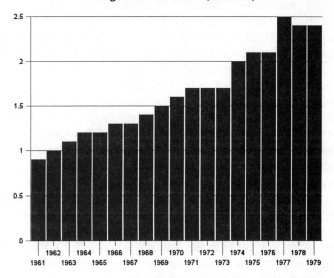

Figure 2
Number of Serious Offences recorded by the Police:
England and Wales (per 100,000 population)

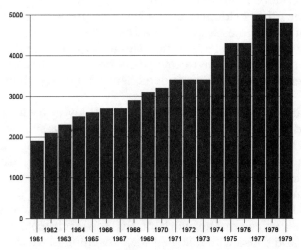

Source: Home Office, *Criminal Statistics England and Wales*, London: HMSO, annually.

The more reliable figures of the British Crime Survey (BCS), available from 1981, confirm this picture of a deterioration in security of person and property before 1979. Utilizing earlier figures from the General Household Survey (GHS), the BCS was able to provide figures back to 1972 on its basis for only one offence, residential burglaries involving loss. On the BCS's count, there were 379,000 residential burglaries involving loss in 1972. This figure had risen to 388,000 by 1979.[21]

Statistics do tend to knock the props from under some of the most cherished and fundamental beliefs of the poverty lobby. It therefore entertains some hostility to them. It has had allies in the universities who have engaged in a successful campaign to establish the belief, not just that the figures of recorded crime are defective (this is so), but that because the defective figures say that crime has risen, it is legitimate to conclude that crime has not risen—an elementary *non sequitur*. The *trend* of the reported crime statistics is confirmed by the 'victim' surveys of the BCS for the short time they take us back into the past. But if the criminal statistics were useless, *other* evidence would have to be adduced one way or another. It is no good the spokesmen for the poverty lobbies and their supporters in the serious media saying (or rather hoping it will be taken for granted): 'The statistics are useless, therefore I can believe whatever I want'.

What does other evidence show? Not just problem families on estates, but problem estates, were already a recognized problem in the early 1970s.[22] In 1979 vandalism and theft was already so rife in dwellings built only a few years before, that many local councils were already having to demolish them or sell them off at any price.

It was easy to take the view that the fault lay in their original quality and design. But so far as their quality was concerned, most had been built to the standards of the Parker Morris Committee of 1961.[23] These were much higher than those of private builders catering for anything like the same market. They were incomparably higher than the standards of the dwellings previously lived in by their occupants. So far as their design is concerned, they were the work of the top architects of their generation and those who followed their teaching in their work as architects with local authorities great and small all over the country. They were built under the control of Labour as well as

Conservative central and local governments. There was steady inspiration and guidance from enlightened civil servants and government experts, and from the professionals of the planning and architecture departments of the local authorities. The designs were welcomed by the local media and many of them received the formal accolades of the leaders of their professions.

I personally have the satisfaction of knowing that I opposed the plans and designs of the planners and architects in the late 1960s and early 1970s, when the consensus of my political colleagues was solidly for them. I wrote two books and several articles at the time about the damage so-called slum-clearance was doing to the people it was supposed to be assisting.[24] I therefore have very little respect for the members of the same Left consensus who after the event blamed the planners and archi- tects. It would have been more honest for them to blame them- selves. 'Blaming the victim' is one of the great mindless slogans of the last few years. If anyone dared to say that the people who inhabited the new dwellings were at fault in the way they conducted themselves in them, 'blaming the victim' would be the first cry. But it was the architects who were to a large degree the victims, not the perpetrators, of the collapse in civic culture in the late 1960s and 1970s. The architects did not invent the block of flats in the 1960s. They had the experience of their use by the well-to-do in England. They had the experience of their use by the working class in Europe. They had the experience of their use in England in, for example, the Peabody Buildings in London, some of which had been occupied for nearly a century. They had the experience of the harmonious living together of the working class in the crowded conditions of all England's great cities and industrial towns. In their designs they assumed that those high standards of civility existed, and would not only continue but be reinforced with better housing and rising levels of income, leisure and education. When the deterioration of those high standards coincided with the construction of the buildings they had designed, the effects were disastrous.

In July 1978, for example, 2,000 modern maisonettes in the Everton district of Liverpool were offered to any takers for 10p each. They had been built 12 years before, but were now known as 'The Piggeries'.[25] Oak Gardens and Eldon Gardens, Birken- head were similar dwellings built in 1958. A combination of bad conditions, 'anti-social behaviour among tenants' and 'appalling vandalism' persuaded Wirral Council to start evacuating the dwellings as early as 1975. They were blown up in October 1979. The dwellings had cost £750,000 to build, and when they were demolished £600,000 was still owed on them. Their demolition cost £150,000. Oak and Eldon Gardens were described as 'once a utopia municipal housing project'.[26] In August 1993 blocks of flats built to replace Gorbals' slum tenements were blown up. They had been designed by Sir Basil Spence, and had lasted for less than 30 years. (They had owed 'as much to the Japanese Metabolists as to Le Corbusier.')[27]

Some feel for the high levels of crime and other forms of social disorder already apparent in 1979 can be derived from the case of Kirkby new town, outside Liverpool.[28] The next chapter will try to give some feel for the low levels of crime and other forms of social disorder in 1961.

In the early 1960s, Kirkby Labour party was told by Barbara Castle, prominent and powerful in the Labour movement: 'This is your chance to build a new Jerusalem'. The local MP was Harold Wilson, who would become Prime Minister in 1964.

But by 1979 in the new estates here, as elsewhere in Britain, vandalism had become the boy's and the male youth's form of self-expression. Nowhere near the inner city, the problems of such areas were described as 'inner-city' problems in order to retain intact the emotional capital tied up in outrage at the city slum and the condition of the working classes in 1844.

Even the immediate presence of the official and formal forces of social control were helpless in the face of the boys' and young males' destruction of the physical fabric of their own community. A four-storey block of flats less than twenty years old stood wrecked and gutted by arsonists a short distance from the police station.

Alan Road's report on Kirkby in early 1979 gives a graphic picture of what he calls the *self-destruction* of Barbara Castle's envisioned new Jerusalem.[29] By then another Labour minister, Gerald Kaufman, had already compared Kirkby's vandalized flats and houses to the aftermath of the Flixborough chemical plant disaster. 'You crunch across a carpet of broken glass in Rough-wood Drive', Alan Road writes:

> past the heaps of uncollected rubbish, the 16 doorless garages strewn with rubble and the obligatory graffiti for ... the 'Roughwood Boot Boys', to a four-storey block of flats that looks as if it might have been

the epicentre of some natural disaster. Scorched rafters are exposed to the grey sky and not a pane of glass remains unbroken.

Whole blocks of flats built in 1970 stood empty and disembowelled. By 1979 Knowsley Council had 1,000 flats in Kirkby under contract for demolition and another 1,300 demolitions awaiting government approval.[30] In May 1982 Knowsley Council spent £330,000 merely to blow up four of these blocks which had been a target for vandals 'almost since they were built' twelve years before. Extra costs were incurred because several homes in the neighbourhood were damaged by the explosion, and the occupants had to be accommodated in a hotel. Four other similar blocks were scheduled to be razed in the course of the following month. The interest and amortization charges, the main element in the costs of building the dwellings, still had to be met for decades ahead.[31]

From his back garden Colin Dumbell looks at the scene of desolation with an expert eye, Road writes, for in 1975 as a 14-year-old Colin had vandalized similar property—dwellings which had not been built when he was born. 'I bunked off from school for two years. I was never getting taught nothing anyway.'[32] Road's article is illustrated with a photograph of a three-storey block containing dozens of such flats, with all their windows broken and their roofs stripped. A 14-year-old boy grins out of a broken window. He is holding a hammer. Building debris and rubbish lies everywhere. In Kirkby only the vandalism is memorable, writes Road, and vandalism, like the Biblical plague, afflicts one home in seven.

Theft and vandalism on construction sites meant that the community's organized efforts to stem the tide of destruction were sabotaged. A foreman of a firm of contractors brought in to repair some of the damage caused by vandalism in Tower Hill, Kirkby said to Alan Road, 'It's not a job. It's a war.'

Another photograph shows barricaded shops.

In Kirkby's main shopping precinct the eight padlocks that secure the shutters of the True Form shoe shop are opened. The steel shutter of the Abbey Building Society are raised. The pubs look like blockhouses, an impression only fortified by the barbed wire round their roofs and the blocked-up windows. In many parts of the town the steel shutters are never taken down and retail business carries on by artificial light.

Shortage of shops is at least partly the result of retailers giving up and leaving the estates to their own devices because of the theft and destruction they have suffered in their trying to earn a living as a shopkeeper.

There is a swimming baths in the middle of the town. Knowsley has the biggest sports' centre in the North West. There are eight youth clubs.

At one voluntary youth club in a new building opened only ten years before by Harold Wilson, thefts were 'an almost nightly occurrence'. £1,000 of worth of disco equipment donated by a Merseyside millionaire was stolen after only two nights.[33] 'We won a silver cup for cross-country running. Even that got nicked.'

It was 'reliably estimated', Road writes, that the unemployment rate in Kirkby in 1979 was 25 per cent, twice the Merseyside rate. 'Despite the lack of work, there seems no shortage of customers with cash to spend in the town's numerous pubs and clubs at lunch time or in the evenings.' This response to unemployment, apparently, is what the Germans came to call the '*Liverpoolized*' response, for this is the term used by the chief of the Labour Office in Bremerhaven when he was explaining to an English reporter why the town had not 'fallen apart' in the face of its economic difficulties.[34]

Alan Road interviewed some members of the Kirkby clerisy (in Coleridge's sense, the people put in an area to uphold the highest possible standard of culture there).[35]

What Road describes as 'a church leader' said, 'Selling stuff that is stolen is part of factory life and club routine.' Either the same church leader or another one (it is not clear from Road's report) said, 'We must disentangle what is Christian from what is middle class'. The people of Kirkby were 'short on corporate responsibility', but they were strong on 'personal morality'. 'It's crimes against property—vandalism, theft and driving away cars—that bedevil Kirkby, and in a society that values property above life, it's no wonder we get shocking headlines.' Another church leader, who had been in Kirkby during virtually the whole of its existence, 13 years, pleaded for 'a sense of proportion', and admitted to a 'certain sympathy' with the youngsters who regarded Kirkby's wrecked dwellings 'a vast adventure playground'. 'It's children playing that we're talking about. ... If you go to Los Angeles you find a drugs problem. If you go to New

York, a murder problem. And if you come to Kirkby you have a vandalism problem.'

Rowntree highlights political extremism. By political extremism I assume the Report means the phenomenon of private individuals and groups turning to righteous violence (in the narrow and strict sense of the term *self*-righteous violence) without a mandate, or with an insufficient mandate. Because they cannot get their way without violence, they assume the right to define for themselves when violence should be used, at what level, and directed at what 'targets', in the interests of their own definition of 'social justice'.

Rowntree gives primacy to poverty and unemployment in the growth of political extremism. If its theory is valid, then political extremism must have been a phenomenon *concentrated* in the period 1979-92, a period within which—according to its 1995 Report—the rise of unemployment, absolute poverty and relative poverty were *concentrated*.

But that was far from being the case. Private violence had hardly been known in England since 'physical force' Chartism fizzled out in the 1850s. But it was in the late 1960s and the early 1970s, not in the 1979-92 period, that it re-emerged and grew rapidly. A turning point of some symbolic significance in the development of British society was the change in policing style, not during the miners' strike of 1984-85, but nearly eight years before, in August 1977. After several years of growing disorder, on the occasion of the confrontation between the Socialist Workers' Party and the National Front at Lewisham the British police came equipped for the first time with special riot equipment—perspex riot shields. Dustbin lids for protection had had their day—before 1979.[36] By the late 1960s 'radical chic', to use Tom Wolfe's lively phrase, was well established among the cultural élites of the United States. Support was given to emerging movements advocating, glorifying or carrying out acts of private violence, as well as to the jokey techniques of nevertheless serious disruption catalogued by Saul Alinksy.[37] Radical chic crossed the Atlantic long before 1979.

Yet the 1960s and the early 1970s was a period during which absolute poverty had been falling, the gap between the rich and poor was narrowing, and unemployment was extremely low. It slipped the Rowntree Inquiry Group's collective mind, apparently, that its own data have the effect of totally discrediting its own theory of social causation.

The origin of the growth in private righteous violence in Britain lay not only or even mainly in the changing *economic* conditions of 1979-92, but in the changing *cultural* conditions of *both* 1961-79 *and* 1979-92.

The first reports on British society did not appear with the first Rowntree Foundation grant, and competent social science was accomplished before, as well as when, the present generation of Rowntree researchers began their work.

Commentators who push the problem presented by the 1961-79 data onto changes in *recording* 1961-79, asserting or requiring for their theory that by 1979 the records had simply been brought into correspondence with reality for the first time, can thus be satisfied that their theory is intact only if they induce in the general population historical amnesia, and if they themselves either suffer from it or feign it.

The implausibility of Rowntree's theory is already apparent. For if they are correct that the 1979-92 *rise* in burglary, robbery, arson, hooliganism, and political and non-political violence was due to *rising* poverty and high unemployment, then crime and disorder could not have *risen* to the 1979 levels during the previous period of *falling* poverty and low unemployment 1961-79. But if Rowntree's theory of the intimate connection between poverty and unemployment on the one hand, and crime and disorder on the other is correct, then during the period of *falling* poverty 1961-79, crime and disorder must have been actually *falling* 1961-79, and they must therefore actually have been *more* prevalent in 1961 than they were in 1979. As the next chapter shows, crime and disorder were certainly *not* worse in 1961 than they were 1979.

4

The Evidence from the Nineteen-Fifties and Early Nineteen-Sixties

T he Rowntree Report's theory is that poverty and unemployment are principal causes of social disorder and self-destructive lifestyles. According to the Report, the period 1979-92 is a clear demonstration of the theory's validity. As poverty and unemployment worsened, so does decency in civil life.

As earlier chapters have explained, *according to the Rowntree theory*, crime and other manifestations of incivility could not have *risen* during the period 1961-79, because most of these years were characterized by *falling* poverty and *low* unemployment. The only way to save the Rowntree theory is for Rowntree to prove that the rise in crime and so forth took place only in the period 1979-92; and for Rowntree to prove also that, in accordance with requirements of its theory, no rise in crime took place 1961-79. Indeed, if the Rowntree theory is to survive, crime must have actually *fallen* 1961-79, in line with very low unemployment and falling poverty of the period, as compared with the 1930s. The Rowntree theory requires, therefore, that the rise in crime shown in the statistics 1961-79 could only have been an effect of 'moral panic', not of any real increase.

The poverty lobby tends to scorn the criminal statistics. It prefers to have its own opinion on what the facts about crime and disorder were in the past. That makes it much easier to make their 'facts' fit their theory. If the statistics are not to be used, what alternative sources of information allow them to say that the statistical rise in crime 1961-79 did not happen? The answer is, none.

The evidence of all reports points in only one direction, and that is away from the assumptions and conclusions of the

Rowntree Report. All reports indicate that crime and other types of incivility were much less of a problem in 1961 and before than they had become by 1979.

A large number of studies of working-class life were published in the 1950s and early 1960s. Sociology was just expanding from very small beginnings. Many of the new sociologists, the majority from the London School of Economics, were from working-class homes.[1] The most able of them, A.H. Halsey, whose father was a railwayman in Kentish Town, became Professor of Sociology and Social Administration at Oxford. Tom Lupton and Duncan Mitchell studied a housing estate in Liverpool.[2] Cyril Smith (who became Secretary to the Social Science Research Council) studied an estate in Sheffield.[3] With Cliff Slaughter, a Communist then and an active and famous life-long Trotskyist since, I studied a coal mining town in West Yorkshire.[4] Peter Collison studied Cutteslowe in Oxford.[5] John Mogey (who became Professor of Sociology at Boston University, Massachusetts) compared St Ebbes with Barton.[6] Ray Morris and John Mogey studied Berinsfield.[7] With Joe Scarrott's help, H.E. Bracey studied council and private housing estates in south Gloucestershire.[8] Josephine Klein reviewed some of these studies in order to construct a picture of English cultural, especially English working-class, life and to fathom out how it and its varieties were reproduced.[9] Michael Young and Peter Willmott from the independent direction of the Institute of Community Studies produced the most read work of them all, the comparison of the old life in Bethnal Green with the new life in Debden.[10] Madeline Kerr's study of a semi-slum area of Liverpool she called Ship Street is the story of the narrow, frustrated lives of people unable to cope with the complexities of the modern city; it is not a description of vicious attacks upon its fabric and public amenities.[11]

None of these first-hand and contemporary studies reports significant problems of theft, criminal damage, vandalism, hooliganism or alcohol or other drug use except cigarettes.[12] To the reader in 1979, no less than to the reader in the mid-1990s, the most striking thing would have been the utter lack of interest in nearly all these reports of the 'bad behaviour' of young people as a social issue, even in those sections where children and young people are especially dealt with.[13]

Leo Kuper's study of the Braydon Road neighbourhood unit and Houghton estate at Coventry may be taken as typical.[14] There is no mention of lone parenthood, vandalism or crime. The study makes an approach to these matters only in its description of the eight of Braydon Road's ninety families who showed 'extreme neglect of home and personal appearance' and who were 'indifferent to refinement of speech' (they used tabooed words in inappropriate company). (One informant did use the phrase 'hooligan element' to describe them, but there is no suggestion of hooliganism as it is understood today.)

The housing estate of Houghton was a mixed working-class district. The worst that was said of the 'lower set' was that it was composed of the 'noisier, rougher, don't care' families. The others were the 'quieter, honest-to-goodness, help-your-neighbour and help-yourself' element.[15] As in the other studies from the early 1950s which did not specifically concentrate on a 'delinquency area', there is no suggestion of a serious criminal element. The smaller lower 'rough' class is composed of the jollier, more neighbourly, less careful husbands, wives and their children. The larger respectable element is less neighbourly, 'standoffish', anxious to keep up appearances and see that their children do not get into the company of the rough children with their strong Midlands' accents.

The 'problems' of the housing estate, therefore, seem very unproblematical today. Unlike in the old terraced streets with the water closets in the high-walled back yards, 'the close proximity of side neighbours may affect the enjoyment of the amenities of the downstairs water-closet'.

'It's embarrassing for women when men are in the next garden.'

'I may only be going to clean the w.c. or wash it, but its all the same to them. For all they know I may be going to the toilet.'[16]

In the new houses there sometimes could be a problem of hearing the neighbours. Informants mentioned the wireless, the baby crying at night, and coughing.

In the worst case,

'You can even hear them use the pot; that's how bad it is. It's terrible.'

But there was 'active adjustment between neighbours'. Hints were dropped, people turned down the wireless, did something to quieten embarrassing sounds. And many who were aware of the 'vicinal noises' did not complain of them. This forbearance, Kuper says is 'an expression of British fortitude, of the "we can take it" spirit'.[17]

In his 313 page survey of these studies, Ronald Frankenberg makes only two references to illegitimacy. It is quite clear that does not mean principally children born out of marriage, but children conceived out of marriage. One of the references is to 'illegitimacy' in Llanfihangel, in this context:

> The chapels frown on drinking and above all on sexual immorality. In practice this moral disapproval is selective. ... It is selective in that 'illegitimacy', while not approved, is nevertheless not strongly condemned or sanctioned.

The word illegitimacy, given in quotation marks in the original, clearly means fornication among the unmarried, which ends in marriage if there is a child.

There is no discussion of crime, delinquency, or vandalism or any of its synonyms. The main discussion of the misbehaviour of young men refers to the fact that they enjoy 'considerable licence' and thirty or forty of them actually 'gather each evening for horse-play, joking, and perhaps drinks'. The girls, however, 'are more closely surveyed'. Their worst conduct is described in connection with the way in which they *uphold* the permitted sexual, and the strict family code of their community. Fornication is permitted between appropriate marriage partners. But when a widow was visited by a young lad, the young men gathered round her house every time he was there, 'stopping up the chimney and throwing dead vermin and other noxious objects in through the doors and windows'. (This indicates that the windows were open, and the doors were not locked.) In another district a married man who was 'associating with another woman' was met by a crowd of youths, plastered with cow dung and thrown in the river for his misdemeanour.[18] Dead vermin and cow dung are far from pleasant, but they break no heads.

Having no premonition of what lay in the near future, Frankenberg had not—could not have had—any conception of the importance of his own casual descriptions *and omissions* as a record of what Britain was like up to the 1950s.

John Barron Mays, the Warden of the University Settlement, studied 80 boys growing up in a slum area of central Liverpool with 'a long history of poverty, neglect and exploitation', a sordid area that 'shows few signs of becoming less sordid'.

But, being socialized to be sensitive to such sanctions, the delinquent boys, Mays writes, 'will respond to the ordinary methods of treatment in the way of punishment and disapproval'. Being socialized to be law-abiding, the delinquents 'more or less quickly become aware of the consequences of their actions both for those they injure and for themselves'. They therefore 'learn to adjust their actions to the minimum moral demands of the law'.

If, in the remote future, delinquency did come to be treated as 'normal' (to Mays in 1954, a cloud no bigger than a man's hand) then the seeping away of ethical standards in the young and the perpetuation of anti-social and self-destructive behaviour would render of no avail even the most spectacular improvements in the urban environment. Mays insists that the differential adjustment to these common sordid conditions means that a wise policy will attempt to deal with the other source of delinquency, 'that is to say, at the level of family relationships'.[19]

But the more the source of delinquency in nineteenth-century slum housing was dammed, the more severely the existing dam on non-family procreation and childrearing relationships was breached. That explains the apparent paradox of improved material conditions and deteriorating social behaviour.

A few years later Cyril Smith did consider the growing problems of law and order in the early 1960s, when the crime rate was moving up quickly, but when no one had any conception of how steeply and continuously it would to rise through the years in which the standard of living of the poor in both absolute and relative terms also rose more or less continuously and unemployment remained low.

Cyril Smith's final thought is that 'the forces making for law and order in Britain are far stronger, and more enduring, than any passing fashions in youth culture'.

> Gather a few Britishers together in a completely novel situation and in less than no time they will have evolved some workable but unwritten rules to govern relationships in the community. This deep-seated respect for law and order which lies at the back of the genius is still successfully transmitted to the young today.

He explains the 'conformity of the young' by saying that these traditions depended partly on their being maintained by the great institutions of the state. But they were, too, 'very much alive in the ordinary affairs of the family'. English young people, he wrote, were overwhelmingly co-operative and law-abiding partly because of the past: these traits have been instilled into them by their elders, from parents to bus conductors. But it is also 'a self-interested response to the opportunities that lie ahead of them in the future'.[20] These were not opportunities that held no challenges for them. How could the notion have arisen among the young in a country that had been plunged into two world wars, the second of which on all objective criteria it was bound to lose after the defeated British army had been evacuated from France just a few years before, that an opportunity was the same as a guarantee; that if the rewards were uncertain, the position was hopeless?

Even if the statistics are ignored, on this and all other evidence there was a profound change in English civility between 1961 and 1979, when the standard of living of the poorest was improving absolutely and relatively and unemployment was low. The decline in civility merely continued into the period 1979-92.

As Smith was writing, the opportunities for the young were being dramatically expanded in new universities and the rapidly growing old ones. The standard of living continued to rise. Unemployment remained low. But 'the forces making for law and order' did not reassert themselves. The emerging culture proved stronger than prosperity; and more enduring than either respect for a common past or self-interest in a personal future.

No one denies that there were crimes. The criminal statistics were not a blank. No one denies that there were unusual concentrations of criminals in particular streets, small areas, or estates.[21] No one denies that there were from time to time dangerous criminal gangs in some of the big cities. By far the worst area for large, fully criminal and dangerous gangs running protection rackets and engaging in organized shop- and house-breaking on a large scale was inter-war Glasgow in the crowded central districts of the Gorbals, Calton and Bridgeton. James Tait was stabbed to death during a gang fight in 'the battle of Albert Bridge' in 1928. There were two more gang murders in 1945, when the problem was otherwise under control. It was the *atypicality* of such crime that made Glasgow notorious between the wars. Even so, by present day standards there were 'only' three gang deaths in twenty years. Nearly all the violence was between the gang members themselves, though the fights did greatly disturb the peace of the people in the neighbourhoods where they took place, waged as they were between the gangs with hatchets, swords and sharpened bicycle chains.

Mack says in a matter of fact way, 'In the course of the 1930s order was restored to the streets of the affected area'.

In the 1950s, the period with which we are dealing here, crime in Glasgow remained high, at about twice the average for Scotland—but both Glasgow's and Scotland's rate was *falling*, Glasgow's more rapidly than Scotland's. Crimes of personal violence known to the police fell from 869 cases in 1947 more or less steadily to 559 cases in 1954. Robberies fell more or less steadily from 313 to 117. All crimes known to the police dropped from the peak figure of 41,000 to which it had climbed in the last year of the Second World War to 26,000 in 1954.[22]

What is denied is that the impact of crime on the lives of the general working-class population reached anything like the magnitudes that accumulated after 1961.

The Angry Young Men of the 1950s were not angry because of the injustices and hardships suffered by the poor. They were angry because they believed that their parents had left them no good causes to fight for. *That* is the grievance of John Osborne's Jimmy Porter, as well as the other heroes of the London stage in that decade.[23] The young were 'rebels without a cause', like the most famous of them, James Dean, who was rebelling in the film against his father's ineffectualness in giving him guidance, and the fact that his father was tied to his mother's apron strings.

It is only the romanticism and politics of the 1960s and later that created the myth of a universally 'rough' working class (much more foul-mouthed, sexually active and sexually permissive than even the rough working class of reality). The poverty lobby was one of the creators of the myth of the 1990s, that it was a criminal one. Both myths are maintained in the only way possible: by pulling an impenetrable curtain down on the real reports of the past.

Were these first-hand researchers, some of them living as participant observers in their areas for years at a time, in a better or worse position than the present-day theorists of the poverty lobbies to say how much crime there was in the inter-war period, and in the post-war period up to 1961?

A friend of mine moved with his family to another house in Sunderland in 1945 or 1946. It had been hurriedly vacated at the beginning of the war by the butcher who owned it, who had gone to live in the country away from the expected enemy bombing. When my friend's family moved in six years later, no-one had broken in. Nothing had been disturbed in the empty house. An unbroken egg from 1939 still lay on the table.

That is not an anecdote that is out of line with the official statistics and common report; it is an anecdote that illustrates them. All the burden of proof to the contrary lies with the those who say that the statistics are useless and that common report was wrong.

Two problem housing estates of the early and mid-1950s famous in the literature at the time were Knowle West and Southmead, both in Bristol. A leading criminologist from the London School of Economics, John Spencer, obtained a grant from the Carnegie Trust to improve matters at Southmead and learn lessons that could be applied to difficult housing estates elsewhere.[24] His Bristol Social Project, as it was called, was partly based on the Chicago Social Projects[25] and on 'community work' and 'social group work' generally.[26] With Peter Kuenstler he was particularly concerned with 'unclubbable boys' and the whole movement towards 'Adventure Playgrounds'. The strongest influence on his thinking then were the projects under way at the Tavistock Institute on psycho-analytically oriented group work.[27]

The causes for alarm look very strange today. For instance, in 1955 there were 1,200 per 100,000 boys aged 10-14 convicted of crime in Bristol as a whole, but 1,600 from Southmead. (The figure for England and Wales was 1,400.) Among 15-19 year-olds the figures for both Bristol and Southmead were below the national figure. Among the 20-25 year-olds the Southmead figure was below both the national and the Bristol figure.[28] The theory was that working-class boys and youths suffered under too much discipline at school, in their homes, at work, and in their leisure associations. If they were given more freedom they would behave more responsibly. As a result, most of the behaviour that gave rise to public objection was that of the young people being given a free rein by the Bristol Social Project itself.[29]

I remember going into Bristol one day in the summer of 1956 on the top deck of a No. 2 bus with the elder sister of 'Mary Johnson'.[30] She was visiting from London. It was known, but politely ignored in the circumstances by everybody for the time being because it was situationally inappropriate for anyone to act in any way as if anyone knew anything about it, that she was a prostitute. No movement had yet started to normalize her as a 'sex worker', and to render perverse my status as a husband bound in life-long monogamy. She and her sister were just as disgusted with and just as filled with contempt for men breaking their marriage vows by the use of her services as was anyone else.

She took out a little tin of cigarette ends, broke them open and rolled the tobacco so obtained in a Rizla paper. Licking it closed, she generously offered it to me, and asked in her best respectable voice, for on that No. 2 bus we were two respectable passengers travelling together, 'Would you lake a feg?' I do not remember that I had any thoughts about the health aspects of the friendly transaction at all. I do not think I had. It was just that I did not smoke, a fact about myself that she heard with the greatest approval and with exhortations that I should never start; it was a mug's game.

The difference between the 1950s and the 1990s, not least the difference in the stance of the social-affairs intelligentsia, cannot be more strongly brought home than by contrasting Lassell's account and assessment of the Johnsons, with the account and assessment given in the *New Statesman* by the former Professor of Social Administration at the University of Bath of the lone mother and her seven children from the Easterhouse estate, Glasgow, and the other 1990s' case studies in his *Children and Crime*.[31]

In the 1970s and into the first years of the 1990s, when the 'moral-panic' school of criminology dominated in the universities and therefore in the national media (though not the local press), the great French sociologist, Emile Durkheim, was often called to the witness stand (so to speak) to testify on its behalf. His argument was that crime was 'normal' in all societies. He classified crime as a 'factor in public health', an 'integral part of all healthy societies'.[32]

He *had* argued that. But he had argued it to make exactly the opposite point to that attributed to him. He was not saying that *crime* was at the same level in all societies and at all times. He was saying that the *strength with which crime was condemned* was at about the same level in all societies and at all times.

Imagine a society of saints, a perfect cloister of exemplary individuals. Crimes, properly so called, will there be unknown; but the faults that appear venial to the layman will create there the same scandal the ordinary offence does in the ordinary consciousness. If, then, this society has the power to judge and punish, it will define these venial acts as crimes and treat them as such. For the same reason, the perfect and upright man judges his own smallest failings with a severity that the majority reserves for acts more truly in the nature of an offence.[33]

According to the view put forward by Durkheim, therefore, it was perfectly explicable that the generally extremely mild misdeeds of some of the young, and the slightly more troublesome anti-social tendencies of a handful of others, made Southmead a notoriously 'difficult estate' in 1956.[34]

But that is also why such a book as the Rowntree Foundation's *Life on a Low Income*, a follow-up to the 1995 Report, designed to put flesh on the bare bones of the statistics, so much missed the point of what was distinctive about contemporary Britain in 1996. Elaine Kempson presumably thought that she was mitigating public anxieties about the underclass by arguing that their values were then just the same as everybody else's.[35]

Viewed as a cultural crisis and not as a problem of poverty, the enormous rise in crime, riot, destructiveness and drug-taking among young people is the result of their being incapable of organizing their sexual, family and other affairs on a basis that is not unduly burdensome to other people in society. They are following the lead (not indeed in following the values, but of the dismantling of values) of the culture-making and culture-destroying élite which can organize their lives on the basis of self-fulfilment and the devil-take-the-hindmost. As Nietzsche said somewhere in somewhat more elevated diction, plebism is bad enough among the plebs; it's when it's embraced by the élites that the real trouble starts.

5

Poverty, Unemployment and Social Disorder between the Two Wars and Earlier

I dleness and aimlessness are social evils. Involuntary poverty is a social evil. Paid employment is one of the most important ways in which they are combatted. These things are not in dispute. What is in dispute is that unemployment as such is one of the main causes of the rise in crime 1979-92, as Rowntree asserts, assumes and insinuates. Unemployment *as such* is quite distinct from cultural ways (or personal ways freed from cultural content and control) of *responding* to unemployment.

During the period of post-war full employment, to which both Labour and Tory post-war governments were committed, national unemployment figures stood regularly at below two per cent. From the mid-1970s they began to rise rapidly, and reached their post-war peak of 13 per cent in 1984. In spite of the fact that the proportion of the men in their late teens seeking work was depleted by the expansion of higher education, unemployment was more prevalent among young men than it was in the general population of males.

The study of unemployment and crime by David Dickinson of the Department of Applied Economics, Cambridge, was published a month or two after the Rowntree Group was convened. His own thesis is the same as Rowntree's. Unemployment is a principal explanation for crime.[1] It is quite easy to show, however, that the data he himself supplies are fatal to his own conclusions. Dickinson shows that in mid-1988 unemployment stood at 1.8 million. It then fell to 1.3 million. In early 1991 the unemployment figure was back to 1.8 million. The crime figure he correlates with unemployment is burglary. But burglary had not followed that fall and rise at all. It had climbed more or less steadily by another 300,000. At the same level of unemployment, that is, burglary alone had climbed by 300,000 in two-and-a-half years. The figures on crime and the figures on unemployment do not correlate at all if a longer time-span than that of the mid-1970s to the 1990s is considered.

Dickinson himself shows (he has no option) that in the period 1961-79 the crime rate accelerated exponentially and smoothly, while throughout the 1960s the unemployment figures fluctuated around a level of only about two per cent. In the days of low unemployment when crime was rising it was consensual to attribute the rise to the fact that unemployment was low. It was 'obvious' that in the 1960s young men no longer needed to be well behaved or socially conformist in order to get or keep a good job. Dickinson dismisses this period as irrelevant to his thesis. He says that unemployment didn't count then because it was 'voluntary'.

What of previous periods, then, of involuntary unemployment? Dickinson does not deal with them. He does not deal with the figures on unemployment and crime in the late Victorian period, when unemployment figures first become available. Nor does he deal with the interwar period of heavy involuntary unemployment.

Sociology was for long the discipline that was interested more than others in the extraordinary capacity of human beings to act in response to what they believe to be true, as well as in response to what is true. What is more, human beings vary in their reactions to what they believe to be true (even when they share the same perceptions of the truth, however erroneous). For their responses to a 'factual' situation depend upon their moral code or lack of one. To know how a person defines his situation factually, and the assessment he makes of how he must properly respond to it, is to have sociologically understood his conduct.

Sociology emphasizes the causal importance of *the definition of the situation by those who are in a position to effectively define it.* The definition of the situation of what options are open to an unemployed young person has altered in recent years. Crime and riot have been increasingly defined by respectable society as the 'expectable' (if not the inevitable) result of unemployment. 'That is how people with no stake in society will act.'

The more that unemployment is publicly declared to be the main explanation for criminal conduct by Chairmen of the Social Security Advisory Committee, Trustees of the Baring Foundation, Directors General of the Confederation of British Industry, Economics Editors of national television networks, General Secretaries of the Trades Union Congress, Chief Executives of the Association of County Councils and others of British society's cultural leaders, the more frequently criminal conduct will result from any given level of unemployment.

Crime and other social and personal disorders among young men began their upward trend very markedly in the period of declining absolute poverty, a narrowing of the income gap between the rich and the poor, and low unemployment 1961-79. Though various important factors have added to the momentum since then, the underlying influences must be traced back thirty or forty years.

Those influences have been cultural. At bottom there has been a sea-change in the way that people perceive and handle adverse economic circumstances. Culture changed from being in all sorts of ways binding. The rules of nearly all institutional structures and informal social intercourse were quickly relaxed 1961-79; this relaxation of institutional rules merely continued 1979-92. The exception was the bureaucratically organized economy. Given the continued efficiency of the economy, relaxation could go on unhindered elsewhere. Society changed from emphasizing cultural duties, to a relatively anomic state of affairs where the claim to rights was paramount. It changed from approving the postponement of gratification; society moved in the direction of becoming a mass of consumers encouraged individually to pursue the ethic of hedonistic immediacy.

'Relative poverty', covering the job prospects of the young as well as income, housing, possessions and so forth, is therefore in an important sense an explanation of the growth of crime after 1955. But it is relative poverty understood in the context of the *definition of the situation* and how the definition of the situation has been changed by the social-affairs intelligentsia. While the economy and the political system have been generally successful in creating more private and public goods and services of higher quality and have avoided the massive employment problems of the inter-war period, the social-affairs intelligentsia has been even more successful in creating discontent.

If Rowntree's and Dickinson's theory is correct, and poverty and unemployment are principal causes of social and personal pathologies then, as compared with either the period 1961-79 or the period 1979-92, the frequency of social and personal pathologies must have been very much higher in the worsening conditions of unemployment and poverty in the 1920s and 1930s, and in a period of generally diminishing inequality, and growing relative poverty for large occupational groups and communities.

National unemployment stood at 22 per cent in 1931. In the whole of the Black Country it was 35 per cent. In Dudley in the Black Country it was 40 per cent.[2] In Sunderland the average rate of unemployment over the whole period 1927 to 1934 was 35 per cent.[3] Yet the only source of figures, the Home Office statistics, show by present day standards extremely low rates of crime in inter-war Britain, and in inter-war Dudley, Sunderland, and other places like them. The inter-war crime statistics, even more decisively than the 1961-79 figures, do not suit the Rowntree hypothesis. Let us forget the last chapter, and let us accept for the purposes of argument Rowntree's necessary assumption that the rise in the 1961-79 official crime-figures was an artifact of 'moral panic' and did not reflect any real rise in crime. Let us grant still more to the adherents of the 'moral-panic' school, and with them reject the inter-war and nineteenth century official crime figures as useless. Even on those two assumptions, the Rowntree theory of the connection between poverty and crime is in no better condition. For there is *no* evidence, from *any* source, that suggests in the slightest degree that crime, vandalism and riot in Britain in the 1920s and 1930s (and, with the exception of nicotine, increasing drug use) was anything like the problem they are today.

In the 1920s and 1930s (not to speak of periods in the nineteenth century) unemployment was higher and increasing, poverty was lower and deepening, the gap between the poor was wider than it was 1979-92, and not (to say the least) perceptibly diminishing.

It is not disputed that, at any given level of the propensity to engage in anti-social and self-destructive activities, poverty and unemployment have a tendency to raise those figures. But crime and other expressions of social and personal disorder are not the inevitable ways in which poverty and unemployment will be handled. Countervailing forces can be already strongly in operation and prevent them rising, or countervailing forces can be activated to direct frustration into constructive channels.

The Pilgrim Trust carried out a study of men who had been unemployed for at least as long as the twelve months from November 1935 to November 1936.[4] Nationally the long-term unemployed—continuously unemployed for a year or more—constituted about 20 per cent of all the unemployed at that time. The interest of the Pilgrim Trust's report to readers sixty years later lies in the relatively small sections where cultural and individualized *responses* to the fact of long-term unemployment and poor employment prospects are discussed.

In Deptford, London, the long-term unemployed were, the Pilgrim Trust report said, so many isolated individuals. They coped with their problems with hope or despair, to the degree that the dilute general culture had been successful or not in preparing them to respond constructively to their difficult circumstances.

By contrast, in both Liverpool and the coal-mining valleys of the Rhondda, South Wales, local cultures provided strong definitions of what the appropriate responses to unemployment were, and institutional structures capable of supplying the appropriate motivations. But those two local cultures were different from one another.

Economically, Liverpool was in a comparatively favourable position. There, the long-term unemployed percentage was about the national average, 20 per cent. In the Rhondda the long-term unemployed constituted no less than 63 per cent of all the unemployed. The seriousness of the economic situation in the 1930s is indicated obliquely by the Pilgrim Trust's favourable comment on the city's economy, that 'at no moment, indeed, even during the crisis, was there a danger of Liverpool becoming a derelict community'.[5] The implication was, that *economic* dereliction was the experience of other inter-war communities. The long-term unemployed constituted only three per cent of the whole of Liverpool's labour force. They constituted 25 per cent of the whole labour force of the Rhondda.

The number of Liverpool's long-term unemployed, 10,300, was similar to the number of the Rhondda's, 11,000, and they were residentially concentrated in the working-class districts of inner Liverpool:

and must therefore, be considered as a mass ... with mass phenomena and community values such as the unemployed community of the Rhondda has.[6]

The proportion of the under-35s among the long-term unemployed was also about the same in Liverpool as in the Rhondda. Of the six towns studied, Liverpool had the highest proportion, 35 per cent, and the Rhondda the next highest, 28 per cent.[7]

But in Liverpool, according to the Pilgrim Trust, the younger men dominated the culture of unemployment. In the Rhondda it was 'the family man of 40 or the widower of 60'. In Liverpool:

the existence of large gangs of young men, fairly stable in their membership (for a short casual job is not always a real interruption of long unemployment), together with the provision of special institutions for the young unemployed men, make it easier for the young unemployed to evolve both an individual and communal pattern of life suited to *his* unemployment.[8]

The Pilgrim Trust does not deal with crime, riot or drug abuse in this community. By the standards of 1961-79 and 1979-92 the communal pattern of life suited to the younger men among the long-term unemployed looks positively benign. It was, according to the Pilgrim Trust, 'easy-going and sociable'. The unemployed man had 'his corner, his friends, his library, and his bookmaker'. But applying the culture-bound canon of good and sensible behaviour in the face of long-term unemployment, and as compared with the adjustment of the long-term unemployed in the worse affected mining and weaving towns it studied, the Pilgrim Trust saw fit to append to this description of Liverpool the word 'sordid'. In providing a family home 'not much is spent on rent and next to nothing on upkeep'.

Figures descriptive of home management, family relations, domestic standards, state of furniture among the Liverpool unemployed, distinguish them clearly from the unemployed in the other five places.[9]

One of the principal causes of this, the Pilgrim Trust says, is that the long-term unemployed man in Liverpool 'lacks what is one of the main resistants to deterioration', a good home and family life. As between the English, the Irish and other immigrant elements, it appeared to be the English worker 'whose domestic life gave way under the strain of this environment.'[10]

Almost the worst that the Pilgrim Trust found to say about the life of the long-term unemployed in Liverpool was that it was strongly oriented towards gambling and football. Football rowdyism, to the extent that it existed, was not important enough to receive a mention. The all-pervading atmosphere of football pools, betting and horses was more conspicuous in Liverpool than elsewhere, says the Pilgrim Trust. The fault of these activities was not so much that they were harmful in themselves. It was that they were frivolous, and over-indulgence in them blocked the way to more constructive activities. It had become such an important local environmental factor, says the Pilgrim Trust, that for the individual unemployed man it was a culturally unassisted effort for him, a matter of exceptional personal character, to develop interests unconnected with them. The extent to which the whole lives of so many of the Liverpool unemployed centred around the pools had to be seen to be believed.[11] There is a world of difference in this kind of sporting interest for the unemployed, says the Pilgrim Trust, and the people of the Rhondda turning out to the last man to welcome Tommy Farr, so nearly heavyweight boxing champion of the world in his fight with Joe Louis, 'with flags and posters and civic honours'.[12]

In County Durham, even more than in South Wales, there was, the Pilgrim Trust observed, 'a sturdy refusal to give up'. 'The Durham miner who has been out of work for five years has not a perpetual sense of grievance, but rather—though he is actually rather poorer than the unemployed man is South Wales—a determination to make the best of things.'[13]

In the second half of the nineteenth century the cycle of economic boom and slump was much more severe than since the 1939-45 War, including the Rowntree period 1979-92. Poverty was indescribably worse than it was in the period 1961-79 or the period 1979-92. But crime actually declined at the end of the nineteenth century. When the population was 20 million in 1861 there were 88,500 crimes recorded. In 1901, when the population was 32 million, only 81,000 crimes were recorded. The text of the 1901 criminal statistics volume goes far beyond the figures and characterizes the advances in civility that had been made in the previous decades in these terms:

> We have witnessed a great change in manners: the substitution of words without blows for blows without words; and approximation in the manners of the different classes; and a decline in the spirit of lawlessness.[14]

In saying this, the author was simply stating the obvious. The greatest economist of his day, Alfred Marshall, observed that the skilled workmen were becoming more courteous, gentle and thoughtful. They were 'steadily becoming gentlemen'.[15] One of the greatest historians of the time, Arnold Toynbee, spoke of the very great moral advances generally in the manufacturing areas, manifested 'in temperance, in orderly behaviour, in personal appearance' and in the diminution in foul language.[16] Beatrice Webb said that the working-class people of Bacup, Lancashire, were 'more refined in their motives and feelings than the majority of the money-getting and money-inheriting classes'.[17]

The crime figures rose after the 1914-18 War, but by present-day standards by negligible amounts. In the five-year period 1920-24 the annual average of serious offences known to the police was 106,800. It was 127,600 in the period 1925-29, 195,000 in the period 1930-34, and 267,300 in the period 1935-39. That is, the number of crimes recorded by the police at the end of the *twenty-year* period was only 160,500 higher than it had been at the beginning of the twenty-year period. Throughout the 1960s and 1970s, not to speak of the 1980s and early 1990s, an *annual* increase of 160,500 crimes would have been regarded as utterly trivial.

A striking feature of many of the statistics that deal with crime in the period before the 1914-18 War and during the inter-war years is the small numbers involved. The numbers fluctuated year by year. During the inter-war period 1920-38, the best year was 1927 (110 robberies) and the worst year was 1932 (342 robberies). Fifty years later the whole period 1970-90 was one almost entirely of steady increase. In 1970 there were about 6,000 robberies. In 1980 there were about 15,000 robberies. In 1990 there were about 36,000 robberies.[18]

208 robberies in the whole of England and Wales, then, in 1931, when the unemployment rate was 21 per cent; 36,000 robberies in 1990, when the unemployment rate was 5.5 per cent.[19]

It makes very little difference to the argument if one assumes that the 5.5 per cent unemployment is 'really' as high as one wants to imagine. Let us say that the 'real' unemployment rate in 1990 was not 5.5 per cent, but 40 per cent.[20] If unemployment in 1990 had been 40 per cent, it would still be only twice as much as the 1931 figure. The robbery rate was 173 times the 1931 figure. In 1995-96 there were 72,275 robberies, 340 times the 1931 figure.[21]

It is the same with related phenomena regarded at the time as having to do with the 'morality' of the British. It is true that from time to time observers thought the indices of bad behaviour were rising steeply. George Dangerfield's *The Strange Death of Liberal England* is an informative as well as entertaining example of works of this kind.[22] When the figures were published showing that in 1928 there had been a total of 4,018 divorces in England and Wales, there was an uproar in all the serious broadsheets at the immorality that had spread since the end of the Great War.[23]

But when viewed against the magnitudes of the period 1961-79 and 1979-92 (the dates dealt with in the Rowntree Report), the figures measuring violations of social conduct, and failure or refusal to live up to former institutional norms, appear remarkably low and the rises in absolute numbers negligible. The total of *all* crimes recorded by the police annually at the end of the 1930s came to less than 300,000. *Violent* crimes alone in the mid-1990s came to more than 300,000. These low levels persisted in slump and boom, in the face of long-term structural unemployment as industries succumbed to foreign competition or technological obsolescence or, like the miners after 1918, in the face of cuts in real incomes and a steep fall down the wages league.[24]

The criminal statistics and other statistics give no credence to the contention (or in Rowntree's case, the necessary implication) that social disorder was as high in 1961 as it was in 1979, and higher between the wars than it was in 1961. But the stock-in-trade of the commentators who argue that crime and other expressions of social disorder did not rise until the 1979-92 period, is that the statistical record is useless.

If that were the case, then other evidence would have to be used. When other evidence is inspected, we find that contemporary and competent researchers give no credence to the contention that crime and disorder were as frequent in 1961 as in 1979 and more frequent in the inter-war period when the standard of living was far lower than in 1961, 1979 or 1992 and unemployment far higher. The implicit content of books, films, plays and popular songs give no credence to this contention.

The taken-for-grantedness of British law-abidingness between the two wars often strike one forcibly when the cultural products of the time reappear.

One of the first English films with a sound track was made with Ronald Coleman as Bulldog Drummond. Bulldog Drummond is an English gentleman bored in civvy street after the excitement of being an officer in the Great War. He advertises in the press for any adventurous and dangerous commission. He chooses the message he receives from what was called in those days a damsel in distress, and goes to meet her at midnight at a hotel in Godalming. It turns out that she is *American*. She tells Bulldog Drummond that her father is being kept against his consent in the big house up the hill. He looks at her incredulously. 'This is England, not the United States. Such things do not happen here.' But she persuades him she is serious, so we have a film to watch.[25]

A standard and admired book on education at the London School of Economics after the 1939-45 War was Lowndes' *The Silent Social Revolution*, which dealt with the success or failure since 1895 of the system of universal and by then free and compulsory education in the work of making slum children useful and civilized. The results, he wrote, had 'triumphantly vindicated' the elementary schools in the way they had prepared 'English men and women' for their life's work. In 1895 Senior Chief Inspector Sharpe had written of the teachers in London's elementary schools who were teaching those who would be adults in the 1920s and 1930s: 'Of one thing I am sure, that so far as their teaching goes, it is thoroughly intelligent and practical'.[26]

Students radical for their time, and some of them by then educated in those very same elementary schools in the slums (not, on that account, slum elementary schools) and whose older relatives, siblings, cousins, former neighbours and friends in working-class jobs had been educated in the same schools, did not find those assessments at all extraordinary.

G.D.H. Cole, a leading historian of the Labour movement in his lifetime, said this about unemployment in the mid-1930s:

The worst areas were a great belt across industrial Scotland, the whole area of the North-east coast, and practically all of South Wales. There were other isolated areas of extreme wretchedness ... In these places not only were there were men who had never worked for years, *there was good reason to believe that they would never work again.* Pit after pit was closed, shipyard after shipyard, factory after factory ... The effects of idleness, poverty and the 'dole' as the sole source of income alarmed every grade of social worker from archbishops downwards.[27]

As there was little or no work in the area, then there was little or no work waiting for boys coming out of the schools or for youths who had already left. Cole says that in such circumstances anger was bound to break out. In 1919 there had been 'almost pitched battles' between the police and strikers in Glasgow. There was unrest in the army, and five men were killed in a riot at Kimmel Park, where the Red Flag had been raised (the faintest echo of what was happening in Germany and elsewhere in Europe and Russia at the time). In 1921 unemployment demonstrators were batoned by the police at Dundee and Sunderland. Cole says that the violence of the army unrest 'looked like' being repeated in civilian life, but apart from Glasgow the only violence came from the police. Of the hunger marchers at that time Cole says that they

were never violent: they paraded in military formation, it is true, and in considerable numbers, but they wrecked no buildings and seized no food; their banners were as often Union Jacks as Red Flags; as a marching song they preferred, for both sentiments and tune, 'Colonel Bogey' to the 'International'.[28]

The form in which that anger at unemployment and poverty was expressed in the 1930s was attempts to 'ginger up' the Labour movement (as Cole puts it) with a campaign for a united front of Labour, the Socialist League, the Independent Labour Party and the Communists. 'Not an inconsiderable number of the most active workers in the provinces wondered whether they would be better advised to quit their old-established organizations and work for this new programme'.[29]

Cole does not record crime, riot, vandalism, school arson or drug-taking as having occurred anywhere in the 1930s to any extent worth mentioning, nor does he record that any Archbishop suggested that these would have been understandable, much less that they would be necessary reactions in the circumstances.

These facts are quite separate from the issue of whether it was a good thing or a bad thing that the English working class was in the inter-war period so docile, or so subservient, or so servile and unrevolutionary in the face of the mass unemployment it experienced.

Social surveys continued into the inter-war period the nineteenth-century tradition and Edwardian tradition of poverty surveys, and surveys of bad housing, disease and so on.[30] Monographs on subjects that necessarily deal with the urban neighbourhood also provide information on inter-war England.

The account by Innes Pearse and Lucy Crocker of the pioneering health centre in an inner-city London borough throughout the inter-war period from 1926, set up to deal with the problems of ordinary people in the area, has no entry in its eight page index under 'crime', 'illegitimacy', 'riot', 'destructiveness' or any of their synonyms, and they are issues nowhere in the text. There are two under 'promiscuity' ('a biologically dangerous procedure', whether casual, or deliberate as in trial marriage, which is 'liable to confuse the developing specificity of each partner'). Sexual adjustment between married couples was a problem: there are eleven entries under 'sex' and 'sex education'. What Pearce and Crocker take for granted as the ideal to which most people were aspiring, even if the could not all attain it, was 'the family working through a living and growing home. ... Family by family, each thus inhabiting its protean home, makes its way among its neighbours, encountering all, acknowledging all, welcoming where it wishes. ... As each family grows, so its society grows with it'.[31]

In the 1930s surveys began to be produced also on the problems of adjustment of slum-cleared families who had been rehoused and other families moving to new areas. Young studied Becontree and Dagenham.[32] Ruth Durant (Ruth Glass) studied Watling.[33] Other studies were undertaken soon after the war.[34]

Most of studies show no interest in crimes, riots, hooliganism, vandalism or drugs, and at best they are the subject of a passing mention with no indication they are regarded as a serious matter by residents. Alcohol consumption had been diminishing throughout the latter part of the nineteenth century and the twentieth century to that time.

The poverty lobby reiterates that poverty (in one ingeniously devised sense or another) equals crime, riot and so forth (as counted in ways that make the equation plausible to the general public). Poverty, according to the poverty lobby, is not to be eradicated or mitigated only for its own sake. It has to be eradicated *because it is the cause of vandalism, hooliganism, crime and drug abuse.*

In the inter-war period as compared with 1979-92 there were higher levels of poverty however defined in material terms. There was a wide gap between the rich and the poor, the diminution of which could be scarcely perceptible to the ordinary family (and that diminution was not pressed upon the attention of the working class by the radical academic élite at that time—quite the contrary). There was a widening gap in the working-class population between those rehoused on the new estates and in the new towns and those who were left behind in the nineteenth century streets. If the poverty lobby is to be believed on this point, then crime, riot, and the abuse of strongly intoxicating substances must have been at least at the same level as in 1979 (when according to present poverty-lobby theory the real rise in crime began), *but none of these researchers noticed the high level of crime and so forth, and nobody pointed out that they had not noticed.* The sheer nakedness of the poverty lobby's case, supposedly attired in all the finery of social science, spun, woven, cut and sewn in York, needs only to be pointed out for the bemused spectators to collapse into gales of relieved laughter.

6

No Stake in Society

R owntree pleads that poverty be ameliorated, training provided, and able-bodied young men earn at least their own living. Those objectives are almost entirely uncontroversial. Controversy rages over the constructive ways in which they can be accomplished without causing more harm than good.

But Rowntree does not only say that. Its case is that it is because of poverty and conditions of low-paid, short-term and insecure work, that all or part of a substantial minority of the population is 'becoming excluded from the mainstream'. They are opting to remain on benefits and not work. Or they are working but not declaring their income. Or they are 'acting illegally' in other ways.[1]

This opting not to work and acting illegally, too, if not undisputed, is widely accepted as probably true. The disparity between the spending power of the bottom ten per cent and the income of the bottom ten per cent strongly suggests that undeclared income, and income from 'acting illegally' in other ways, are factors in the standard of living of some families in the bottom tenth. What *can* be strongly queried on social policy as strongly as on factual grounds is the reason Rowntree gives for their opting not to work; opting not to declare income; opting to represent themselves as separate households in order to maximize benefits from the state while *de facto* pooling their resources in the dwelling of the woman; opting to act illegally through riot, drug taking, theft, and random destructiveness.

Since 1982 their cash income guaranteed by the state has been protected only against inflation, instead of rising in line with earnings. For this reason, among others, 'They have little or no stake in the prosperity of the country'. Rowntree does not say

72

that it is this substantial minority's erroneous *perception* that they have no stake in the prosperity of the country. It says they *have* no stake in the prosperity of the country.[2]

It is implied that, that being true, no one can complain of their conduct. Without any stake in 'what is going on' (as Rowntree puts it) young people see their own localities as places to be 'ignored, vilified and vandalized'.[3] They owe neither work, nor allegiance, nor honesty. Indifference to their fate on the one side, riots, drugs, crime, political extremism, destructiveness, loutishness on the other.

Rowntree does not find it sufficient to say (much less demonstrate) that the criminal, gratuitously destructive and riotous boys and youths are poor. They do not simply say that they are poorer than previous generations of young men; or that, although they are richer than previous generations of young men, they see other people richer still. They do not find it sufficient to say (much less demonstrate) that the riotous, drug-taking and criminal boys and youths lack skills; or that it is objectively more difficult for them to acquire skills than it was for their predecessors. They do not say simply that, in industry and the services, there are so few unskilled jobs that there is a hard core of young men who have not the ability ever to acquire a marketable level of skill; that it pays no employer to have them on his workforce. All of these already either are cause for general concern, or are subjects that investigation might succeed in showing that they ought to be cause for public concern. For Rowntree adds an altogether stronger statement. It says that young men 'in recent years' have been rioting, taking drugs and committing crimes because they have 'no stake' in society; they have 'no stake' in the economy for which they have no skills that the economy wants to use.

This is the point from the Rowntree Report 1995 highlighted a year later by another Rowntree Foundation publication, Elaine Kempson's *Life on a Low Income*, even though her language is more guarded. The Rowntree Report 1995, writes Kempson, 'identified the dangers of social dislocation if such a large section of the population continued to be denied a stake in national prosperity'.[4]

The Rowntree version of the facts and its researchers' interpretation of them are routinely endorsed by the social-affairs intelligentsia. In itself it would be of no significance that someone who had undertaken 'research of tough council estates' should then report that 'nobody' had a job, and that it was 'impossible' for anyone to 'survive' on state welfare benefits. What is significant is that in this age of satire such a statement should be made by an 'award-winning film-maker', that it should be reported seriously in *The Times*, and that it should be the basis of a BBC film version of *Macbeth* in which (*The Times* tells us lest we are so dull as to miss the point) 'the parallels are emphasized'.[5]

There are young men who have 'no skills which are valued' and who have no legal income but welfare-state benefits. They constitute the potential material for riot, crime and drug abuse at contemporary levels. They have an incentive to riot. But to assume riot, crime and drugs is the only option open to people who 'have no skills that are valued' and no income from legal employment is to ignore the enormous constructive adaptations to similar and worse problems made by previous generations.

For previous generations operated in a cultural context that, for over 100 years, had far more successfully excluded riot, drugs and crime as an alternative to economic adaptation. The options of riot, drugs and crime always exerted more or less pressure on all the poor and unemployed, strongly appealed to some of them, and sometimes they were adopted.

But the options of crime, drugs, and other social and personal pathologies had not yet been introduced into the cultural and (more importantly) into the non-cultural, hyper-individualized, repertoire of boys and young men by the churches, the research foundations, the Shakespearean theatre, the serious media and the educational system. Until the 1960s there were hardly any elements in the cultural élite in this country that allowed the factual and moral situation to be defined in such a way that *childhood and youth* rioting, crime and drug-taking was even a possible reaction to, much less a necessary effect of being poor and having 'no skills that are valued'. The culturally dominant definition of the situation was that the necessary skills had to be acquired.

There are 'homeless' young men and women. There are young men and women who make nothing of the training facilities available. But it is not true even of them (much less of riotous and criminal children and youth in general on the Marsh Farms, the Ragworths, the Meadow Wells) that, just because they and their advocates in the poverty lobby say so, it is true that they have 'no stake' in the society and the economy. Society and the economy provides them with (to mention only a few things) educational facilities, accommodation and household amenities, health services, transport, water supply, household rubbish disposal, mains drainage, electricity, public libraries, leisure facilities, social workers, baked beans from Kwiksave in 1996 at 9p a tin and milk at under 25p a pint, and otherwise at least day-to-day subsistence either through the state or voluntary organizations, either directly or through their parents or guardians. They may complain about law enforcement, but they have a stake in keeping it at least as efficient and fair as it is. They would know they had a 'stake' in law enforcement as it exists in their localities and towns if they lived in many other countries of the world. They have a stake, if they did but know it, in the culture, institutions and personnel of the criminal justice system that processes them.

> A businessman ... said that he had been driven to taking direct action because a string of 30 break-ins within a year were crippling his business in Kettering, Northampton. He had lost £20,000 of stock ... 'I asked the police to protect my business, but they said they didn't have the manpower.'

Northampton Crown Court were told that Mr Rodwell and his workers had caught a Mr Love climbing through a window at the Kettering Auctions warehouse in August last year. They had tied his hands behind his back and held him captive for three hours, during which time they took him to a room and made him hand over the stock stolen in previous burglaries. Mr Rodwell then flagged down a police car. One of the policemen said, 'Well done. We have been looking for him for a year'.

Mr Love, who had 14 previous convictions for burglary and 19 for theft, admitted the August burglary. He was sentenced to 120 hours community service and was currently working in a charity shop.

The Northampton trial, however, was not to protect the man who was burgled, Mr Rodwell. It was to protect burglars like Mr Love from false imprisonment and assault at the hands of their victims. When the police had seen that Love's hands were tied and his face was bloody and swollen, they had arrested Rodwell. He and his workmen were tried because although Mr Love was caught red-handed violence had been threatened, the incident was premeditated and it was carried out by a group with a ring-leader.

Mr Rodwell, a married father with five children, had no previous convictions. He was locked up for 23 hours. He was under the strain of the impending trial and the trial itself for ten months. 'It took me seven years to build up this business. I built it up from nothing. Now a burglar has taken two shops away from me.'

As it happens, mitigating the deterrent effect on others but not removing it, the jury refused to convict either Mr Rodwell or any of the three workmen who had helped him. The estimated cost of the Rodwell trial was £230,000.[6]

For an annual fee of £4.50 any unemployed youth in Sunder-land—anyone unemployed at any age—is entitled to free swim-ming each weekday morning at the swimming baths in term time; free skating on two weekday afternoons; free squash and badminton two weekday afternoons if unbooked courts are available; free indoor tennis Monday to Friday mornings; free outdoor tennis every weekday morning in five of the city's parks; free use of bowls facilities at ten centres in the city; free use of selected items of beach hire equipment; and free entry to all the city's sports' complexes. He or she is also entitled to discounts and concessions on food purchased at the leisure complexes, on seats at the civic theatre, as well as other discounts offered by local businesses. If the unemployed person has a family, then the fee is £8.30 a year, and all the free facilities and discounts are available to all the members of the family, however many. The same facility is available for anyone receiving incapacity benefit, income support, family credit, council tax remission, or housing benefit; full-time students including members of sixth-form colleges; youth trainees; registered disabled; and old-age pensioners.

If young rioters, thieves, ram raiders, users and dealers in illegal drugs think, that because they have no skills that the economy can use, they have 'no stake' in the existing imperfect system of production, distribution and law and order—that they have 'nothing to lose but their chains'—it is either because they know no history and they know no comparative anthropology, or because someone is telling them lies. To say that even the young beggar sleeping in a shop doorway in the Strand has 'no stake' in society is mere hyperbole, factually incorrect, scientifically absurd and therefore a most insecure basis for social policy.

'Regardless of any moral arguments or feelings of altruism, everyone shares an interest in the cohesiveness of society.' It is in the interests of all, the Rowntree Report 1995 continues, 'to remove the factors that are fostering the social diseases of drugs, crime, political extremism, and social unrest'.[7] That is so. The question is, however, does the Report identify correctly what the key factors are, or point us in the right direction?

Of course receiving the lowest income, being exposed to the highest chances of unemployment or any of a variety of other handicaps and frustrations 'foster' crime, riot and drug-taking if those are culturally available options. But Rowntree's theory is that these factors do not just 'foster' riot, crime and drug-taking, but are the principal contemporary explanation for them. This assumption of principal cause and effect—there is hardly any attempt to demonstrate it—stems from universities and flows down through the Foundations. It seeps into news reports and into serious newspaper analyses; into the body language and *obita dicta* of 'impartial' TV presenters; into radio programmes; into songs; into fiction; into the pulpits; into teacher-training colleges and school rooms—and into the set definition of the situation of boys and youths who can least afford to hold it. I owe you nothing. Up yours.

Hobbes wrote that:

> civil societies are not mere meetings, but bonds, to the making whereof faith and compacts are necessary; the virtue whereof to children and fools, and the profit whereof to those who have not yet tasted the miseries that accompany its defects, is altogether unknown; whence it happens that those, who know not what society is, cannot enter it; these, because ignorant of the benefit it brings, care not for it.[8]

It would have been beyond Hobbes' imagination that intellectual life would deteriorate so far in the late twentieth century that the point of view of what he called children and fools would be put as their own by England's great and good.

7

The Consumption Levels of the Bottom Tenth of Income Receivers

Up to this point I have assumed for the purposes of argument that the only contentious issue is Rowntree's assertions about the connection between, on the one hand, any fall, absolute or relative, in the standard of living of the poorest and, on the other, disorder and self-destructive behaviour. *I have accepted so far that what Rowntree has to say about rising absolute and relative poverty 1979-92 is true.* But—avoiding Rowntree's use of this question-begging language of 'poverty', which is calculated to make its case criticism-proof—*did* the standard of living of the poorest people in Britain deteriorate between 1979 and 1992?

Rowntree shows that between 1961 and 1979 the general level of cash-incomes, as reported, rose by about one-third in real terms. The reported cash-incomes of those in the bottom tenth of the distribution rose by over a half in real terms. Thus the absolute standard of living of the bottom tenth measured by cash-income was substantially improved. The fact that their standard of living had increased by just over 50 per cent in real terms while the general standard of living had increased by 33 per cent in real terms meant that their relative standard of living 1961-79 had also considerably improved.

So far as state benefits were concerned—the safety net below which no one's income need fall—before 1982 there had been a period when state cash benefits had been tied to the rise in earnings. Over the relevant period up to 1982, when earnings rose faster than inflation, this meant a standard of living that did not fall at all in absolute terms, and at worst could only fall a little in relative terms. From 1982 state benefits were tied to the rise in prices. This meant that the absolute standard of living of people on benefits would not fall.

In the face of those facts, before 1979 (and indeed for a long time after 1979 until the widening of the gap became apparent and knowledge about it spread) commentators on poverty mentioned cash income very little. They emphasized the low standards of public services for those at the lower end of the income scale as compared with those at higher up it—the hospitals were worse for the poor, there were worse old-people's homes for the poor and so forth. 'In keeping with evolving theories of poverty', as Elizabeth Gittus said, emphasis changed to the 'social income', that is, to the 'command over resources of the *collectivity* of households living in an *area*', such as the quality of the dwellings, the state of the schools, and other 'benefits and disbenefits' *common to the locality*.[1] In the 1970s British urban sociology was almost totally colonized by followers of Manuel Castells, who put at the centre of his theory the overwhelming importance for the working and unemployed proletariat of these and other items of 'collective consumption'.[2] Since 1979 demands that more money be spent on the NHS, on education and so forth have not diminished. But these demands have been presented on behalf of the whole community, not especially those on the lowest incomes.

Gradually over the 1980s and into the 1990s, less and less was heard of the non-cash social services as an element in combatting poverty. Rowntree curtly dismisses non-cash social services in an appendix. 'People receive other kinds of benefits in kind ... These can be considerable.' Adding them, Rowntree admits, would give a 'much more' equal distribution. For the poorest tenth of households, average benefits from education and the NHS alone were estimated at over 70 per cent of their disposable cash income. The argument used by Rowntree to enable it to ignore this income as an element in the standard of living is that the needs of the poor for health services are also greater. The example that is supplied is not of the difference between a poor youth and a rich youth, the category crucial to the argument about social disorder. The example is of the money spent on 90-year-olds by the NHS. The NHS element of the 90-year-olds' social wage does not contribute to their having a higher standard of living than the fit young person upon whom less is spent. Their needs are simply greater. Characteristically, Rowntree falls out of the frying pan into the fire.[3] For poor and ill 90-year-olds, compared with their predecessors, *do* have a much higher standard of living, *as* ill and frail people, as a result of state health expenditure and the improvement in the quality of accommodation and care in old people's homes.

By the time of the Rowntree Report 1995, nearly all the attention of poverty publications was directed away from the share of the poorest in collective consumption (what in the 1970s had been heavily featured as 'the social wage'), to the fall in the cash-income, the money-in-the pocket, of those at the bottom of the income distribution. It was also directed at the widening of the cash-income gap between the bottom of the scale and the top.[4]

What is just as striking as the shift from the social wage to money-in-the-pocket is the emphasis on reported cash *income* and the neglect of cash *expenditure*. That this is purely a propaganda choice is sufficiently proven by the fact that, following B. Seebohm Rowntree's report to the effect that poverty had already been virtually abolished by the early 1950s,[5] from the very earliest days of the attempts to reinstate poverty as a major social problem it had been known that expenditure *substantially* exceeded income, and that the proportionate excess was greatest for the lowest income group. It was known that it was notable also for all other income groups except the highest. This was clearly stated in Abel-Smith and Townsend's 1965 survey, financed by the Rowntree Memorial Trust. They pointed out, indeed, that already in 1965 social scientists had been aware of this 'for many years'.[6] The Final Report on the concept of poverty to be used by the European Community decided on expenditure, not income, as the variable with which to measure and analyse poverty.[7]

The Family Expenditure Survey (FES) itself—it is clear from its title—is strong on expenditure, and much weaker on income. The FES, carried out annually since the 1950s to ensure accuracy in the weights in the calculation of the retail price index, is a survey of expenditure, and only incidently of incomes. Yet it is from the income data of the Family Expenditure Survey that much of the poverty-lobby's data are drawn. There is one simple reason for this. The income data suit its case far better than do the expenditure data.

Clearly the standard of living of households is not only a question of the level of their reported income. At least as significant, quite apart from the public benefits that are free at the point of delivery, is the actual consumption of goods and services that the household pays for. In the Rowntree Report 1995 the question of expenditure levels is raised only in a brief, dismissive discussion of under-reported incomes. Its comments on the difference between the income and the expenditure distributions, such as they are, specifically refer only to the small group reporting no income or reporting losses. As these cases constitute only 0.4 per cent of the distribution, the Report says, they can be discounted. Otherwise the Report invites its readers to assume that misreporting is the same throughout the income distribution. 'Therefore' (i.e. if that assumption is correct!), it says, the true income distribution will be similar to the expenditure distribution. The extremely weak formulation it uses to give this impression is, 'If—in the extreme case—all respondents were hiding something' the shape 'could be' unaffected.[8]

But the differences between, and the significance of the income and expenditure distributions were distinctly and clearly *not* simply a matter of this one group, the self-employed, reporting just this one tranche, zero income and negative income—four per cent of the bottom ten per cent of households, and only 0.4 per cent of all households, who could be ignored as insignificant.

For by 1992 the proportion of the bottom ten per cent of income receivers who were self-employed was not four per cent but 13 per cent. This was only four percentage points below that of the pensioners. After housing had been paid for (the measure Rowntree prefers) the proportion of the bottom tenth represented by the self-employed was five percentage points *above* the proportion of the bottom tenth represented by pensioners.[9]

Taking all those in the bottom tenth of the income distribution, not just the self-employed, their *reported income* was about *15 or 16 per cent lower* than it had been in 1979.[10] But their *average cash expenditure* was *30 per cent higher*.[11] That is, on a realistic measure of their standard of living, what they were actually buying, the absolute standard of living of the poorest tenth had not fallen. It had improved by a third. In both years, 1979 and 1992, about 50 per cent of those reporting negative income (and appearing therefore in the *bottom tenth* of the *income* distribution) appeared in the *top half* of the *expenditure* distribution.[12]

The expenditure level of households in the lowest income group in 1992 in relation to their reported income was not explicable by the fact that they had been sinking into debt significantly more than their predecessors in the group in 1979. 'Whereas about 30 per cent of the bottom income decile reported some credit expenditure in the early part of the period, this had only risen to 35 per cent by the early 1990s'.[13] For the most part, however, we have only very sketchy information on how the gap between reported income and reported expenditure *was* bridged. The use of savings was one obvious way. The contribution made by savings was not known, but the Institute of Fiscal Studies, the best source for such data, suggested that it was considerable. Contributions from relatives, in kind perhaps more than in cash, released the reported cash income for additional expenditures. The size of contributions from the 'black economy' to the bottom tenth of the distribution of income or expenditure was also an unknown quantity, though Ray Pahl's study of families on the Isle of Sheppey showed that, there at least, households without open paid work also did very little concealed paid work.[14] Also unknown were contributions from other irregular sources. Such supplementary sources of income are not, obviously, disclosed by the households concerned.

The fact remains that—in the words of Goodman and Webb—this growth in expenditure at the bottom of the income distribution is 'startling' when juxtaposed to what were supposed to be the income changes of the same group.[15]

In 1992 only about *one-third* of those who are in the bottom *income* tenth were in the bottom *expenditure* tenth. Nearly one in five of the households (19 per cent) in the *bottom tenth on income* fell into the *top half in expenditure*.[16] The Goodman and Webb figures show that in 1992 two per cent of all those in the *bottom ten per cent* of *income* recipients were actually in the *top* ten per cent of *spenders*.[17]

But the bottom tenth of the income distribution is more peculiar when its expenditures are examined than even the above figures suggest. Both in 1979 and 1992 the highest spenders in the lowest income tenth had higher expenditures than the *highest* spenders in the second-lowest income tenth. In 1979 that had not been true of the lower groups in the bottom tenth. But by 1992 this strange feature had spread throughout the expenditure figures of the whole bottom tenth: the median spenders of the lowest income group spent more in 1992 than the median spenders of the income group above them. When income and expenditure are measured after housing costs the lowest spenders of the lowest income groups, too, spent more than the lowest spenders of the income group above them. The bottom tenth of the income distribution is the only one displaying this pattern.[18]

The solution to this puzzle can be found in the change in the composition of the bottom tenth between 1979 and 1992. In 1979 the main component of the bottom tenth had been old-age pensioners. In addition to their state benefits they normally had other sources of income from post-office savings, building-society accounts and so forth. Although they were the poorest in society, they were not so poor as they would have been if they depended solely on state benefits. As Goodman and Webb point out, the composition of the bottom group of *spenders* in terms of household type remained relatively stable over the 1980s. In 1992 pensioners still comprised 40 per cent of the bottom spending group even though pensioners were by then only a small part of the bottom income group, eight per cent.[19]

In the course of the 1980s pensioners had been replaced by people who were *solely dependent on state benefits*, that is to say, never-married mothers and the young unemployed. Benefits themselves kept up with inflation and the *basic benefit* standard of living was maintained. But the new poor in the bottom tenth had no *reportable income* to supplement their benefits, unlike their predecessors, the pensioners. That is why as compared with the poor in 1979 the *income* of the bottom tenth *dropped* by 15 or 16 per cent after they had paid for their housing, even though benefits at least kept pace with inflation and prevented any fall beyond what would also have been the minimum in 1979 but for the rewards the pensioners enjoyed from their thrift.

A significant proportion (by no means all) of the new occupants of the bottom declared-income tenth had adopted a lifestyle, such as a previous anti-school mentality or unmarried motherhood, that made them poor on nothing but basic state benefits as declarable income. Old-age pensioners were now in the second-bottom instead of the bottom tenth, not because they had significantly more income than their predecessors of 1979, but because the new poor had less. But in one way or another the new poor were able to *spend* more than the old people who had been moved into the category of the second-bottom tenth on declared income. In 1979 fewer than one in three of the households in the bottom tenth of income receivers had a fridge-freezer. By the mid-1990s 84 per cent of them had one. In 1979 40 per cent of them had a car. By the mid-1990s 57 per cent had one. Very few of them indeed had the new consumer product, a video. By the mid-1990s nearly 75 per cent had one.

Late in 1990 the *Guardian* carried a report on Drumchapel, a Glasgow housing estate and 'not the worst' of them. Almost one household in three had only one parent. Why was this so? Why, says the *Guardian*, because of lack of money. 'People on benefits cannot afford romance. A single woman with children can just about manage. Woe betide her if she is caught out with a man. Her benefit will be cut because, the law says, a man must support his woman and children. However, the law also says that if a woman has a job, she must support her man.' (His woman and her man: husbands and wives must not be mentioned.)

Norrie was a married man with three daughters. He worked as a heavy-goods driver. His wife had a part-time job in a hospital kitchen. He lost his job. The strain of keeping the family on *her* tiny wage was more than his wife could take. But she refused to take 'the easy way out' of giving up her job. 'Instead she moved out, taking the girls with her, to fend for herself.' She just did not think keeping a husband was worth such a struggle. Another lone-mother household had come into existence. The *Guardian's* message was clear if subliminal. Cash was at stake. The most natural thing in the world was to prefer it to the family.

The picture that illustrates the article shows a young man called Alan. As a 17-year-old he falls into the age group that since 1988 makes him ineligible for his own state benefits except under stringent hardship rules. In effect, he must stay at home and share his parents' income—which might be entirely composed of state benefits, including benefits for his presence in the household as a dependant. The report says that he left home of his own accord after a row with his step-mother. He is now in sheltered single-person's accommodation, but still depends for food on a government-funded Young Persons' Benefit Scheme. The *Guardian's* caption tells its readers what to make of all this. 'Alan was forced to live on friends' floors and in doorways, eating from food parcels handed out by the Young People's Benefit Scheme.' Of course, given both the cultural weakness of the family—so clearly demonstrated by the language and judgements of the *Guardian*'s article—and the supreme importance of cash, Alan was 'forced' to do what he did.

A former shop steward interprets Drumchapel's problems differently, including alcohol and drug abuse. 'We don't live together', he says, 'we just self-destruct.' People at Drumchapel 'no longer identify with their partners and wains'. How could they then, he asks, identify with anyone else?[20] A part-time worker with the Young People's Benefit Scheme also focuses on the weakness of the family and the priority of cash values. Parents cannot afford to keep their older children, so they 'just throw them out'.

But the article itself inadvertently demonstrates that alternative *evaluative* environments produce different results. A woman called Anne Marie was interviewed. Her father is a bus driver. Her mother has stayed at home. But they had brought up 12 children. Every one of them had proceeded into further education. Anne Marie and her twin sister were two of the five from her Drumchapel school who went to college in her year. In 1989 her younger brother was one of just two from the Drumchapel school who were admitted to a university. The *Guardian* reporter writes, 'She could not tell me what the magic ingredient was'; and her readers, if they continue to depend on the *Guardian*, must remain forever in the dark.[21]

8

The Young Unemployed
in the Bottom Tenth

W hen B. Seebohm Rowntree carried out his second survey of poverty in York in 1935-36 he wanted to find out the *different* as well as the common factors which contributed to various households being in the lowest categories of income. Those in poverty in York were homogeneous in not having enough weekly income for subsistence; more money, sensibly spent, would ease all of their crucial subsistence problems. Sensibly spent or not, it could make a scraping life that little bit more bearable.

But they were heterogeneous in the reasons for their poverty. Unconditional money for the aged sick, whose motivation to join the labour force was quite irrelevant to the question of state benefits, was one thing. Unconditional money for the younger able-bodied was quite another. Their motivation to get up every morning of the week and be at a particular workplace at a particular time and work under strict instructions for set hours before being allowed to come home was a factor to be considered. Work had to contend with the temptation to spend their time in better ways. They could stay in bed all the morning before going to the Institute for a few free or cheap games of snooker, or gambling a few ha'pennies on 'killer' in the park, or having a game of 'brag' in an open-air card school. In a place like Sunderland there was always the pull of the sea and the sea-shore, the cliffs and the bays to compete with a day cramped among the noise and fumes of a ship's boiler under construction, or in the pitch black of the mine, taking stone- and coal-dust into your lungs with every breath.

The issue of motivation did not apply only, of course, to the existing generation of the able-bodied unemployed. It applied with perhaps even more force to the viable ways of life that would lie before children not yet of employment age. The issue of motivation applied also to the parents of future generations of children, their relatives, neighbours and school teachers, in terms of the urgency and seriousness with which they inculcated any work ethic.

When the long process of the equalization of reported cash incomes was reversed and became one of growing inequality, the poverty literature lost virtually all interest in *the flow of different people* and families or other households through the category of the lowest ten per cent.

The implication was planted that the households and individuals who were in the lowest ten per cent of the income distribution in the late 1970s were the same households and individuals who were there in the 1990s. According to the picture presented in the poverty literature, the same individuals and families who had been poor at the earlier date were not only still poor at the later date but were actually substantially poorer. *They* had endured a further decade of poverty and *their* standard of living had fallen absolutely and in real terms by 16 per cent after their housing costs had been met. If the money spent on housing them is included as part of their income (until very recently it was automatically assumed that people bought their housing out of their income) then their income in absolute terms remained the same as in 1979. But their static incomes *as a percentage* of the rising incomes of higher groups was less—in that strained sense only had their incomes 'declined'. In the language of the poverty lobby, they had been 'deprived' of the same percentage increase as groups above them. But the particular people in the lowest income category are not the same from one year to the next, much less in 1992 as compared with 1979. Steve Webb's analysis for the Institute of Fiscal Studies showed that nearly half of the individuals whose incomes were in the lowest tenth in one year rose to a higher band in the next year.[1] A study of National Insurance records by the Department of Social Security for the years 1978-93 showed that about 75 per cent of employed men aged 25-44 in 1978 had higher earnings in 1993 than in 1978. But among the men who had been in the lowest tenth in

1978 a higher proportion than this, 90 per cent, had higher earnings in 1993.[2]

In the course of the decade the entrants to the lowest tenth were partly the self-employed. But they were partly the 'new poor'. Some were the households of unemployed young men and unemployed young women living alone. Others were the households from which fathers had excluded themselves or had never been admitted. Either they had never married the mother of their child (whether by their own, the mothers' or by mutual choice), or had been divorced in their early married life. For legal income both these groups depended much more on the minimum benefits of the welfare state than had the pensioners they replaced. For that reason and in that sense they were a poorer poorest tenth than the previous poorest tenth. It was their new dependence on the state minima that placed them there. Their bare dependence elevated their predecessors in the bottom tenth, the pensioners with their largely unchanged incomes, into the tenth above them.

Heavily represented in the new bottom tenth of income were the unemployed young men and women who had left school without qualifications. They therefore lacked skills which were sought by employers. Some of them were capable young people who were under-achievers at school, and therefore their low levels of literacy, numeracy and other skills indicated to potential employers that their attitudes towards work was suspect.

Angela Phillips provides an example of one of the new poor, Sam, a 23-year-old woman living in a council flat on the Orchard Farm estate in Hull. Her poverty, Phillips tells us, 'is not apparent'. Sam is unmarried. It seems from Phillips' account that Sam is living alone in her flat, but perhaps she is living with her child as a lone mother. She was brought up by her mother and 'a series of step-fathers' on Orchard Farm.

Five years ago Sam 'asserted her independence' by moving into a privately rented flat with her boyfriend. The boyfriend now lives and works in Bath. 'His job doesn't pay enough to support us both', Sam says. 'If I went to join him I might not like it and I would lose my flat and have to go on a lower rate of benefit.' Sam has never had much money. 'But then nor has anybody else. We are all in the same boat so it doesn't really matter. We hardly spend any money on food ... We eat a lot of chips and crisps and beans on toast, and then spend the rest of the money in the pub.

... We have to make a choice and what we have chosen is to spend what we have on leisure things, like cigarettes rather than food.' Sam continues: 'What's the point of getting a job and doing all that work when the pay is so low? I would end up with no more than I have now and if I didn't like it and left, my benefit would drop for six months.' She has considered going to college, but now that is 'out', because students can no longer claim housing benefit.

> I've done nothing since I left school. I don't think I could do a job. I'd be sacked in a couple of weeks. But it doesn't seem bad to me to be on the dole all my life. It's what I've always expected.

Phillips comments: 'What hope, I wondered, is there for the health of a future generation born of young women who live on crisps, beer and fags?'

The headline (which cannot be attributed to Angela Phillips) interprets this all for the reader. It is not an account of a deficit of self-help. It is the result of too much self-help. It is the 'underside' of 'the enterprise culture'. Sam is 'trapped' in Hull.[3]

Where low skill levels and poor motivation are the result of handicaps that cultural attitudes cannot touch, there is every argument for providing generous benefits, and a way of life as comfortable and satisfying as money can provide to the young men and women affected, as well as to their carers. But it is the strangest of all perversions of left-wing doctrine to maintain (as has been increasingly maintained by distinguished professors of social science and social policy, the most senior of church leaders, and feature writers in the serious media) that most young English men who have poor school records have failed to perform better because of money. If they are 'victims', they are victims not of defects in the cash-benefit system, but of their cultural environment. They are the products of a cultural environment within which the messages of responsibility, striving, self-help and self-improvement have been progressively weakened. The weakening of these culturally inculcated and socially maintained constructs was not the work of ordinary people: it was not the product, to use Ortega y Gasset's phrase, of a 'revolt of the masses'.[4] It was a product of what Lasch called the revolt of the élites.[5]

Neither the people who propagated them nor their children suffered in the short term from these anti-culture, culture-destroying, cultural messages. Absolutely to the contrary. Whole tranches of competition for middle-class jobs that were once produced by schools educating working-class boys have been removed. Principled propaganda to destabilize and 'deconstruct' Western social institutions lay behind much of the reiterated messages of hopelessness, pessimism, self-centredness, and the connivance in the low achievement of boys in schools with low-income catchment areas. The favourable reception of these cultural messages, however, was not primarily the result of a conspiracy. It was the result of misguided good intentions. Yet had there been only a conspiracy, this is what would have been invented and fostered to achieve its ends. Gertrude Himmelfarb has correctly called this the de-moralization of society: the cultural work of élites designed to undermine all cultural values and replace them with the freely-chosen lifestyles of self-regarding individuals.[6] Only now are the foul fruits of this pernicious process in the schools being recognized for what they are, and the axe hesitantly and belatedly lifted to root and branch.

9

The Fatherless Household in the Bottom Tenth

Motivational problems applied also to the man's long-term commitment to fatherhood in the household of his child and its mother. As youths say today when they hear that someone has been married for forty-five years: 'That's *three* life-sentences!'

Closely connected with the Rowntree Foundation's interest in poverty is its interest in the household that contains no father. The Foundation's publications and the published work of other researchers associated with the Rowntree Foundation have in recent years attacked poverty, yet defended lone parenthood, one of poverty's prime recruiters.[1]

The extremely small contribution lone parenthood made to creating poverty in York in 1936 is shown by the fact that, in B. Seebohm Rowntree's classification of the principal causes of poverty, lone parents (however labelled) do not appear in a separate category at all. They are only a small part of what is itself a small group of 153 families which in total account for only 2.5 per cent of those in poverty. Others in this small group of 2.5 per cent of all those in poverty were the 35 households where the husbands were working away from home in, for example, the Army, Navy, or Mercantile Marine. Some of the families of these men were in poverty because they 'were not allotting a fair proportion of their income for the support of their families'. But some of them just did not have the money to support two households, and sent as much as they could, even though it was inadequate.

Among these lone parents in poverty in 1935-36, divorcees do not appear at all. There were 41 households where the mother was legally separated from the husband and 38 households where the wife had been deserted by the husband.

The only suggestion of households containing children which were not, or had not been, households of married husbands and wives were the *five* households where the principal cause of poverty was 'women with illegitimate children'. In total 19 persons were affected.[2]

The expansion of absent-father households had its origins in the late 1950s. Many trend lines which indicate the weakening of the family *as an institution*, that is, as a dense and complex network of mutually supporting rules and roles, began to move distinctly upwards from 1955. From being supported and enforced by nearly everybody in society from top to bottom, even by people who violated them (especially in the cultural élite), they begin from about 1955 to be subtly undermined and dismantled (especially by the cultural élite). The birth pill came onto the market in January 1961, and for that reason 1961 was a notable year for the changes in sexual and family *mores*.

Technical developments in work and the home also began to affect family life. The late fifties saw the beginnings of a marked diminution in the rationale for early specialization in earning money for one's children by hard and often dangerous physical labour in forge and mine, in the shipyard, at the docks and at sea—and a working life-time's hardening in it. An excellent picture of the continual and pervasive inculcation of the 'virtues' of 'manliness' (as they were thought of then) in family, street ('within a ship's-biscuit toss of Clive Street, North Shields') and workplace (the merchant ship) is drawn by the Professor of Law at the University of Newcastle upon Tyne, who served as a foremast seaman during the Second World War. According to Professor Elliot's first-hand account, anyone saying he intended to quit the service when the Control of Engagement Order enabled him to leave was a rarity, and was regarded 'with suspicion and contempt'.[3] It is difficult to conceive how Arctic convoys in winter could have delivered munitions to Murmansk or how cargoes of petrol could have sailed for Malta on what were realistically suicide missions in the absence of such a strong and specifically 'manly' *culture*. The problem does not arise to that extent in workplaces such as mail-order businesses, teacher training colleges, potato crisp factories or radio or television studios, and therefore it is easy for people in those occupations to believe the culture never existed, or if it did, that it was at best unnecessary.

Where it was still required, the physical efforts of lifting and pulling formerly supplied by manual labour was quickly being transferred to machines. Many of the heaviest and most dangerous jobs disappeared altogether. In 1961 there were 149 collieries in the North Eastern coalfield. By 1996 there was one. (In 1928 there had been 304 working collieries in County Durham alone.)[4] In 1961 116,000 miners were employed in the North Eastern coalfield. In 1981 32,000 miners were still employed there. Within a few months of the end of the miners' strike of 1984-85 the number had been cut to 14,000. By 1996 only a few hundred mining jobs remained, nearly all of them on the rural Northumberland coast, far outside the range of the old pit villages and towns of Wearside and Tyneside.

Sunderland had produced from the late nineteenth century and for many decades of the twentieth century a bigger tonnage of ships than any other town in the world. By the 1980s it had ceased to build ships altogether, and shipbuilding in Sunderland was banned by the European Union into the indefinite future.

Within a short time on the sites of the Sunderland shipyards, forges, foundries and heavy-engineering works there was provision for almost the lightest physical labour of all, a university campus for 18,000 students.[5] This number vividly illustrates the scale of the changes in the employment, educational and sexual conditions of young people since the early 1960s. For in 1961 18,000 was the total number of undergraduates in the Universities of Birmingham, Manchester, Liverpool, Bristol, and Durham combined, with the addition of all the undergraduates at the college which became the University of Newcastle.[6] The colliery site had been cleared of all traces that it was once a workplace, and was being prepared as the new stadium for Sunderland AFC. The Labour politician Aneurin Bevan had said to an early post-war Durham Miners' Gala, to thunderous applause, that he looked forward to the day when nobody would have to do the terrible work of the pitman. Thus had a long-standing dream been fulfilled.

The rationale diminished, too, for the early inculcation of skills and motivations for a life-time's commitment to preparing food for them, repairing their clothes, and keeping disease and vermin at bay through the cleanliness of the home.

The long-existing trend to smaller families continued. From the point of view purely of housekeeping as a task (as distinct from wider matters of childcare), progressively fewer dependent children concentrated into a shorter period of an adult's life made it less demanding and arduous. The house continued to be less crowded. The number of children born to each woman dropped steadily to below the population replacement level. The population of Britain which had probably been growing ever since the Black Death in the middle of the fourteenth century was predicted by the Office of National Statistics (ONS) to be in decline by 2026 if the trend towards a smaller number of children per woman continued. Among women born in 1944, only 10 per cent had no children at the age of 45. The ONS prediction in 1996 was that 20 per cent of women born in 1964 would have had no children by the time they were 45.[7]

Nearly every dwelling came to be provided with the facility for tapped hot water, with its own bath, its own built-in kitchen sink, its own pipes for the disposal of waste water, and an internal water closet. Refrigerators became commonplace.

In the 1970s and 1980s ready-to-eat or easy-to-prepare meals multiplied with improved techniques of freezing foodstuffs, transporting them and storing them in the shop and in the home. An enormous variety of restaurants, cafés, and so-called 'take-aways' (sandwiches at mid-day, curries late in the evening) spread on the streets of the great towns. For more and more people, therefore, whether to be skilled or not in time-consuming shopping, food-preparation and cooking became nothing more than another leisure option.

New materials and cheap imports made darning and patching, knitting and dress-making, matters of choice rather than necessity. In comparison with bars of soap and washing soda, modern detergents had already transformed the washing of clothes and dishes. The electric smoothing-iron and the vacuum cleaner, already widespread, became as common as the flat iron and the broom had been forty years before. The tumble drier became commoner, and the electric washing machine more sophisticated. By the 1980s the coal-fired boiler, the poss-tub and the poss-stick of the 1950s 'wash-day', the whole street's newly-washed, coaly-flecked family clothes drying on the lines in the back lane, had faded into a scarcely credible memory.

The proportion of jobs had thus declined that required workers who, especially the unskilled, were strengthened and hardened by long usage of specialized muscles and who were in character prepared, roughly if necessary, to accomplish their tasks at sea, or in the mine, the quarry, the forge or the forest. Housework had thus been made easier in the dwellings that had largely replaced the nineteenth-century terraces. The contribution of women to the income of the household from paid outside work was therefore made easier. But in the 1980s and 1990s it became also more important. For the 1980s was a decade in which manufacturing labour, following labour in the primary and secondary heavy industries, also began to be shed in large numbers. The General Household Surveys show that male employment among 24-55 year-olds fell in Britain from 95 per cent in 1979 to 86 per cent in 1991. Schmitt and Wadsworth attribute this to declining labour market opportunities available particularly to the unskilled man.[8] Chinhui Juhn argues the same for the USA.[9] In the same period unskilled men with jobs experienced downward pressure on their wages.[10]

Quite as striking, and in its effects on the family just as important, was the changing nature of the cultural reaction to these changes.

Historically the attack on the family was not a very prominent Marxist or Trotskyist concern. But when the central bourgeois institution of the family came under attack from other quarters in the 1960s and later, there was plenty of anti-family sentiment in both movements, and Trotskyists in particular could feel that destabilizing marriage was at least a supplement to their own transitional programme.

Shortly after the appearance of Trotsky's 1938 manifesto,[11] France was defeated by the Germans. The complicity of the Vichy regime in the German occupation after 1940, and the complicity of the French intelligentsia with Vichy, gave a great boost in that country to earlier movements of hatred for bourgeois society's existing institutions and personal codes of conduct. The 'tired remnants' of such fringe movements as Surrealism and (the creation of Germans taking refuge from military conscription in Zürich in 1916) Dada allied themselves with Marxism and the prestigious and powerful French Communist party. They suddenly acquired, as Marc Fumaroli wrote, an altogether disproportionate significance as descriptions of the supposedly real world and as prescriptions for the moral response to it. Together with a coterie round the egregious Jean-Paul Sartre and one of the early ideologists of feminism in its present-day form, Simon de Beauvoir,[12] with their camp following of nihilistic anarchists, they became accomplices in producing the early literature of what was to become contemporary post-modernism. Nothing in society is worth preserving; everything social is to be defined as stunting and restrictive, everything personal as primary and liberative; all cultural elements that are viewed by the uninitiated as elevating are to be unmasked as meaningless; everything is the proper object of destruction—or, to use the cant term, of 'deconstruction'.[13] A key element in personal emancipation was liberation from the old sexual and family morality.

In the 1960s, as German students began to come to terms with their parents' possibly wilful ignorance of, passive reaction to or active participation in the Holocaust, and as American students reacted to the Vietnam War (more or less influenced, like the Dadaists, by anxiety personally to escape the draft and death) the curious 'Marxism' of the Frankfurt School exerted its tremendous influence.

'Respectability' in all its forms, *especially* working-class respectability, was mercilessly attacked. The ways of the respectable working class secured their place as the particular focus of hatred because it had signally failed in the bloody revolutionary mission revealed to it by Marx,[14] to emancipate mankind from all oppression and exploitation, and to usher in the faultless social system of communism. Due to the affluence it had enjoyed since the Second World War, from being the ferment of social change (as Marcuse said) the Western working class had become the cement of the bourgeois social order. The revolution now had to look for its recruits in 'the substratum of outcasts and outsiders', including the unemployed and 'the unemployable'.[15]

Keenly attractive to the restless students in the newly expanded universities was Marcuse's amalgamation of Freudian theory and Marxism which claimed that modern society engaged in quasi-Marxian 'exploitation' both young and old by 'expropriating' an unnecessary amount of sublimated sexual energy and burdening them with a surplus of sexual repression.[16]

The example of China under Mao also greatly appealed to this generation of students. Mao's 'Cultural Revolution' was deconstructionism *par excellence*. The old culture of China was to be eliminated. The joy of it was, that before the Western students' own eyes it was being eliminated by students in Communist China, where it was not the work of pupils still at school. A Maoist jacket and the *Little Red Book*, along with the ability to quote from Marcuse, Horkheimer, Adorno or Habermas, were the symbols of academic soundness in the social science, social policy and politics departments of Western universities of the late sixties.[17] The best-remembered slogan of the time, the 'long march through the institutions' is, of course, a direct reference to Mao.[18]

In the economic and technological circumstances of the 1980s and 1990s three possibilities were available to men who would become fathers and women who would become mothers. The choice made by the father or the mother would have specific implications for the income on which the mother and her child would have to depend. The choice made would have implications, in particular, for the chances of the household containing a child ending lower down, rather than higher up, the income scale.

The first possibility was to adopt *as a personal lifestyle* the old *mores* of the family. That is to say, a man and a woman could voluntarily conform with the essential old rules, even though the enforcement of them was much weakened. They could refrain from sexual intercourse until they were each committed to being a parent, in the event of a child being conceived, during the period of the child's dependency and beyond. They could go through a public ceremony of marriage. They could promise, and keep the promise, to be life-long partners, and to engage in sexual activity only with one another.

The other two possibilities involved the man not being present in the household of his children. The likelihood that fathers would make either of these two possible absent-father choices at some stage or another (i.e. including the situation of marriage and then divorce) was greatly enhanced by the success of the various camps of deconstructionism. The deconstructionist's world-view on income levels, sexuality and childrearing spread through wide sections of academia, the media, and increasingly even the Christian churches (especially the Church of England).[19] It sometimes just seeped through undetected.

The first of the two absent-father possibilities was for the mother to combine work and home without the father or a substitute adult male being present in the household, either of her own accord or because the father refused or failed to live with her.

Men and women found it increasingly possible to envisage this alternative. The mother could cope both with children in the home (which was easier to manage than in the past) and with employment in the paid economy (which was providing more opportunities where physical strength and brute determination developed over a period in the workplace were irrelevant). From this point of view, the child's father need not be a part of the family at all. He could be done without as a wage-earner. He was not needed in any capacity that required his presence in the household.

That this adaptation had become objectively easier for women themselves to manage, meant that when men or women did consider it (either as fathers not marrying or divorcing the mother, or as never-married or as divorced mothers of dependent children) there was less incentive for parents, siblings, cousins, friends and neighbours to condemn the father (or the man who by his sexual activity could become a father), or warn the mother against it (or the woman who through her sexual activity could become a mother).

When the difficulties for the woman associated with a home that did not include the father of the child were discussed on the radio or featured in the press or TV, not only could a more reasonable case than previously be made out for fatherless households; the entertainment value, the *frisson*, of speaking against the traditional family far exceeded the entertainment value of defending it. Agony Aunts had a field day in filling their columns with extremely interesting, because hitherto 'shocking' cases, and interestingly normalizing them. Advertisements could feature independent women, dynamically in control of their own lives; that is, not locked and suffocated in and never to be locked and suffocated in marriage. In films it became anomalous to see family life portrayed on the 1950s' pattern. Soon bespectacled school-girls of 14 could be observed on the train to school solemnly reading in their respectable women's magazine how they could help their clumsy and ill-read boyfriends to adopt the newest experimental posture of the series; this week's position happened to be the sitting one.

Conceptions outside marriage, abortions of the conceived children, births without the father marrying the mother, men living with women without marrying them, and divorces, have all strongly changed pattern since 1961, and taken on entirely unprecedented magnitudes in the 1980s and 1990s.

That is, Dutschke's long march has made most progress through the institutions which, before 1961, governed who could engage in what kind of sexual intercourse under which socially defined circumstances with whom; what protection the conceived child would have against the personal preferences of the child's mother, father, or other individuals who might be inconvenienced by its birth; what the structure of the household would be under which the child should be brought up, and so forth.

The original route of the long march had been dictated by Marxist theory. It was to have been through the crucially important institutions of the economy. Unfortunately for that strategy, the adverse effects of disruption and deconstruction of economic institutions rapidly showed up in bread shortages, power cuts, three-day weeks, and general and obvious discomfort all round. The long march through the economic institutions did not appeal to the general public at all.

The family was much more promising terrain. The advantages for the independent father and mother were immediate and obvious, even if in divorce it might be only the advantage of getting into a bad situation from a worse one.

The pay-off in sexual liberation had immediate appeal to the young men and women at the forefront of their generation, especially on the new, large university campuses. From being among the most strictly controlled of all activities, sexual intercourse became one of the activities freest from social control. The content of sexual activity, which had been the most important basis of social approval and disapproval, and 'morality' without a qualifier generally meant 'sexual morality', almost ceased to be a moral issue. The sole criterion of morality came to be, increasingly, consent. Where there was consent between sexual partners of whatever description, or free choice of auto-eroticism, then the sexual activity was increasingly judged to be the legitimate private concern of the person or persons concerned. By 1996 the Law Commission was able to advocate the liberalization of the law that criminalized serious acts of consenting sado-masochism: short of inflicting permanent handicap, 'the law ought not to prevent people to consenting to injuries caused for ... sexual purposes'.[20] Public censure was appropriate only in cases of unwanted sexual interaction—strict disapproval extending beyond coercion into unprovoked signals which explore the possibility of mutual sexual interest, 'sexual harassment'.

The doctrine of consent stretches progressively further down the age range of partners who are both sexually mature. For a time in the 1970s these principles were openly claimed by paedophiles to apply to their own sexual preferences. But in terms of the inability of children to give genuine consent to an adult in these matters (a view that sits uneasily with many other pressures to give even very young children the full panoply of 'human rights')[21] paedophilia came to be, and is, one of the few firmly excluded sexual lifestyles.

The adverse consequences are much less obvious, and those who suffer from them are the least articulate of those having a stake in the family as an institution. The difficulties for the dependent child are covert and long term. The dependent child takes the initiative less often in bringing its problems to the public's notice; and it is rarely invited to the TV studio to put its point of view. The younger the child is and the more vulnerable, the less its voice is heard.

The proportion of children in the nineteenth century who were born without their father having married their mother fell from low rates (by 1996 standards) to very low rates (seven per cent in 1845 to four per cent in 1900).[22] Gertrude Himmelfarb has shown an even more striking picture for the East End of London, an area dominated at that time by casual dock labour, poverty, slum housing and unemployment. In the middle of the nineteenth century the illegitimacy rate in the East End had been only 4.5 per cent. At the end of the nineteenth century it was even lower, three per cent. Both of these figures were below the national average prevailing at the time. The stability of the working-class family in those times of stress and change, and the contribution the family made in enabling its members to make the optimal adaptation to their difficult situations, is in striking contrast to the informal chaos of uninstitutionalized, private sexual and childrearing arrangements of their economic equivalents today.[23]

As late as the early 1960s the rate was still only six per cent. Today's rate of children born without their father having married their mother is in excess of 30 per cent.

Women have indeed entered the labour force in large numbers. One of the most striking changes in the labour markets of Western industrialized countries over the last twenty or thirty years has been what Harkness and others, partially financed by the Rowntree Foundation, call the 'dramatic' increase in female labour-force participation. Various issues of the OECD's *Economic Outlook* show that in the United Kingdom the labour-force participation rate of women aged 15-64 rose from 46 per cent in 1960 to 65 per cent by 1991. Typically, the rate of change in family patterns has been more rapid and far-reaching than in otherwise comparable European countries (though not so rapid and far-reaching as in the USA). The increase in France was from 47 per cent to 57 per cent; in Germany from 49 per cent to 59 per cent. Among British women in the age range 25-49, 60 per cent were participating in labour force by the late 1970s. A little more than a decade later, in 1991, the proportion was 75 per cent.[24] Full employment has been joined, where it has not been partially eclipsed, by the equality of female with male participation in the paid economy as a principal feature of labour-market policies (as embodied, for example, in European directives).[25] For various reasons, furthermore, pressure-group agitation has concentrated on increasing the labour-force participation specifically of mothers with children under school age.[26]

For women at work, too, the successive databases of the government's General Household Survey show the substantially improved capacity of women aged 24-55 to meet budgets through their own work. Between 1979 and 1989 the ratio of women's to men's median hourly earnings in full-time employment in the UK rose from 70 per cent to 75 per cent. Where they were mothers, the improved earning capacity of women mainly applied to those whose income was high enough to allow them to make full-time arrangements for the care of the home and the children, for the ratio for part-time female workers rose only from 55 per cent to 57 per cent. (In the UK in 1991 44 per cent of women in employment worked part time.)[27] Between 1981 and 1991 the real monthly earnings of men at work increased on average by 23 per cent—£214 a month. But the real monthly earnings of women at work increased on average by no less than 92 per cent—£219 a month.[28]

But if we look not at the general population of women, and focus rather on lone mothers only, one feature immediately makes itself conspicuous in the figures. The lone mother's adaptation to the new possibilities of (for whatever good or bad reason) doing without the father's contribution from within the home, by engaging herself in paid employment outside the home, is that it is much more readily available to the sort of well-off woman who comments on these matters in the university lecture-room, the press, and on TV and radio shows, and influences the next level of opinion formation in the local press and the class-room, than it is to the woman low in the income scale who follows her lead. For the former is much more successful on average in finding that she can combine paid work and mother-hood in the home than is the latter.

Thus, in the *upper* half of the income distribution, both at the beginning of the 1980s and in the 1990s, about 93 per cent of lone mothers with dependent children were working—with a slight rise during the period. Simone de Beauvoir herself (rather curiously) levelled the accusation at liberated women that their emancipation was at the expense of other women. Poorer women had to maintain their services to their own families while serving also the rich families of their liberated sisters. In contrast to the lone mothers in the upper half of the income distribution, in Britain at the beginning of the 1980s only 41 per cent of lone mothers in the *lower* half of the income distribution were working, i.e. handling the demands of both looking after a child at home and generating income by her own efforts. By the beginning of the 1990s the proportion of lone mothers in the bottom half of the income distribution handling both home and outside employment was still lower, 39 per cent.[29]

A second absent-father possibility was increasingly opened to the mother. She still did without a father or substitute male in the household (either by never marrying anyone or by divorcing the husband). But she did *not* depend upon her own paid work in the labour market. She had the improved option, instead, of depending on state benefits in meeting her own and her chil-dren's housing and other living costs.

By 1996 there were 2.7 million children in lone-parent households, 1.8 million of whom were in households dependent upon the main form of unconditional social security, Income Support. Lone mothers were entitled to state supplements to this state income which were not available to a married mother.[30]

Clearly, any woman who has a child in a rich society like Britain, under any conditions whatsoever, has a powerful claim on the community. Other people might deplore the action of the mother who has either deliberately or through carelessness conceived a child without being able to care for it from her own or her own and the father's resources. The fatherless child's part in the problem of resources for its care could not have been controlled in the slightest degree by public disapproval. Nevertheless, most communities in the past have used harsh treatment of the child, through social stigma no less than through withholding resources, to control the conditions under which adults engage in sexual intercourse and reach decisions about the household arrangements of their biological child. Social stigma has been progressively lifted from the illegitimate child. Modern society has almost completely rejected the option of punishing children already born in order to deter the mother or father, and (even remoter from the child actually suffering the stigma and social neglect) to deter unspecified adults in the future from engaging in the actions that create fatherless households.

The necessary corollary has been the improvement in state benefits for lone-parent households. The necessary corollary of that in turn, however, has been the improvement in the conditions for the biological father who chooses not to be part of his child's household, and for the mother who chooses not to have the father as part of his child's household. That is to say, shortly, that it makes those choices more likely. In referring to its assertion that since 1979 the number of people in Britain living on low incomes 'has trebled' to 14 million and 'income inequalities have increased', the Rowntree Report of 1996 states that this has been a phenomenon 'of lone parent families in particular'.[31]

What the churches used to clearly distinguish as pastoral problems concern the care of the person who has fallen into difficult circumstances or a self-destructive lifestyle, whether due to circumstances entirely outside his control or circumstances created by his own choices. What sociologists used to clearly identify as institutional problems concern the ramifications of choices attractive to individuals in the here-and-now through the structure of a society's *mores*. Some of these ramifications end by widening the area of attractive choices, some of them end by narrowing them.

The churches, which have historically been institutions that peculiarly had to deal with both pastoral and structural issues, were once therefore peculiarly sophisticated in keeping the distinction clear. As Archbishop William Temple said, there is an important class of acts which may be harmless or virtuous in the individual case, but which it is the Church's task to identify as wrong because they tend to destroy social well-being, 'even though the agent is quite ignorant of this tendency'.[32] 'How but in custom and in ceremony/Are innocence and beauty born?'[33] Social science and social policy faculties of one sort or another in the universities were largely set up in the first place with the aim of studying (in the setting of life-time security of tenure in return for responsible work) the long-term effects of measures that under the pressures of politics and business 'seemed like good ideas at the time'. To say 'the responsible press' was to refer precisely to its concern with the total effect on human welfare of current practices and policies.

As Oakeshott put it, human life is a gamble. But while the individual must be allowed to bet according to inclination (on the favourite or on an outsider), society always has to back the field. The individual might win or lose. If he loses and is penitent, he may hope to fall back into society's forgiving arms. For a society, on the other hand, the penalty is a chaos of conflicting ideals, and the disruption of the common life within which, and only within which, a proportion of individuals can do risky things without too much damage to themselves or others.[34]

In the past forty years the crucial distinction between the pastoral and the structural has been eroded, partly by neglect, partly by design. In 1993 a journalist from one of the major BBC news and current affairs programmes, 'P.M.', came to interview some residents of Booth Street, in a working-class area of Sunderland next to Sunderland Forge and the Pyrex Tableware glassworks. She had been given my name as someone who could perhaps arrange for her to interview some people who had been brought up, and who had lived, under those institutions of neighbourhood and civic life that the Hammonds said in 1917 were by then the 'positive forces' that were 'so pronounced a feature of artisan civilization'.[35]

The journalist was anxious only to produce an accurate and balanced report of her assignment, which in my opinion makes the point about 'pastoralism' all the more important. The old residents had been talking about the peacability and trust of neighbourly relationship until the 1950s, and that led on to how order was maintained, and that led on to family *mores*, and the very low numbers of illegitimate children.

'But it must have been terrible, it must have been horrible, for a girl who *did* have an illegitimate baby!'

Jenny Heron said: 'O, yes, it was *terrible*. It was the *worst* thing that could happen to you. [Name] had a baby. It was *awful*.'

'She was pushed out? She was ... ?'

'O, no!', replied Jenny Heron, horrified. 'Me Mam used to make her a hot dinner every day, and things for the bairn, and take it down to her. The ladies in the street used to make the baby all her clothes.'

The way she was treated by her family, neighbours and friends provided at no time any trace of an *incentive* for her or any other woman to become an unmarried mother. She was 'looked down on' by people in other respectable streets, just as unmarried mothers in other streets were looked down on by the people of Booth Street. 'Getting the street a bad name' was bad business for all the residents, and all the residents knew it. Employers, shop-keepers, potential husbands and wives in the town had not (and do not have) the time and the knowledge to 'judge everybody on their real merits'. They have to sort out the best from the worst prospects in the first instance by rough and ready guides. But the system within the street was: it's happened now, we'll make the best of it for the mother and baby. The people in Booth Street understood the distinction. Do everything by acculturation and social control that you can to stop it happening. But when it does happen, then there is no question but that pastoral care must be unstinting.

I do not remember exactly, but I do not think that much of that was broadcast. I do remember that after vivid descriptions of life in Booth Street from the older residents the journalist said, 'But that is *middle-class* morality!' (She maybe had a sociology degree.) I expostulated, and the expostulation was broadcast.[36]

Pastoral care is only possible in a society which keeps a clear head, so to speak, about the distinction between it and the maintenance of well-founded structures of grace (as the Church used to call them). The indispensability of both the institutional and the pastoral was summed up in the old aphorism, 'Hate the sin, love the sinner'.

But the social-affairs intellectual has become increasingly the person who obliterates distinctions instead of pointing them out. All people on the lowest incomes are basically the same. They are all simply the amorphous 'poor'. All households with children are basically the same. They are all simply 'families'. All women bringing up children by themselves are the same, whether widows or never-married teenagers. They are all simply 'lone parents'. All social problems are the same. They are all the problems of 'victims'.

When we study the work of social-affairs intellectuals over the past forty years, we see a remarkable example of role-reversal between them on the one hand, and politicians and popular journalism on the other. It has become the latter (who have to be more in tune with common sense, the actual general experience of a society over an extended time) who have had to do the work that the churches, the universities, the research foundations and the 'serious' press formerly did, and are still paid by society to do.

Such role reversal applied to the *Sun*, the *Daily Express* and the *Daily Mail* with their need to remain in touch with the constantly attenuating common sentiment, as against the *Guardian* and *The Independent*. It applied to the Leader of the Labour Party as well as to the Secretary of State for Social Security, as against the social-affairs experts on 'the family' and on 'poverty' in the universities, the research foundations and the respected lobbying groups.[37]

Harkness, Machin and Waldfogel, using the data archive of the General Household Survey, analyzed for various years the work, benefit, and income patterns of the 3,000 or so sample households containing dependent children. The mothers were in the age range 24-55. They found that 59 per cent of lone mothers in the lower half of the income distribution either chose lone motherhood and state benefits without work; or else, having chosen lone motherhood, had no further choice then but be without work, and to depend on state benefits.[38]

The consequences for the standard of living of these mothers and their children can be most clearly seen by contrasting both their employment prospects and their household income with mothers who choose to live in the same household with their spouse. The figures do not distinguish between *married* couples with dependent children and *cohabiting* couples with dependent children. Any advantages of marriage itself as a strategy for keeping a family higher rather than lower in the income scale are therefore concealed in the general figures for couples of any sort. But for brevity just here I shall refer to married/cohabiting mothers with dependent children as 'married mothers'.[39]

In 1981 only the same percentage of married mothers with dependent children in the bottom half of the income distribution were working as were lone mothers in the bottom half. But in the 1980s the presence of another adult, permanently part of the household and integral to it, enabled married mothers with dependent children *flexibly to take advantage of expanding employment opportunities for women, and to combat the declining employment opportunities for men*, to a far greater extent than lone mothers. The percentage of the lower half of lone mothers in employment dropped by nearly two per cent 1981-91. Lone mothers were less likely to be working in 1989-91 than in 1979, and even those women who were working were more dependent on 'non-labour income' (principally state benefits). By contrast, in the lower half of the income scale, the percentage of the married mothers who were in employment *rose* by over 20 per cent during the same period, so that by 1991 59 per cent of married mothers were working, but only 39 per cent of lone mothers.

The effect on the chances of mothers and their children being lower rather than higher in the income scale, depending on the mother's choice of lone parenthood as never-married mother or divorcee (again, for whatever good or bad reason) is shown in the figures for household income.

Over half of all families with dependent children with the *married father* present in the household enjoyed, in the early to mid-1990s, a gross income of more than £350 a week (56 per cent). Only nine per cent of *fatherless* households with dependent children had that income. At the other end of the scale, only five per cent of married couples with dependent children had less than £100 week gross. Nearly half of all fatherless households had less than £100 a week gross—in the cases where the fathers never married the mothers, and the mothers married no one else, the figure is 60 per cent.[40]

In 1981, standardized at 1991 prices and standardized also for the family's size and composition ('equivalized' in the jargon), the real monthly income of married families was £1,050. The standardized real household income of lone-mother households was £873. The monthly gap was therefore £177. By 1991 the average monthly income of lone-mother households had risen in real terms to £917. But the standardized real income of married families had risen far faster, to £1,540. The monthly gap was now £623.

In terms of the real standard of living of the fatherless household and the married family this gap was partly closed, of course, by the many state social benefits to which the non-working lone-mother (but not the working married woman) was entitled in addition to the cash of her benefit income, and for the financing of which the earnings of the working married woman were taxed.[41]

As the Rowntree Report says (with some exaggeration) there was a 'rapid growth in the 1980s in the numbers living in low-income families with children, particularly lone-parent families'.[42]

The lower income of the household without the father present is intrinsic to the average experience of the one-adult as compared with a two-adult family. Instead of the flexibility of the arrangements allowed to two people, there is only one potential earner who, because of the dependent child, is restricted in the employment opportunities available. In its pseudo-scientific propaganda the poverty lobby uses the low income of lone parents as a grievance, without dealing at all with the contribution of lone parenthood to the fact of low income.

This the poverty lobby does on two bases. One is that shortage of income is a substantial cause of the other differences between households where the married father is present and those where he is not. The other is that the state ought to remove substantially the lone-parent family's income disadvantages. The poverty lobby normalizes the fatherless household as a household arrangement, on the inarticulate major premises (i) that the only disadvantage of being brought up in a lone-parent household is shortage of money and (ii) that the state can be persuaded to make up the shortage of money. When the state has been so persuaded, then there will be no significant differences between lone- and married-parenting. That is the implicit logic that has led to the progressively deepening indifference of the cultural élite to the departure of fathers from the households of their dependent children. In setting up a large and costly survey in Newcastle upon Tyne in mid-1996 to investigate the causes of the failure of certain children to thrive, no questions were included to ascertain the marital status of the child's parents. Such a question would be 'stigmatizing'.

The emphasis is on relationships. A headmaster of a comprehensive school in an urban priority area, struggling with the burgeoning consequences of lone parenthood for more and more of his pupils, recalls taking part in a group discussion in the mid-1980s in the course of which the Director of Social Services of a large borough talked about the need to replace the term 'family' with the term 'centre of intimacy'.[43]

Relationships are good in so far as they express the qualities of love, faithfulness, commitment and mutual responsibility. These and their opposites, the argument goes, are *possible* under any private arrangement or within any structure.[44] The *non sequitur* is that if there is intimacy we need not concern ourselves with issues of arrangement or structure which favour benign and stable intimacy, and still less arrangements that maximize the chances of benign and stable intimacy being underpinned by the group's economic viability.

Marriage (not just cohabitation of any sort) had proved over the period the child's best defence against being in a household lower rather than higher in the income scale. Fathers and mothers had been advised, by countless people of good will, and by the former guardians of morality in the universities, the churches and the serious media of communication, that the growing numbers of families without their fathers, whether on the initiative of the man or the woman, were no indication that the family was deteriorating. It was only changing.

That home and the lone mother's outside work could be combined with high income was largely true for those higher in the income distribution who gave the advice. It was patently untrue for those lower in the income distribution who took it.

10

The Loss of Poverty as a
Salient Social Issue

T hat the Rowntree Foundation should emphasize poverty as a major contemporary problem, blighting the lives of millions of Britons in the mid-1990s; that serious commentators should follow its lead; and that the Rowntree view should go virtually unchallenged in the universities, would not have been predicted by the Rowntree Inquiry Group's predecessors in social policy and social research. For even in the 1890s, poverty had seemed to Charles Booth to be a tractable problem that would be soon solved. Booth had concluded from his study of the East End of London in 1891, the most impoverished large urban area in Britain, that over two-thirds of its population lived in what he called comfort or affluence. One quarter of its population were not living in comfort, but their income was sufficient for what he called a decent, independent existence. Those 'in want' accounted for 13 per cent of its population. What we would now call the underclass accounted on Booth's reckoning for only 1.25 per cent of the population of the East End: those who provided the ready material, he said, for civil disorder when occasion served; who rendered no useful service and created no wealth; who degraded all they touched, and fouled the reputation of the unemployed and the whole working class.[1] At about the same time Beatrice Potter (later Beatrice Webb) came to the same conclusion from her first-hand research. British manual workers were not in a state of chronic destitution. The poor were not getting poorer. She deplored the tendency to exaggerate the penury, the incompetence and the helplessness of working people. Marxian socialists, she said, overlooked the independent working class, and when they talked about the hardships of 'the proletariat' their subject was really the 'ne'er do wells'.[2] As early as 1907 the great economist Alfred Marshall was protesting at the misuse of Booth's work by the very scaremongers whom Booth had refuted with his data. The one thing that every German 'knew' about England, Marshall wrote, was that one million Londoners lived 'in poverty'. 'But they open their eyes when they learn that under this misleading title are included all families with less aggregate income than 21 marks all the year round.' Not one-third, as in London, but three-quarters of working-class families in Germany lived on less.[3]

In 1935 B. Seebohm Rowntree decided to repeat his earlier investigation of York,[4] and to find out what changes had occurred in the living conditions of the workers in the thirty-six years that had elapsed since 1899. He conducted a house to house investigation of 'practically every working-class family'—over 16,000 families in all the streets in York where it was likely that the chief wage earners were earning £250 a year or less.[5]

For data about income he did not depend upon his household informants, as the General Household Survey and Inland Revenue do. He did not think it was reliable enough. Being himself a senior figure in the Rowntree family, and Rowntree being one of York's largest employers, his personal influence gave him access to the wages books of large firms and information on scales of pay, pensions, unemployment benefit, health benefit, and so on. Neither income from benefit fraud nor from the black economy were investigated. (These never appear in the social surveys of the time as a problem worth considering in arriving at an accurate general account.)

He adopted as his 1935-36 poverty line the standard of living attainable by a family of man, wife, and three children. Rowntree then made calculations to take account of different sizes of family, and the presence or not of dependent children. His poverty calculation allowed for whatever housing was costing the family. He then allowed an income that was sufficient to meet the minimum subsistence diet and other essentials of clothing, cleaning materials, transport and so on, that he had worked out in his own book, *The Human Needs of Labour*.[6] Every ha'penny had to be spent wisely and well.

Rowntree thought it was inappropriate to mix an empirical description with a moral crusade. The whole point of his work, he argued, was to establish as accurately *as possible* with the resources he had what was factually true of a particular aspect of social life. He chose to try to establish the following particular facts, clearly as facts and nothing else: how many people lived in families in York which received an income that enabled them to meet his measured, specific, very low subsistence standard without any leeway for either wilful, accidental or incompetent waste.

In trying to be as clear and plain as possible within the limits of his ability, time and resources at the stage of establishing the facts, therefore, he preferred the term 'Class A' to the term 'living in abject poverty'. He preferred the term 'Class B' to the term 'in poverty but not abject poverty'. *First* try to establish what is true to the best of one's ability and as well as resources allow. *Then* the moral crusade.

This *attempt* to separate *as far as possible* ideology from data, words from agitation, is anathema to post-modernists in all their many manifestations. To more and more social reformers of Rowntree's day his seemed the only way forward. To more and more social-affairs intellectuals educated in the university departments of sociology, social work and social policy after the 1960s the distinction became simply incomprehensible.

Rowntree found that in York in 1935-36 eight per cent of the total population were in Class A—14 per cent of those living in working-class streets. An additional 10 per cent of the total population were in his Class B—an additional 17 per cent of the working class. In total 18 per cent of the population of York were on his definition receiving a weekly income below his subsistence level, and 31 per cent of people in the working class.[7] There were 5,800 children under 14 in poverty, 3,200 in Class A, and 2,600 in Class B. Living in York's 22,700 inhabited houses were just over 2,000 Class A households, and just over 3,000 Class B households.[8]

Rowntree studied the composition of these lowest of York's income groups, classified 'under what appeared to be the principal cause'.[9] The largest single group of persons in poverty were there because of the low wages of the wage earner in regular employment, 33 per cent. The unemployed group accounted for a smaller proportion, 29 per cent. The next largest group were the old, accounting for 15 per cent of those in poverty. The 'inadequate earnings of other workers' was the principal cause in another nine per cent. Widowhood was the principal cause in eight per cent of people in poverty. Illness accounted for four per cent. Only five households, containing in total 19 persons, were in poverty because the women had illegitimate children.

Rowntree, again in the interests of an accurate record, whatever use might be made of the accurate record in due course, regarded it as '*most* important' to be able to measure accurately what had happened to the poor in the thirty-six years since 1899.

He therefore calculated the number in 1935-36 who would have been in poverty if they had been measured, not on the standards he had set in *The Human Needs of Labour*, but on the subsistence level he had used in 1899, in which, for example, he had selected a diet that was 'more economical and less attractive than was given to paupers in workhouses'.[10]

In 1899, 10 per cent of the total population and 15.5 per cent of the working-class population of York were below the 1899 standard. By 1936 both of these percentages had been more than halved: four per cent of the total population, and seven per cent of the working-class population of York were below the 1899 standard.[11]

Rowntree, having established *that* fact, commented on *that* fact. He called it a 'striking reduction' in the amount of primary 'poverty'. He allowed himself a further comment, a broader judgement. The fact that in 1936 nearly seven per cent of the population in a typical provincial town in England, he said, were still living below the poverty line he had set in 1899 showed how great a task still lay before social reformers. But he had this to say about the processes of social reform that had brought the progress about: they had been processes of orderly government, serious intellectual effort and honest research in the universities; in the trade unions; in the friendly societies; in the Labour party and other parliamentary parties; in wards and in the local council chambers; and in the national and local civil service. These processes of intellectual work and democratic change took place against a background where optimism did not come easily. The incentives to give up hope were as strongly present in the economic environment then as in the 1990s and hopelessness developed; but those incentives were not reinforced, they were largely repudiated by the culture, of which the BBC 'became perhaps the central agent'.[12] The incentives were as strong then as in the 1990s to conclude that the workers had 'nothing to lose but their chains', that they had 'no stake' in society, and it was a matter of indifference at best if the whole structure was torn down. But the minority movements that espoused that view, though they gained some ground in the élite universities, gained little in the English working class. 'Only a few figures are needed to show', says the review of the year 1929 by the English and Scottish Co-operative Wholesale societies, 'that the process of trade deterioration was continuous, and not a mere fluctuation'. Of the miners: 'The tragic situation in the coalfields ... since the slump began in 1920, grew steadily worse'. Twenty-two per cent were wholly unemployed, and another 43 per cent temporarily stopped. 'It could be fairly assumed, at this time, that *very few* of the totally unemployed had *any chance* of getting back into the industry.' The reports from the railways, the mines and the cotton mills are of wage *cuts*. But it was the number of members of the cooperative movement that grew (from 3.8 million members in 1918 to 5.5 million members in 1927), not the number of burglaries, riotous arson and looting or acts of vandalism.[13]

In the face of all that, and all the more because it was in the face of all that, the success that had attended 'the efforts made by the community' since 1899 to improve the conditions of those living in abject poverty, Rowntree said, was 'a tribute to those who have been striving during the present century to raise the standard of life of the people'.[14]

From 1904 to 1940 in York the average number of cases of wounding with intent and assault reported to the police was 10 a year. The annual average in the decade before the 1914-18 War was eight. The annual average in the 1930s was eleven. There were only four such crimes of violence against the person reported to the police in the whole of the year 1906. But there were only four in the whole of the year 1931 as well. The highest figure ever reported in the 36 years of the decade before the 1914-18 War to the outbreak of the 1939-45 War was nineteen, in 1929.

York in 1935-36, like the rest of the country, was just recovering from the difficulties of post-war readjustment of the 1920s (which culminated nationally in the General Strike and the seven-month miners' lock-out of 1926), the Geddes Axe that had been taken to social security benefits, the unemployment of over one million men in the latter part of the 1920s, and the mass unemployment of the early 1930s.

B. Seebohm Rowntree interpreted the thirty-six years of change 1899-35 in a quite different manner from the way in which the Rowntree Group interpreted the thirty-one years of change 1961-92. B. Seebohm Rowntree saw the improvement in the absolute standard of living of the poorest tenth of the population as a matter for pride in the country that had accomplished it. From 1899 to 1935, he wrote, 'more far-reaching steps had been taken to raise the standard of life of the workers than during any previous period of similar length'.[15]

By contrast, in 1961, the beginning of the period on which the Rowntree Income and Wealth Inquiry Group of 1995 mainly focuses, the total *gross national product of the United Kingdom* in real terms was almost exactly the sum of *government expenditure* in 1995.[16] Notwithstanding this, the Rowntree message in 1995 was that on income grounds (not on the grounds of religious or philosophical asceticism) and because of 'economic forces' there were 'groups of disaffected young men who have no role in and no stake in society'.[17]

B. Seebohm Rowntree hardly mentions, and does not raise the option of violence. When vandalism, theft and violence did appear on a large scale in British society, their driving force must have been something different from low levels of income, and high levels of inequality and unemployment. These had all been powerfully present when vandalism, theft and violence were rare. What changed was the factual and ethical definition of the situation. And that was the work, and it cannot be otherwise, of the social-affairs intelligentsia.

A sub-heading in the Beveridge Report is somewhat bewildering to a reader in the mid-1990s. The figure of, for example, 14 million people in poverty is quite regularly reported to the reader in the 1990s in the serious press. Yet Beveridge's 1942 Report says, *Abolition of want as a practicable post-war aim.*

Beveridge observed that the 'social surveys made by impartial investigators' in the 1930s showed that 'want could have been abolished *before* the present war by the redistribution of income *within the wage-earning class*, without touching any of the wealthier classes'. He did not make that point to suggest that only the working classes should be taxed to pay for the abolition of poverty. He said it simply as the most convincing demonstration that abolition of want just before the 1939-45 War was '*easily* within the resources of the community'. In every town surveyed, substantial percentages of the families examined had less than the bare minimum for subsistence. But 'the great bulk of them had considerably more than the minimum'. Furthermore, the inter-war social surveys, Beveridge wrote, yielded 'unquestionable proof' of large and general progress.[18]

In London, the New Survey of London Life and Labour, commenced in 1929, 40 years after the beginning of Charles Booth's great and famous survey, showed that for an hour's less work a day the average London workman could buy one-third as much again. The infant mortality rate had dropped from 159 to 58 a thousand in 30 years.[19] In York the infant mortality rate had dropped from 161 to 55 between 1899 and 1936. School children had gained two inches in average height and five pounds in weight. 'What has been shown for these towns in detail applies to the country generally'.[20]

George Orwell, writing in 1943, at about the same time as Beveridge, also makes statements about the tractability of poverty that surprises the reader in the 1990s:

> All that the working man demands is what politicians, priests, literary men and whatnot would consider the indispensable minimum without which human life cannot be lived at all. Enough to eat, freedom from the haunting terror of unemployment, the knowledge that your children will get a fair chance, a bath once a day, clean linen reasonably often, a roof that doesn't leak, and short enough working hours to leave you with a little energy when the day is done.

The problem of poverty was capable of being completely eliminated by 1963. 'How *easily*', Orwell continues, 'that minimum could be attained if we chose to set our minds to it *for only twenty years*'.[21]

After Beveridge's recommendations had been largely implemented, B. Seebohm Rowntree conducted a third survey of poverty in York in 1950.[22] Under five per cent of the working class were in his 'poverty' classes A and B. He found that abject poverty, the poverty of his Class A, had almost totally disappeared: only 0.4 per cent of working-class families, and of course a much lower percentage of all families in York, were in that class. Only 4.2 per cent of working-class families were in Class B.

For his 1950 poverty line he had used the dietary recommendations of a commission of the British Medical Association. This had been set up in 1947, and it reported in 1950. A man, wife and three children under 15 were accordingly in poverty if they did not have the household income to buy the following for their weekly consumption (or their dietary equivalents at the same cost):

2½ lb. breast of mutton
2 lb. minced beef
1½ lb. shin of beef
1 lb. liver
1 lb. beef sausages
1 lb. and a quarter bacon

1½ lb. herrings
1 lb. kippers

14 lb. potatoes
½ lb. peas
6 lb. swedes
4½ lb. onions
12 oz. lentils
2 oz. barley

4 lb. apples
½ lb. stoned dates
1s. 6d. worth of extra vegetables and fruit

10 oz. rice
4 oz. sago

1 lb. 4 oz. flour
2 lb. oatmeal
3 lb. sugar
10 oz. cooking fat
1 egg
9d. worth of extras including salt, seasoning

10 oz. cheese
14 pints full cream milk

23½ lb. bread
2½ lb. margarine
1 lb. jam
1 lb. treacle

4 oz. cocoa
½ lb. tea

That could strike no one as a starvation diet (least of all families in Third World countries). It is a measure of how prosperous Britain has become since the war that it bears no relation to the enormous *variety* of food that was being retailed in the 1990s, and it would probably be quite difficult to persuade children to accept menus that would constitute an adequate diet for them based upon those items.

In order to establish the weekly income that would be counted as keeping a family above the poverty level in clothing, a woman investigator interviewed twenty-nine women to ascertain how much they spent on clothing for themselves and their children. As he was anxious to establish a poverty line that no one could reasonably claim was too high, Rowntree based the minimum weekly income needed for women's clothing at the average expenditure of the three women whose expenditure was the lowest.[23] The same procedure was adopted for children's clothes and household sundries.

Similar interviews were held with thirty-two men, taking the average of the three men whose expenditure on clothing and fuel and light were lowest.

Rowntree allowed small expenditure on the following 'personal sundries':

> sick and burial clubs
> trade union
> travel to and from work
> stamps, writing paper etc.
> daily newspaper
> wireless
> beer, tobacco, presents, holidays, books, travelling, etc.

(As an indication of the penny-pinching of the income calculations, he included the net value of vegetables grown in allotments or gardens. He also included the value of pre-school and school free milk and free meals at school. As an indication of the penny-pinching of the expenditure that was allowed, the fivepence he allowed for the wireless in 1950 was actually a penny less than he had allowed in 1936. In 1936 wirelesses had used batteries. In 1950 they used mains electricity.)

In addition, there were the family's housing costs.

Where the father was under 30, Rowntree allowed an additional weekly sum for one child, and smaller per capita sums if there was more than one child, to help the family set itself up with furniture, bedding, and other expenditure of a non-recurring nature.

The Labour governments of 1945-51 were committed to full employment (which Beveridge put at an unemployment rate of three per cent because of people voluntarily changing jobs etc).[24] But more important than that verbal commitment were the demands of post-war reconstruction, and unemployment was negligible in York in 1950.

Rowntree regarded such full employment as an historical anomaly. He wanted to know what the poverty levels would be under more realistic employment conditions. He therefore calculated what the poverty percentages would have been if there *had* been normal unemployment levels, as giving a more realistic picture of poverty in British society in the post-war period. The unemployment rate in York in 1936 had been nine per cent. He therefore took the interview schedules of all the *employed* men and took a nine per cent sample. He then notionally allocated to them, instead of their actual earnings, the current national insurance benefits they were entitled to.

Rowntree was able to conclude that, as compared with 1936, a much *lower* percentage of the working-class population, eight per cent, was in poverty 1950 *even at the same level of unemployment* and even though the 1950 poverty standard was *higher*. Putting the same point the other way round: a much *higher* percentage of the working-class population, 31 per cent, had been in poverty *at an unemployment rate of nine per cent* even though the 1936 poverty standard was *lower*.[25]

The development of welfare legislation since 1936, he wrote, had certainly not ensured that men can *normally* be unemployed without their families falling into poverty. But the new National Insurance Act itself, together with other measures of the post-war welfare state, had *substantially* reduced both the amount and the severity of the poverty that would occur even if there were unemployment at 1936 levels.[26] As it happens, the national unemployment level of the mid-1990s was in fact about nine per cent.

The old, at 68 per cent, were by far the biggest constituent of the group of those actually in poverty in 1950. Sickness accounted for another 21 per cent. Widowhood accounted for six per cent, large numbers of children for three per cent, and low wages now for only one per cent (the low wage group had been the *largest* group, 33 per cent, in 1936).

What had struck Rowntree was the absence of unemployment as a cause of poverty in 1950.[27] What just as forcibly strikes the observer looking back on the period is the fact that in 1950, as in 1936, poverty due to 'chosen' lone parenthood (for whatever good reason or bad reason) through the father not marrying the mother or through divorce, had not yet put in an appearance.

But in the overall picture of poverty as drawn by Rowntree in 1950 these were trivial details. Poverty itself had been reduced to proportions that showed that the problem was nearly at its end, and abject poverty (i.e. Class A) had been reduced in York, a city with a population of 105,000, to only 81 households in total. The actual situation in York, not the situation in York if unemployment *had* been nine per cent, was that there were only 864 families—864 families too many—who did not have the weekly income which could pay the rent, and buy the food, clothing, household and personal sundries on Rowntree's list if not a penny was wasted.

In April 1951 it was announced that the retirement pension was to be raised. Rowntree quickly calculated what the percentage of families would have been in poverty in 1950 if the new 1951 rates had applied. If the 1951 rates had applied, then poverty as Rowntree understood it would have all-but ceased to exist. For the number of families in poverty in York would have been only 351, a manageable number for charities, for what were not yet generally called social workers, and for future improvements in the benefit rates.[28]

The welfare state, in a still strongly family-oriented society, appeared from the data of research studies to be accomplishing its aims. Dorothy Wedderburn in her study of poverty among old people found that in the family-centred culture still dominant in 1959 this had indeed been the effect:

> A large number of old people whose financial resources alone would have put them below subsistence levels were not living in poverty because of subsidy from the children with whom they were keeping house. As I commented in my report, 'some of the old people in our sample *with the very lowest money incomes* felt *better off than they had ever done in their lives before*, since they were keeping house with relatively well-paid and generous children'.[29]

By the 1990s one of the poverty lobby's main arguments was that poverty was harsher than it had been in the 1930s, because in the 1930s everyone had been poor, and to be poor was therefore then not such an oppressive experience as it became. But in the 1950s and early 1960s contemporary poverty researchers reported the opposite, that the experience of low income was *not* so likely to be a 'poverty' experience now that people were *no longer* 'all poor together'. The mechanism explicitly singled out to explain this phenomenon, however, was one the utility of which had been greatly weakened by the 1990s, namely, 'the family as an agent of income redistribution',[30] rarely through direct weekly cash payments, but through presents, hospitality, 'treats', subsidies for holidays, fares for long journeys and so forth.

Thus, in the Sixth Eleanor Rathbone Lecture, given at the University of Birmingham in 1955, Richard Titmuss discussed the consensus that the social benefit system and the other social services should aim at being 'self-liquidating' as more and more people were 'raised above a minimum standard of living to a position of freedom in which they could purchase whatever services they required'.[31]

> On this view it could be supposed that speaking generally, Britain is approaching the end of the road of social reform ... This would seem to be the principal implication of much public comment on the social services during the past few years, and one which has received endorsement in the policy statements of the Conservative and Labour parties.[32]

An analysis of the more important writings since 1948 showed, he said, that the dominant message, far from being that social needs had been neglected, was that the welfare state had been established too quickly and on too broad a scale, threatening the 'moral fibre' of the nation.[33]

Several years later two of Titmuss' associates, Brian Abel-Smith and Peter Townsend, still had to recognize that during the twenty years that had passed since the end of the 1939-45 War the consensus had been that poverty had been 'abolished', and that Britain had become a much more equal society.[34] Partly financed by the Rowntree Memorial Trust, their report *The Poor and the Poorest*, was the first to feel its way towards the new consensus that poverty was widespread and had been increasing.

From the point of view of the Rowntree Report 1995 that was premature and an embarrassment, for the essential argument of the Rowntree Report 1995 was that poverty and unemployment increased only in the period 1979-92.

11

The Search for a Substitute

T he first reaction to the fact that poverty had been pushed down the agenda was to admit that a preoccupation with financial means of procuring food, shelter and clothing was no longer the overwhelmingly dominant feature of life for a large minority of the working-class population. As the existence of poverty had been lost as an issue to the Left, then the Left wanted to see to it that the abolition of poverty had been lost as an issue to the Right as well. There were more important grievances than money.

The Affluent Society by the American economist and Left-intellectual John Kenneth Galbraith was one of the best-known attempts to tackle the problem of the apparent near-disappearance of the problem of people not having enough money for necessities. From time immemorial, he wrote, this is what had been meant by 'poverty'.

Galbraith argued that throughout history nearly everybody had been very poor. For most people in most human societies poverty had been and was the unedifying mortification of the flesh—from hunger, sickness, and cold. Those who were temporarily freed from such a burden could not know when it would strike again.

Presumably mocking people in his own circle of dons and diplomats who pleaded poverty for themselves, Galbraith pointed out that such poverty 'was not the elegant torture of the spirit which comes from contemplating another man's more spacious possessions'.[1]

But with general affluence, he says, envy loses its sting. The class struggle is over. The concern for inequality had vitality only so long as the many suffered privation, while the few indulged in excess. 'It did not survive as a burning issue in a time when the many had much even though others had much more'.[2]

Western Europe, the United States and a very few other countries had become the only exceptions in a world of poverty. The wealth enjoyed by their populations was great and 'quite unprecedented'. It was a recent experience even there, 'almost insignificant in the whole span of human existence'.[3] At the turn of the century Alfred Marshall had written that the chance to succour the people in England who were 'overworked and undertaught, weary and careworn, without quiet and without leisure' gave to economic studies 'their chief and their highest interest'.[4] Writing of the United States, but in the context applying his remark also to all Western European countries, Galbraith says decisively, 'No contemporary economist is likely to make such an observation'.[5]

But in the more backward of the social sciences, in social policy and politics, the ideas by which they interpreted the existence of people in this favoured part of the world, and therefore in measure guided their behaviour, had not been forged in the world of wealth. It was entirely inappropriate, Galbraith wrote, to use the ideas that had been evolved for a world of grim scarcity in order to make sense of a world of widely-spread affluence. Galbraith was dealing with the definition of the situation, and therefore with an intelligentsia that was not doing its job properly. 'We face here the greatest of vested interests, those of the mind.'

Faced with a new situation the social-affairs intelligentsia resorted to devices and arguments 'some elaborate, some meretricious, some in a degree dangerous' by which in vital matters it tried to maintain its association with its older intellectual commitments. Society therefore suffered collectively from an 'uncorrected obsolescence' in its cultural life. 'As a result', Galbraith said, 'we do many things that are unnecessary, some that are unwise, and a few that are insane.'[6]

Poverty, Galbraith said in 1958, can no longer be presented as a massive affliction in the USA or Western Europe. 'It is more nearly an afterthought.'[7] The general preoccupation with the material standard of living supplied by markets and expressed in the cash income of families was therefore founded upon a myth—the myth of material scarcity. Poverty had been called 'a file provided for the teeth of the rats of reform', Galbraith says; and adds, 'it is no longer'.[8]

It would be quite affordable in a modern society to give everyone who cannot earn a living in the economy, money from the state sufficient for decency and comfort. But Galbraith says that this would not solve the problem of what he calls 'case poverty' in its entirety. For giving people sufficient money for decency and comfort did not mean that they would spend it so as to make themselves decent and comfortable. 'To spend income requires a minimum of character and intelligence even as to produce it.'[9]

The broadest effect of the defeat of poverty is that, properly conceived, it had highlighted the necessity to raise society's sights above material things. The motto of his book is that everyone must concern himself with 'the ultimate aims of man'. He must get himself out of the rut of the highly irrational worship of production and ever more production.[10]

At the next level, the problem must be conceived as one of *public* poverty:

> The children ... subject in the playgrounds to the affectionate interest of adults with odd tastes, and disposed to increasingly imaginative forms of delinquency, were admirably equipped with television sets. ... The family that takes its mauve and cerise, air conditioned, power-steered, and power-braked car out for a tour passes through cities that are badly paved, made hideous by litter, blighted buildings ... They picnic on exquisitely packaged food from a portable icebox by a polluted stream and go on to spend the night at a park which is a menace to public health and morals.[11]

At the level of poverty itself Galbraith is equally insistent that the solution no longer lies in cash income to individual families. The children must have first-rate schools and school attendance must be rigorously insisted upon. Badly fed at home, they must be nourished at school. Law and order must be well enforced. 'Poverty is self-perpetuating because the poorest communities are poorest in the *services* which would eliminate it.'[12]

In putting these arguments Galbraith acknowledged his debt to the English socialist R.H. Tawney. He had already said these things in the 1920s and 1930s.[13] Tawney's main attack had been levelled at the degrading passion of the upper and middle classes for more and more things that money could buy. He praised the virtues of the English working class for the high value it put on the family home and on fidelity to principles and promises in sport, work and community life. Tawney emphasized the importance not just of 'the social wage' represented by tax-provided social amenities and services. His was the wide view of the free enjoyment of the goods of the natural world. Public affluence would take the form of equal access to the activities of voluntary associations of all kinds; of equal access to common facilities of the highest standard such as hospitals, schools and colleges, public libraries, art galleries, theatres, swimming pools and parks. His view of the adequate standard of cash income guaranteed by the state or even allowed to be paid by industrial firms was by present-day standards astonishingly low.

Common goods and the common good had an importance for Tawney far beyond the family's cash income. In the words of J.A. Symonds' socialist hymn, 'These things shall be! A loftier race/ Than e'er the world has known shall rise/With flame of freedom in their souls,/And light of knowledge in their eyes. New arts shall bloom of loftier mould,/And mightier music thrill the skies,/And every life shall be a song,/When all the earth is paradise.' Symonds, like Tawney, pictured people in this country 'humble' in their homes, but 'glorious' in the equality of their common life.

Galbraith's notion of 'private affluence, public squalor', now that poverty was 'an afterthought', was paralleled or taken up by social-affairs intellectuals in the 1950s to 1970s in Britain, in their many studies of the institutional and structural deficiencies of the social services and public utilities upon which the working class depended—hospitals, old people's homes, public transport systems and so forth. The transformation of urban sociology from the early 1970s has already been referred to in Chapter 7. Social geography moved in the same direction, as the politicized academy switched its attention to these problems of 'collective consumption'.[14] In due course the notion of private affluence and public squalor was taken over comprehensively and diversely by the many strands of the environmentalist movement.

Stripped of its reformist optimism, it is basic to sociology of the Frankfurt School, the most influential set of ideas on students during the later 1960s and 1970s. According to the Frankfurt School (I follow Offe's account)[15] modern technology, enterprise, and social organization have abolished scarcity of consumer goods. But consumption *for everyone* has been severely curtailed.

The very plenitude of material goods and services means that the system must produce not only the goods and services but also the motives for possessing them. Like everyone else, the proletarian now gets plenty to consume, but he does not consume what *he* chooses. 'Choice becomes merely the reaction to a pre-established supply that brooks little resistance.'

Needs that can be effectively supplied by the capitalist system are imposed by the market—many of them 'false needs'. The needs that the market cannot supply are suppressed. *All* classes suffer from the discrepancy between the most advanced production of marketable commodities, including intangibles such as marketed artistic products (films, concerts, games of football, records), the stagnating organization of transport, health and education, and the pollution of the environment.[16] The system of class inequalities, according to the Frankfurt School, had been strongly modified. There was now crucially for everyone a system of disparities between areas of vital human need. The whole population is the net loser in this balance of private affluence and public squalor. (Castellian urban sociology is nothing but an application of these ideas to the city.)

Given the conventional wisdom on poverty today as represented by the Rowntree Foundation, it is a curiosity that Offe uses the concept of 'relative deprivation' *only* to explain the *unreasonable contentment* of the general population, including the proletariat. Modern man does not perceive himself as being deprived. Offe writes that his objectively justified dissatisfaction is '*softened* by perceptions of relative deprivation'.

Of course this is the way in which Runciman mainly used the idea, to explain the quiescence of the poor, not their criminality. The poor were contented, Runciman discovered from his survey material, because they compared their present standard of living with the standard of living of their equivalents in the social structure in previous years. 'Manual workers and their wives were much more likely to compare their lot with that of themselves and their parents during the Depression, and by this comparison to count themselves fortunate.'[17] For the Frankfurt School the proletarian, along with every one else, was suffering from a 'false consciousness of *plenty*'.

Paul Johnson, who became editor of the, in those days, important journal of the Left, *The New Statesman and Nation*, agreed strongly that low money incomes were no longer the main problem to be addressed by the Left:

> I have no illusions that anything of real social value is going to emerge from current policies, based as they are on the fallacy that the attitudes of human beings to each other can be transformed merely by changing the amount of money in their pockets.[18]

But his answer to the problem of the remission of classical poverty was to come up with a new version of the theory of class polarization.

The issue of poverty was no longer available (or so it seemed at the time). What was the significance of that in the 1950s for Left-inclined intellectuals?

A career as a Labour politician, where competition would be less intense for them, was always also an alternative to a career in the Conservative party for public schoolboys. But obviously they would feel better in themselves, and be more convincing as candidates, if they did feel genuinely upset by the injustices which were salient in the lives of working people.

They themselves could only have a rough and ready idea of what those salient injustices might be, and there was always a time lag. Such an inevitable time lag has meant that the saliency of youth crime, riot and fathers without families in working-class areas, a working-class fact of increasing importance since the 1960s, began to penetrate only slowly to their latter-day equivalents in the universities and the responsible media, more belatedly to the higher reaches of the churches and more belatedly still to the senior judiciary.

But what was the situation of public schoolboys at the end of the 1940s and in the 1950s who were turning their minds to a political career? Even if they had wanted to be Labour, a Labour government had done them the disservice of leaving them nothing to be indignant about on behalf of Labour.

What is more important, if they wanted to be Labour, it gave them nobody to be indignant against. Their friends could feel superior on social-class grounds without even thinking about it: they were better than working people because their fathers employed working people, or did not have to work very much at all except at the game of *being* superior; they were richer; they had better jobs or a better non-working lifestyle; they spoke properly; they were well educated, well dressed and had good manners.

If you wanted to be Labour you could not feel superior on grounds of your social class. But you *could* feel superior on grounds that you were *morally indignant* about the right things and they were not. That was in some ways even better than social-class superiority. However minor your public school, you could now look down on the whole of the aristocracy that was not morally indignant about the right things, and nearly the whole of the English middle class.

There was a further benefit of moral superiority over mere class superiority. It did not stop you looking down on most of the English working class as well. Most of them were not morally indignant about the right things either.

You could feel superior to almost the whole of the respectable working class. You could smile at their polishing their door knockers, attending their allotments, going sequence dancing, stunting themselves with their absurd exaggeration of the importance of heterosexuality, being faithful to their husbands and wives for years on end, never swearing in the family or in front of a member of the opposite sex, not understanding that their repressive attitudes was what was to blame for crime, worrying all the time about 'a point of order, Mr Chairman!'

Paul Johnson gives a first-hand account of an important Left-intellectual's search for an issue to replace poverty. In conceding the poverty issue, money income had to be replaced as an explanation of either good or bad behaviour in society.

Paul Johnson was born in 1928, and was educated at Stony-hurst and Magdalen College, Oxford. Coming to political con-sciousness in the later 1940s, he says, he had no sense of outrage. When he left Oxford he still lacked a sense of outrage.[19] He did his National Service as an officer in Gibraltar. Still no sense of outrage. He returned to England in 1951.

He does not say that he came across B. Seebohm Rowntree's 1951 report on poverty in York, but it was a major book on social science in itself, and part of the intellectual and political atmo-sphere of the time. Here was Rowntree himself, exact, laborious, who had carried out careful research in York, with the long-dead Charles Booth one of the two most famous 'poverty' researchers of all, as good as proving that, give or take a few score families in York, and a few tens of thousands of families in the country, poverty had been abolished. Even if unemployment came back it would stay as good as abolished. That was obviously no basis for a life-time of moral indignation and superiority. I think the phrase public schoolboys use is that somebody had shot the fox.

But then he went to France. He spent a year on the Left Bank. While he was in Paris the French Communists staged a big demonstration against the installation of General Ridgeway ('the germ-warfare monster of Korea') as head of the Allied forces in Europe (SHAPE):

> Every day for four days huge battalions of workmen armed with clubs assembled ... Police and *gardes mobiles* were brought from all over France and there were bitter fights even on the Grands Boulevards.
>
> The students were also active on the Left Bank, and the day the rioting reached a climax ... I watched a head-on clash between students and a battalion of *gardes mobiles*, wearing steel helmets and carrying rifles ...
>
> The police descended with a ferocity I would not have believed ... From that moment I possessed the *capacity for outrage*.[20]

His outrage was not against the workers wielding clubs on behalf of the Stalinist Communist party of France. It was not against students who were rioting and having 'a head-on clash' with the *gardes mobiles*. It was a sense of outrage against the French police and against the *gardes mobiles*, 'wearing steel helmets and carrying rifles'. (I myself was in the youth hostel in Cambrai in about 1957 or 1958. I remember how amazed I was to see armed French troops and tanks in the streets. They were not controlling anything. They were just on exercise. But coming from England I was shocked.)

Paul Johnson makes it clear that although he now had a sense of outrage, it did not do him much good in England. In England, he writes, 'the worst fighting word was "groundnuts"', and 'political passion was muffled in the foggy boredom of the House of Commons smoking room'.[21]

It was no good even '*pretending* that current political issues *are* important', Johnson said. Toryism tamed and timid, whose one desperate gamble in political savagery, the Suez war, might have done wonders for moral indignation, but it had been brought to 'an ignominious close within a week'. It had not given students time to riot, nor workers the chance to wield clubs on behalf of the Communist party. Even if they had rioted and wielded clubs, the British forces of law and order would probably have been so disobliging as to refuse to appear wearing steel helmets and carrying rifles.

Public schoolboys could go to the Left Bank for their sense of outrage to be stimulated in support of club-wielding Communists and rioting students. The drawback of that was that they might have to wait for several weeks before rioting students, club-wielding Communists and *gardes mobiles* wearing steel helmets and carrying guns all turned up at the same time outside the café where they were sitting.

> What, then, [Johnson asks], of the thousands of young Englishmen, of my age and education, who lack this emotional impetus? ... They have no personal experience of how Franco subdued the Asturian miners in March 1958, of how the French parachutists tortured Henri Alleg in March 1958, of how Salazar ended the Portuguese salt-mine strike in October 1956; they know nothing of conditions in the Belgian coalpits, of the *latifundia* farming system in Southern Italy, of those little-heard-of concentration camps on the Greek islands.[22]

Paul Johnson, then, had his sense of moral outrage already. But other people had not been to Paris at all, never mind in a café on the Left Bank. As he rightly said, many had not been in Portugal in October 1956 to have personal experience of Salazar ending the salt-miners strike, and there were a lot more people, even students, who did not know what a *latifundia* was, or even whether it was singular or plural.

What of outrage, then, at the English class system? 'The history of all hitherto existing society is the history of class struggles' is one of the best known sentences from one of the world's best-known pamphlets, the Communist Manifesto.[23] But in England even class seemed unpromising to Johnson. 'First, it is finely graduated. The yawning chasms which breed violent jealousies have never been allowed to emerge. Secondly, individuals have always been allowed controlled movement in the social hierarchy. The new graduates of the Welfare State were slowly and carefully digested.' Nevertheless, Johnson concluded, he had to do his best with what was at hand. 'To put it bluntly, I think it is about time we destroyed the British class system'.[24]

It is essential to the Rowntree Group's theory in the mid-1990s that class differences narrowed before 1961-79 (and that affected people's conduct, i.e. they knew that they had) and widened after 1979, and as a result of them widening after 1979 crime, riot, and illegal-drug taking increased.

In the mid-1950s Johnson had to use similar data of income changes since the Second World War, namely, the fact that income differences were narrowing. Crime was not in his mind, only righteous indignation. But for the purposes of righteous indignation and not crime, he uses those data to claim that a proper object of Left outrage was that the *narrowing* of the *income* gap had in fact *widened* the gap between the social classes. It was worse to be working class in the 1950s, he maintained, than it had been in the 1930s.

The social-class gap, he said, had been narrowing during the 1930s. Certain features of the British class system were in that decade 'in perceptible decline'. In the 1930s the dominance of Oxford and Cambridge was being successfully challenged by the provincial universities. In the 1930s there had been a distinct move away from the public schools. In the 1930s snobbery was becoming a social handicap.

But, Johnson continues, in the 1950s class divisions had widened, and they had widened because of the much less important income equalization. 'Hence the class system flourishes *as never before*.'[25] The 'limited' redistribution of income in the years 1945-58 'had the opposite effects to those aimed at'. As income differentials were lowered, 'the middle and upper classes erected fresh social barriers, largely immune to legislative attack'.[26] The British class system has not merely survived the 1945 experiment but is now actually stronger than it was before.[27]

From the point of view of the validity of the Rowntree theory, that crime is principally a function of relative deprivation, a factor of which is the gap between the different classes, Johnson's analysis actually contains the germ of a better idea than its own. If the Group had been able to follow Johnson, and prove that 'real' class differences had widened in the period 1961-79 as well as in the period 1979-92, that would explain, using its theory, the rise in crime throughout the whole of 1961-92.

It could not prove that 'real' class differences did widen 1961-79. But if it were able to prove it—if it saved its theory by making it apply to the period 1961-79 when crime was rising steadily during a period of a marked reduction in the income gap between rich and poor—it would be at the expense of its contention that the problems of class polarization and crime coincide specifically in the period 1979-92. Unintended and innocent, or calculated and covert, the actual and obvious political impact of the theory would be lost: that crime, poverty, class polarization and all the rest are the fault of Tory governments 1979-92—for all practical purposes the fault of the Tory government in power when the Rowntree Report 1995 was published. Personally and politically I do not mind that in the slightest as party-biased propaganda, pressure-group politics and media knock-about. But I do object to it very much as social science.

12

Unconditional Rights

O ne strategy by which 'poverty' was restored to the radical agenda was that of defining state benefits as rights to income divorced from any conditions of conduct. Struggles against the low standards and harsh conditions of the 1834 Poor Law had been carried out since its inception. These struggles had first culminated in the so-called 'principles of 1907' being presented in the Minority Report of the Royal Commission on the Poor Law.[1] (The Minority Report had much more influence on subsequent government policy than the Majority Report.) The 'great leading principle of 1907' was that there was '*mutual obligation* between the individual and community'. As part of that mutual obligation every individual was entitled to bodily maintenance at a standard of living adequate for 'a civilized life'.

But it was not all give by the community and all take by the individual. There was a 'joint responsibility of an indissoluble partnership'. The partnership placed 'new and enlarged' responsibilities on the individual, unknown to *laisser-faire* society. It placed an *obligation* upon each young person, for example, (a) to learn, and (b) to be well conducted. The young person was in a compulsory partnership with other people—'the community'. Their freedom was limited. They had to provide the resources to maintain him and to educate him through the agency of the state. In return he necessarily forfeited some of his rights to do what he liked. The community which provides the benefits is entitled, according to the principles of 1907, to enforce these obligations if they are not willingly fulfilled.

There is thus not just the principle of 'Universal Provision'. The partnership combines three principles. If there is to be universal provision then there must also be 'Curative Treatment' for those who reject their obligations. A third principle must also operate on those who do not respond to curative treatment—'Compulsion'. Using these three principles, the community 'deliberately weights the alternatives of volition'. Everybody is entitled to the basic minimum of a civilized existence—but under conditions appropriate to the case. A guaranteed pension for an old person no longer able to work, or long-term state support for a widowed mother or a married mother deserted by her husband is one thing. Unconditional and long-term support for able-bodied young people who prefer not to work; or are unable to work through alcoholism; or for anyone who has a child without a father to provide for it in its home, is quite another.

Thus, for example, 'the labour exchanges and the farm colonies make it easy [sic] for a wage earner to get a situation; perhaps the reformatory establishment, with powers of detention, is needed to make it disagreeable for him to neglect them'. This doctrine, the Webbs said, 'inspires every detail of the Minority Report'.[2]

Beveridge's ideas were not significantly different on these points:

> The plan is not one for giving to everybody something for nothing and without trouble, or something that will free the recipients from their personal responsibilities. The plan is to secure income for subsistence *on condition of service and contribution*.[3]

The older arguments for a guaranteed subsistence income had been based upon the notion that they improved the prospects of people to lead a life in which they would be less, not more dependent on others. Subsistence income was the starting point from which they could play their part in that process of give and take that balances itself out over the years—the process infused with what the famous anthropologist Bronislaw Malinowski called 'the principle of reciprocity'.

Churchill in his Liberal days before the Great War had famously said that a guaranteed standard of subsistence was a better basis upon which to build an independent life within a framework of mutual aid than was despair. He became Lloyd George's lieutenant in the drive for a system of *thrift* that was 'national, compulsory, and organized'.[4] Everybody had to be *made* to save for the emergencies of sickness, unemployment and old age. The 'miracle of numbers', the insurance principle, would do the rest. He saw the welfare state as an unbroken causeway along which the whole body of the people could move with a certain assured measure of security against hazards and misfortunes.[5]

One of the arguments that Charles Booth advanced for pensions, conditional only on the age of the recipient, was that it strengthened independence within a system of mutual aid within the family. If they had 5s. a week to contribute to their own keep, someone in the pensioners' own family would be more likely to look after them, and thus keep them out of the workhouse. 'Thousands of old people with 5s. a week in hand might find a home with some son or daughter.'[6] For before the first Old Age Pensions Act, 1908, a working man who became too old to work (there was no question of 'retirement') had as a rule to choose between two alternatives, either to live with a married son or daughter (often as an unwanted guest) or go into the workhouse.[7]

Harold Laski, one of the Labour party's main intellectuals in the 1930s and 1940s, emphasized that 'rights are correlative with functions'. In return for the conditions of well-being that the state provides, the beneficiary must make a contribution that 'enriches the common stock':

> I have, therefore, no right to do as I like. My rights are built always upon the relation my function has to the well-being of society; and the claims I make must be claims that are necessary for the proper performance of my function. That does not mean that I must, to use Mr Bradley's phrase, accept without repining the duties of my allotted station. ... I win, or ought to win, the station in which I may best fulfil myself.[8]

The whole emphasis of these old arguments was that state cash benefits were the friends of virtue, as virtue was conceived at the time: independence; hard work; mutual aid; pulling your own weight at least, and more than your own weight if you could; prudence; pride; and so forth.

The 1950s' welfare state was very far, then, from being a charter that would invite, for example, a young man to have children (or do the things that might mean that he did have children) before putting himself first under a very heavy obligation to bring them up together with the mother in the family household. The 'village' (to use Hillary Clinton's image of the national community) had duties towards all children; but (contrary to the implication of Hillary Clinton's at least earlier use of the phrase) that did not mean that the duties of the father were lessened at all.

But continuing its historic struggles against the Poor Law, the poverty lobby began to reassess its position. In rethinking and reorganizing its arguments, it gradually settled on a number of ways to protect poverty from ever being cured. To say that permanent poverty was 'invented' is perhaps putting it too strongly. Like Topsy (as they say) it just growed.

The first adjustments were well in line with the tradition of the subsistence minimum. One part of the Labour government's welfare state was National Assistance. Administered by the National Assistance Board (NAB), it remained closer to the old nineteenth-century poor law than the rest—not, indeed in being remotely *laisser-faire*, but in its parsimonious application of the principle that nobody should be tempted into state dependency by the generosity of the benefits.

National Assistance had been designed as the measure of last resort to protect people's subsistence standard when all else had failed—work, sobriety, sexual continence, personal savings, friendly society benefits, immediate family, state insurance benefits. As the harshest feature of the welfare state, National Assistance therefore became the centre of attention of people interested in ameliorating hardship caused by shortage of income.

The NAB commenced its work with a scale of allowances roughly in line with the recommendations of the Beveridge Report. The NAB standard was below B. Seehohm Rowntree's 1936 standard, so there was some work to be done in the 1950s on the issue of raising it to Rowntree's subsistence level.[9] But new arguments began to be put forward that seemed to give the poverty lobby a more secure life-line, and these new arguments gradually coalesced into an attack no longer on the principles of the old Poor Law, but (with the exception of universal provision) on the principles of the 1950s' welfare state itself and on all its roots in pre-1914 Liberalism and the English ethical socialism of the Labour party.

National Assistance, unlike National Insurance, was, at the point of claim and payment, purely a matter of need and income.

There was no contamination of conduct in the sense of how the claimant had put himself in that position in the first place, 'no damned nonsense about merit'. There was therefore scope for expanding the clientele by increasing the acceptance of the notion that citizens were entitled *unconditionally* to a subsistence level of housing, food, clothing, household and personal sundries and so forth, both for themselves, whatever their way of life, and their children, under whatever circumstances they had chosen to have them.

The move towards unconditional entitlement to social security benefits began quietly enough. Cole and Utting showed that one in three people *over retirement age* with entitlement to National Assistance were not receiving it:[10]

> A couple. I suggested that they should apply for National Assistance, *but they wouldn't hear of it*. He is 74 and worked past retiring age. He has a pension of £4 10s. a week, no other income and no other assets. ... The rent for the tenement is 15s. a week. It must be a struggle for them to manage.[11]

Some old people did not apply out of ignorance, some because the sums were too small for the trouble of having officials 'nosing into their affairs'. Some of them did it because memories of the 1930s remained alive, particularly among the old who were the main sufferers 'and this may lower the line by which they define poverty'—they *thought* they had enough.[12] A proportion did it out of the negative sort of pride that involves avoiding feelings of shame and disgrace. Those feelings of disgrace of not being able to manage on your own, or not having been able to manage well enough in the past, were from now on to be broken down.

The poverty lobby in the early 1960s was able to justify this approach by showing that the danger of encouraging dependency in groups who had no option but to be dependent was very low. Recipients of National Assistance were predominantly the old, widows, the sick, and people who were long-term unemployed through disability. Over two-thirds of the households with low expenditure in the 1953-54 General Household Survey had retired heads.[13] The figure was much the same a decade later: two-thirds of all individuals covered by weekly NAB allowances in the late 1950s and early 1960s were over retirement age. Three other groups of applicants were very likely to have a continuing need for help: widows and deserted wives with children; the disabled and blind; and the unemployed without benefit, a high proportion of whom had some degree of physical or mental disability. These three groups, too, raised no problem or only a slight problem of voluntary dependency.[14]

Brian Abel-Smith and Peter Townsend, in studying the Family Expenditure Surveys of 1953-54 and 1960, discovered that poverty had after all increased during the period. But it had increased among clearly 'deserving' groups. First, the proportion of the population aged 65 and over had risen, they reported, from 11.1 per cent to 11.7 per cent. Secondly, it had risen because there had been 'an appreciable rise in chronic sickness among men in their late fifties, and a very substantial one, amounting to 30 per cent, in men in their early sixties'. There had also been a very small increase in the total population of the proportion of families with four or more dependent children.[15] Abel-Smith and Townsend emphasized the large number of children in poverty as 'possibly the most novel finding', for it had been generally assumed, they said, that poverty existed overwhelmingly among the aged. For every three pensioners in poverty in 1960, there were two children in poverty, and there were considerably more children in poverty than adults of working age.[16]

The stigma attached to the receipt of state benefits had therefore to be removed. The pride connected with doing without help from others *even if you were entitled to it* had to be dissipated. In their 1965 study Abel-Smith and Townsend's first 'implication for policy' is that the 'legitimacy of the system of national assistance' was called into question by the fact that a substantial minority of the population were not receiving it even when they appeared to be entitled to it. Crucially if the dependency argument against easier access to state benefits was to be successfully combatted, the substantial minority was found particularly among the aged, where the dependency argument was irrelevant.[17]

In order to protect it from stigma the name for non-insurance benefit was changed from time to time. Within a remarkably short span of years, the movement that had started to help virtuous old, widowed, deserted, and disabled people not to feel ashamed about the impossible external conditions that had made them now dependent on others, had spread as far as university students. In the 1970s not only did 'Claimants Unions' spring up within the poverty movement, but young radicals from the new sociology and social policy departments went into government-funded 'community action programmes' and openly advocated 'ripping off the state'.

Its near equivalent was Income Support, which at last had very little stigma attached to it. As compared with what had emerged by the mid-1990s, in retrospect it could be seen that the old cultural forces had been relatively successful in endowing low-paid work with honour. That was the case at any rate with the people who did it—the pride in being a good and reliable tram driver, the pride in being a strong and effective navvy. The obverse was, on the one side, contempt for the sloven and the slacker, for the able-bodied man who was letting himself, his workmates, his neighbourhood or his family down; and on the other, feelings of shame at failure to maintain one's own family. It was better to work decently for enough money than get more money in dishonourable trades or by depending on charity or the parish or state.[18]

These cultural assessments were progressively undermined. As a source of income pornography was as good as a professional service. The issue then hinged not on self-esteem or duty, but solely on cash. Perceptions were permitted and encouraged that living on benefit was as good as being in a low-paid job, and it gradually became consensual that it was reasonable and proper for a person not be able to 'afford to work'.

Another, not very promising, idea that began to be introduced was that having to be careful with the household budget was itself an imposition on people that the state ought to assist in mitigating. The problem of people not spending their money wisely had already been recognized by Rowntree in his first survey of York. He had defined secondary poverty as the state of affairs where the 'total earnings would be sufficient for the maintenance of merely physical efficiency were it not that some portion of it is absorbed by other expenditure either useful or wasteful'. But Rowntree was somewhat more interested in the problem of improvident expenditure on drink and gambling than the burdens of budgeting, even though such wasteful expenditure was 'often the outcome of the adverse conditions under which too many of the working classes live ... in sordid streets, frequently under overcrowded and unhealthy conditions, compelled very often to earn their bread by monotonous and laborious work, and unable, partly through limited education and partly through overtime and physical exhaustion, to enjoy intellectual recreation'.[19] As Hagenbuch suggested in 1958, 'The problem of secondary poverty, although it cannot be measured ... comes into greater prominence as primary poverty recedes'.[20]

Here is an example of the way in which the idea that management was itself a burden to be lifted made its early appearance. Cole and Utting found that among poor old people there was a feeling that they now had a reasonable standard of living.

'The rent is paid, and by and large food is adequate.'

'My children don't have only bread and jam for their tea.'

'We have butter, not margarine.'

But, Cole and Utting note, to get adequate food meant that they had to be careful to do their shopping at the cheapest shops, search for cheap cuts of meat and cheap (they say 'throw-out') vegetables and fruit. This bore particularly hard upon the old. It also bore hard on anybody who was not very mobile or, as in villages, had restricted shopping facilities.

Fuel is sometimes [sic] consciously economized upon ... Cleaning materials, prescription charges for those without National Assistance, and other semi-medical and toilet items are also regarded as a prime charge upon income, together with insurance.

Few clothes are bought; among the young with children jumble sales (an important agent of redistribution in a society in which far more people have good clothes to throw away), the WVS or relatives are the providers. Among the old it is more often the family—or just managing to do 'with what we have'. The fact that many appear so relatively well-clad is a reflection of the affluence of the rest of society.

The suggestion appears for the first time in the early 1960s that it is not merely inappropriate for a family to have too little to manage on. It is inappropriate that they should have to have a 'constant preoccupation with managing'.[21]

The older poverty researchers had been especially interested in the question of what *improvements* had been made on the past. By 1936 the old age pension of 10s. a week, supplemented by grants from the public assistance committee and charity, was enough for mere existence, but there were far fewer in that position than there had been in 1899.[22] There were still people in abject poverty in 1949, but there were far fewer than in 1936. By

1959 the national insurance pension was below National Assistance levels, and the National Assistance level was still somewhat below Rowntree's 1936 level, but fewer old people (perhaps five per cent) were actually living below the National Assistance level than in 1948.

This constant improvement meant that comparisons with the past were leading people to believe that things were getting better. Historical knowledge, therefore, gradually became professionally *infra dig*, whether in the sophisticated form of anti-positivism, or in the simpler form of honest ignorance.

13

Relative Poverty

A new, much more durable idea of poverty began to form. The benefit rate was quite quickly redefined, not as the sum of money that kept a person *out* of poverty, but the proof that he was *in* poverty. Another refinement was stumbled upon. In order not to disadvantage the prudent, a person was entitled to National Assistance even if he had a few savings or a small income from some other source. As the *average* 'disregard', as it was called, added on average 25 per cent to the National Insurance scale rate, and was therefore the average income of the poorest, (Wedderburn was one of the first to suggest) 'it would not be unreasonable' to take resources of not more than 25 per cent above National Assistance scale rates (after rent was paid) as being resources at the poverty line.

On that basis it was estimated that two-and-a-half million British old people were living at or around the poverty line.[1] Once that idea entered the fund of ideas of the poverty lobby, it proved a powerful yet simple way to increase the number in poverty. For why stop at 25 per cent above social security benefits? Why not 40 per cent above? Why not 50 per cent? From 1953 a random sample of over 3,000 households supplied records of income and expenditure for two consecutive weeks each year.[2] Its unpublished tabulations were soon recognized as a magnificent source for the study of the effect of deriving different proportions of the population in poverty by applying different definitions of poverty to them. 'The higher the poverty line the more we draw in a sizeable pocket of wage earners.'[3] This allowed much more scope for righteous indignation by inflating the figures more or less at will, rather than following the tedious procedures of the poverty surveys up to the 1950s, of trying to arrive at some empirical measure of what was actually happening over time.

What also began to emerge in the early 1960s was a conceptualization of poverty that was to prove even more fruitful (at least so long as the general standard of living rose). 'If we remember that real disposable income has increased by twice as much as the real increase in National Assistance since 1948, it cannot be thought unreasonable to say that National Assistance rates are a reflection of pre-war thinking about subsistence.'[4] That was not yet 'relative poverty' in the modern sense. But it was coming close.

It is an anomaly that its really effective take-over dates from Runciman's *Relative Deprivation* of 1966, for (as we have seen) Runciman himself still used the concept principally in the sense, damaging and retrograde to the poverty lobby, of working people comparing themselves with their parents and grandparents, or their present conditions with their own previous, lower standard of living. Runciman had been impressed by the *failure* of the poor in Britain to be resentful of the rich. The results of his own survey research had led him to the conclusion, indeed, that at the standard of living they enjoyed in the post-war 'affluent society' and under the other cultural and structural conditions of British life, 'there was, in fact, no occasion for manual workers to make the sort of cross-class comparisons likely to suggest themselves to academic investigators examining the statistical evidence'.[5] To make the poorer members of society aware of their relative deprivation in the here-and-now in the cross-class sense, and to abandon their feelings of relative well-being in the historical and cross-cultural sense, became, therefore, the objective of the emerging poverty lobbies and their academic supporters. Relative poverty in its modern form means *only* the income and possessions of the poorest in the here-and-now relative to the rich in the here-and-now. One of the main uses of the modern concept is to *obliterate* any comparisons with the past not, as in Runciman's usage, to point them out.

In 1992 the Rowntree Foundation published the results of the work of the Family Budget Unit of York University.[6] The standards set up were purely relative and quite immune to any improvements in the absolute standard of living. One, what half the population had, was a 'modest but far from luxurious' lifestyle. The other, lower standard, was what three-quarters of the population possessed. Launching the report, Professor Jonathan Bradshaw, who led the research, said the low cost budget would buy an 'extremely mean' standard of living.[7] Clothing was budgeted at £29.27 a week, based on the cheapest items available at C&A. Food was budgeted at £58.67, based on 300 basic items priced at Sainsbury's. There could be no car, the budget covered public transport only. Nothing was allowed for either drinking or smoking. Nothing was allowed for an annual holiday; only for a day trip to Blackpool.

In order to reach this 'low' and 'extremely mean' standard of living, a household of two adults and two children (whose weekly state cash benefits amounted at that time to £105 a week) would need another £36 a week.

By the time the 1995 Report was published, insufficiency of income could be defined in these relative terms so effectively and naturally that *The Times*—not to speak of the *Guardian* or *The Independent*—could headline the 'fact' that the average family needed £21,000 a year for 'basics'. Keeping a family provided with what most people regarded as the 'necessities of life', Jeremy Laurance's report said, cost £300 a week. Benefits provided by the state amounted to only £100 a week.[8] As £21,000 a year was £5,000 above average *earnings* in 1992, the scope for further employment in the poverty lobby was assured.

Relative poverty was, then, the really fruitful invention. By 1995 it was (to again use Laski's term) 'the inarticulate major premise' of the Rowntree Report. It was not a notion to be thought about, much less justified. It was simply taken for granted. It was by then also very generally taken for granted by serious journalists as the correct (or only possible) view of the meaning of life for the poorest people in any society, no matter how rich that society might be or become. The United Nations' Development Programme's annual report 1996 featured the fact that while there had been a dramatic surge in economic growth in 15 countries since 1979, economic stagnation or decline had affected 100 countries. The economic decline of some societies had lasted longer and in some cases had been deeper than the Depression of the 1930s. In many countries of Eastern Europe and the former USSR *average* income had declined by *at least* 20 per cent. Great Britain was ranked sixteenth out of 174 countries in citizens' quality of life, above both Denmark and Germany.[9] The grip of the notion of 'relative poverty' was so firm, however, that *The Times*' report treated its readers to the headline 'Richest 358 People "Own as Much as Half the World"'—treating, absurdly, the industrial and commercial assets that the rich control as if they were the same as the income that the poor have to spend. In Britain (*The Times* reported the UN document as saying), the poorest 20 per cent had an average income of less than £2,600 a year while the national average was £11,100. This gap, *The Times* says, was similar to that in Nigeria. The report in *The Times* gave the income of the poor in Britain. It did not give the income of the poor in Nigeria, for whom £2,600 a year would be beyond the dreams of avarice. In any other context the implication that £2,600 a year was not enough for the British, but more than enough for the Nigerians, would have been called 'racism'. Relative poverty was everything.[10]

Relative poverty breaks away altogether from the idea, not just of a satisfactory minimum standard of living that the community through the state, or private benevolence, or a combination of both must afford each of its members, but from any idea of a 'satisfactory' minimum standard of living at all.

The concept of relative poverty is a weapon of agitation that the Left wields. But as it has been used so far, it is more effective in securing benefits for the well-to-do in society than for the less well-to-do. For the idea of the ever-rising cash standard of living, the limitless pursuit of commodities, provides a great and continuous stimulus to the economy, providing the well-to-do with the goods, and leaving the poor with the discontent. As an ideological concept, therefore, relative deprivation is far better adapted to modern industry and commerce than any of the old Christian or ethical-socialist notions of what is 'sufficient', either for one specific purpose or another, or for 'a good life'.

14

Short-term Changes and Long-term Trends

T here is an old story about an ant who liked to sit on the axle of a cart. Every now and again it would move its legs like a clown walking on a barrel around the circus ring. When the cart did then trundle off, the ant thought it had made it do so. When the cart did not move, the ant did not alter its opinion. It simply thought that it had not tried hard enough that day, or that the condition of the ground was against it.

But anyone who shared the ant's exaggerated sense of its own importance, and spent his time feeding it leaves, would not go as far as the driver who fed oats to the horse. That the ant is easier and cheaper to deal with, that dealing with the ant is more feasible than dealing with the horse, and so on, may all very well be true. But when the cart moves, it is the horse that is doing most of the work, not the ant which is only doing some of it.

If social problems are to be solved, the correct underlying causes must be addressed. It is not helpful from the point of view of even beginning to tackle the problems presented to society by young men to claim a false cause-and-effect between poverty and anti-social conduct, so that the poorest will receive or earn more money, and so that the gap between the poorest and the richest will be narrowed. The fact that the poverty lobby has embraced a 'good cause' does not entitle it to a free rein as against other good causes. The poverty=crime propaganda may help to solve the problem of low incomes for those who ought to have more. What is wholly damaging is the effect of the ceaseless propaganda that explains *away* the growth of the anti-social conduct of boys and young men as the necessary result of their material circumstances in comparison with those of other people, and which therefore affects the way in which boys and young men define their 'legitimate' responses to their frustrations.

Whatever the background of the person using this theory, and whether he is aware of it or not, this is the most vulgar of vulgar Marxism. It is not sophisticated dialectical materialism. For it simply explains conduct in terms of the volume of commodities a person can purchase. All social evils stem from shortfalls of cash, and all social problems can be cured by money.

Marx himself was extremely hostile to this view.[1] For Marx, even as early as 1848, believed that capitalism had *already then* produced enough overall for an adequate material standard of living for the whole population of Britain. Indeed, in his view, that had been the case 'for many decades past'. The weight of his attack was *against* the way in which all things were being calculated in cash-income terms, and being turned into commodities by the capitalist bourgeoisie. Capitalism had left remaining between man and man no other nexus, he wrote, 'than naked self-interest, than callous cash payment'. The family relation had been reduced to a mere money relation. Capitalism had resolved personal worth into exchange value, and all the virtues that would flourish after the Communist revolution were being drowned, by capitalism's over-valuation of money, in the 'icy waters of egotistical calculation'.[2]

But as distinct from Marx's apparently genuine and heart-felt fulminations against what he called the fetishism of commodities are his views on the strictly tactical mobilization of existing, and the creation of new, bases of discontent. The groundwork for the revolution could be laid, he recommended, by the communists making demands on the existing system that it could not possibly meet. If demands were made, and it proved that the system could meet them after all, then new 'impossible' demands must take their place. In the mid-nineteenth century the impossible demands that occurred to Marx were taxation demands. He had said that if the bourgeoisie agreed to the taxation of the rich, the communists should demand proportional taxation. If the bourgeoisie agreed to proportional taxation, the communists should demand progressive taxation. If the bourgeoisie agreed to progressive taxation, the communists should demand crippling progressive taxation. British capitalism survived all of those.[3]

Nearly a century later, in Trotsky's own updating of the 1848 *Communist Manifesto*, his *Death Agony of Capitalism* of 1938, this strategy, the so-called 'Transitional Programme', was elevated to a central tenet of Trotskyist Marxism. The over-riding purpose was to destabilize existing society by whatever means came to hand, and attack and weaken all bourgeois institutions. So long as the demand was in principle compassionate and worthy—and the more closely it coincided with the ideas and sentiments of bourgeois society itself, the better—it did not matter much what its precise content was. All you had to do was ask for more. As Professor Sassoon reminds us, that was her 'up-the-ante' strategy in the political game she played 'in an earlier Trotskyist incarnation'.[4] The only point of being a player is to be able to raise the stakes, and then denounce fellow-players as cowards and traitors. Trotsky listed as an impossible demand the tying of wages to the rate of inflation. British capitalism survived that demand.[5]

In 1938, that state benefits should be secured against inflation was not just an impossible demand; it was unimaginable one. But a Trotskyist did not have to have much imagination in the 1970s to realise that British state benefits were a transitional programme's ideal subject. 'If the bourgeoisie agree to the guaranteed subsistence benefits, the Trotskyists must demand subsistence plus 40 per cent. If the bourgeoisie agree to subsistence plus 40 per cent, the Trotskyist must demand one-third of average earnings. If the bourgeoisie agree to one-third of average earnings, the Trotskyist must demand what three-quarters the population own and consume. If the bourgeoisie agree to what three-quarters the population own and consume, under stipulations of work and good behaviour from the able-bodied, the Trotskyist must demand what three-quarters of the population own and enjoy, without any conditions. If the bourgeoisie agree to what three-quarters of the population own and consume, without conditions, the Trotskyist must demand what half of the population own and consume ...'

Clearly, many people, from quite different viewpoints than that of the Trotskyist, could and did formulate the same demands quite independently. Some did so out of sheer good will. Some did so out of the modified good will of those who expect others to pay totally or in part for their generous sentiments. Some did so because they are potentially the direct beneficiaries. Very few people would want to oppose them. What possible arguments *can* there be against giving the poor a higher standard of living? Most people, myself included, would rather be in the top tenth than in the bottom tenth of the income distribution. Were I in the bottom tenth, I would greatly prefer that the bottom tenth of incomes generally were close to the incomes of the top tenth.[6]

'Poverty' is therefore on all fronts an excellent battle cry. But that does not make the 'Poverty!' of the battle cry a scientific concept. Even less does it prove that the rise in social disorder is due to the rise in poverty as such, nor does it validate the definition of the situation that says that poverty is a justifiable reason for engaging in acts of social disorder.

In statistics there is the very familiar 'base line problem'. Stepping back from the details of a time series there is a clear long-term upward trend (say, of the prices of shares on the stock exchange). If a segment of a few months is looked at in detail, prices can be going up, down, or staying still.

The movements up and down in the short term have, of course, their causes. They have, of course, effects. People can win and lose fortunes. But to explain what is happening to share prices over the longer period requires that causes that are operating over a long period be identified. In the 1930s the great economist J.M. Keynes said that capitalist growth was at an end. Investors could no longer look forward to an income from either capital growth or dividends. They would just have to save their sovereigns, put them in a box under their beds, and in their old age take them out when they wanted to go shopping. The long-term rise in the stock market that Keynes thought was impossible has been the result of the growth in industrial and service productivity.

At any given level of the propensity to riot, 'the light nights' partly explain why a particular riot has taken place. Superintendent Dick Spring was saying something perfectly sensible and true about the boys and young men on the Villa housing estate at Sunderland in the summer of 1996. At a given level of the propensity to express oneself at someone else's expense the invention and marketing of the can of spray paint explains the multiplication of graffiti in recent years. Poverty and unemployment—far more important as causes—are nevertheless like them in that, given the propensity to anti-social conduct, they cause variations in the level of crime and self-destructive ways of life.

But they are like them, too, in that neither light nights nor spray paint nor poverty nor unemployment can explain the *change in the level* of the propensity to deface buildings, to commit crimes, to riot and to take drugs. Crime, rioting, acts of hooliganism and several other forms of social pathology were low and falling in the second half of the nineteenth century and the first decade of the twentieth. They were rising but were still at very low levels from the Great War to the mid-1950s.

They rose sharply in the period 1961-79 as well as the period since 1979. How can poverty and unemployment explain that pattern, however many redefinitions and shifts of ground are permitted to the people who say they do?

Clearly it was affluence that had grown in the straightforward sense, not poverty in the straightforward sense. Unemployment had been very high for extended periods when crime rates been very low, and unemployment had been low for extended periods when the crime rate had been accelerating upward. The strong long-term trend in this country had been the growth of affluence for most people in work, and rising basic benefits for nearly everybody dependent upon the state. Clearly individualistic values had increased in their appeal enormously at the expense of communitarian values, ideas of personal rights at the expense of social duties. But this strong long-term trend had also affected everybody over a long period. A long-term change in one direction can only be explained by other long-term changes in one direction. A long-term change that had affected all the population in a particular direction cannot explain the exceptional speed and distance of the change in that direction of a particular part of the population.

The expanded problems of crime, riot, vandalism and drugs had not been the work of nearly everybody over a long period. The rise had been the work of *men* over the forty years from the mid-1950s. (At the beginning of the period as at the end, mainly boys and young men.) The important causes must be discovered by studying what had happened *in this country* to *them* over *the relevant period.*

In addition to sharing the general pressures towards self-regarding behaviour (which lay at the base of all the changes), what had happened to boys and men, from 1961 to 1979 as well as from 1979 into the mid-1990s, had been the enormous *additional* influence towards self-regarding behaviour of their progressive release from the expectation and requirement that they should make a permanent home with their children and the mother of their children—whether it suited them personally or not.

15

Fathers Without Families

T here is one key aspect of the growing independence of the individual from cultural controls which links it specifically with growing crime and disorder among men. That key aspect has been their growing sexual liberation—men's freedom to engage in sexual intercourse without being powerfully constrained by social pressure to become, under the same roof, (a) life-long monogamous husbands to their sole sexual partners, and (b) life-long fathers to any children that result.[1] Legal regulation was only one part of that pressure. The law touches us, as Burke somewhere remarked, 'but here and there, and now and then'. Sustaining or undermining effective law are 'manners' in the broadest sense, from the rules of politeness to society's most important *mores*. 'Manners', he said, 'are what corrupt or purify, exalt or debase, barbarize or refine us, by their constant and steady operation, like that of the air we breath. According to their quality, they aid morals, they supply them, or they totally destroy them.'

In part the connection between men's sexual liberation on the one hand and crime on the other is the greater empirical likelihood that a child from a household from which the father is absent will engage in criminal conduct. That connection, with absent fathers, is more conventionally but erroneously described as 'putting all the blame for crime on lone mothers', 'scapegoating the lone mother', and so on, and is therefore dismissed out of hand.

But *much more important* in its criminogenic effects for *all* young men is the growth in young men's freedom to handle their frustrations in a self-regarding manner. They are much freer than they were before the 1960s to cope with their grievances, *as they themselves define and are led to define their grievances as legitimate*, without regard to the adverse consequences for their responsibilities as actually or potentially key adult members of their own families, or for that matter of their families of origin.

The progressive release of men from *sociological* fatherhood, as Malinowski called it, is only one expression, but one of the most important expressions, of the general movement from cultural control to individual licence. It is the most striking and important change of the past forty years. Nothing else has been transformed at the same rate and in the same direction, in lockstep with crime, spread over the entire forty-year period. Sexual access to women without a lifetime's commitment of the father (or of a designated kinsman, to whose children the biological father in turn was sociological father), in close domestic contact to the mother and the child, had been throughout history the prerogative only of the rich, or the powerful, or the famous—a Solomon, a Renaissance Pope, an American President, any dissolute man temporarily notorious. Such access without such commitment was suddenly extended in principle to all English males.

Certainly over that period neither a worsening stock of houses, nor rising unemployment nor deepening poverty come anywhere close to being as likely candidates for the role of crucial cause of the steep *rise* in boys' and young men's vandalism, hooliganism, drug use, and criminality in England and Wales 1961-79 and 1979-92.

What, first, of the matter of a man becoming a father without accepting, or being made to accept, the responsibilities of spousehood and fatherhood, and under the same roof as the mother and child so long as he is not kept away by work or war?

If the question of the change in the cultural conditions of boys and young men is addressed to the period since 1836, when the record of births and marriages first begins to becomes reliable, and becomes increasingly reliable, the picture is quite clear. From 1836 up to the early 1960s in this country, even in war time, the ratio of men not marrying the mother of their child by the time the baby was born had fluctuated only two or three percentage points above and below seven per cent. But between 1960 and 1984 the rate had suddenly risen from this century-long norm of well under 10 per cent to 17 per cent. In the mere twelve years after 1984 it doubled again to a third of all births.[2]

If we consider men occasioning a conception outside marriage (as distinct from a birth outside of marriage) the figure rose from 40 per cent to just under 60 per cent from the early 1980s to the early 1990s.[3]

Family researchers, theorists and media commentators associated with the poverty lobbyists, or used by them, maintain that men have always engaged in just about as much pre-marital and extra-marital sexual activity as they did in the mid-1990s. To keep the theory that growing crime is due to growing poverty in play, it is essential for poverty lobbyists to maintain that nothing else has happened that could cause crime to rise *except* the increase *since 1979* in the relative incomes of the rich as compared to the poor, the declining real incomes of the bottom tenth, and rising unemployment. Men, they allege in particular, have always 'really' had just about as little to do with their children, and been as free of their families, as is was the case in the mid-1990s.

'Cohabitation, births outside marriage, lone-parent families, repartnering and reconstituted families, were common in earlier centuries', said a major Church of England report on the family in 1995. The difference between 1995 and the past was not in male conduct, the report said, but in the fact that 'previously these things were hidden'.[4]

Running parallel to the 'moral-panic' school of crime from the 1960s to the early 1990s was the 'nothing fundamental has changed' school of sex and childrearing. The two schools reinforced one another's point of view. Crime was not increasing. The family was not fundamentally changing. How, then, could the non-existent breakdown of family life be responsible for the non-existent rise in crime?

Exponents of the 'nothing much has changed' school of family thought refer vaguely to 'previous centuries'. Lawrence Stone is a writer whose work on the family is authoritatively used by many academics and media commentators to justify the proposition that men's sexual and family situation has not significantly changed over the centuries. Yet in the Elizabethan period, according to *him*, the ratio of children whose fathers were not married to their mother when the child was born ran at the level of under four per cent. During the period of Puritan control, *he* tells us, the ratio fell steadily to a low point of one-half of one per cent in the 1650s. It was still under two-and-a-half per cent in the 1720s. There was then what he calls a 'remarkable rise', a 'striking increase', to four-and-a-half per cent in the 1760s and to six per cent after 1780.[5] That these are underestimates I do not for one moment doubt. But these are the figures that Stone supplies.

Stone himself, therefore, writing as he was before 1977, still saw a rise of *two* per cent in the figures from four-and-a-half per cent to six-and-a-half per cent, a rise of *two per cent* over a period of *forty* years as being 'remarkable' and 'striking'. Yet while he was writing his book he was in the midst of a rise from seven per cent in 1964 to 32 per cent in 1994, a rise of *twenty-five percentage points* over a period of *thirty* years.

The social effort aimed at attaching the man to his family through (if necessary) 'shot-gun' marriages and disadvantages in law, as well as the shame *suffered by his child* if he did not marry the mother, has been gradually relaxed. The effect on the *man* of stigmatizing the *child* gradually disappeared. In 1972 Lord Hodson was able to say that 'the legal incidents of being born a bastard are now almost non-existent'. The Family Law Reform Act 1987 in effect abolished the legal category of 'illegitimate child'. A child's relationship to other people was now to be construed without regard to whether or not the father or mother had ever been married to one another.[6] It removed the 'separate and disadvantageous' treatment that had been accorded to children born outside marriage under all previous legislation.[7] The terms 'legitimate' and 'illegitimate' were banned from government publications from 1988.

I am not of course recommending in any way the restoration of a social device so cruel and unjust as to make the child pay for his father's freedom from responsibility for it. I am only saying, as a matter of fact, that *as a control on men's conduct* it (like his own social disgrace in 'letting the girl down' or the insistence that if he was the father, he had to marry the mother) has almost ceased to operate.

The Children Act 1989 is quite clear on the unmarried man's liberation from his biological child. 'Where the child's father and mother were not married to each other at the time of his birth, the mother shall have parental responsibility for the child; the father shall not have parental responsibility for the child ...'[8]

Stone's figures refer to a time when contraceptive technology was poorly developed. The conception/fornication ratio must therefore have been very high compared with today. We have had the modern sheath since 1928. We have had the contraceptive pill since 1961. There was never much restriction on knowledge about or use of the pill. The taboos that surrounded discussion about and the sale and use of the sheath were dissipated from the late 1970s onwards. By the mid-1990s the last traces of taboo had been dissolved.[9] The dramatic reduction in the conception/fornication ratio therefore makes the rise in the figures of conceptions outside marriage an index also of the increase in men's freedom to fornicate.

Men's sexual liberation from the late 1950s onwards was largely a demand made upon British society, not by the products of the mines and factories, or the secondary modern and grammar schools, but by establishment figures in the higher civil service, ex-public-schoolboy entertainers at and from the élite universities, and senior politicians who came from the same social background (or those from puritan working-class backgrounds who had assimilated themselves to the *mores* of the sexually enlightened upper-middle class and aristocracy). The Wolfenden recommendations, and the attacks on the public notion of 'obscenity' in the *Oz* and *Lady Chatterley's Lover* trials, were all part of the middle- and upper-class spirit of the times, which owed to 'the working class' nothing but the absurd adolescent fantasy that the working class was already sexually libertine.

By one historical accident television was on the scene by the 1960s to celebrate and disseminate the shedding of men's sexual inhibitions and controls. By another, a vast constituency receptive to such ideas was contemporaneously created. The expansion of the universities after the 1963 Robbins' report put unprecedentedly large numbers of sexually mature young men with other unmarried young people, away from their own homes, kinship networks, neighbourhoods and towns.

The exponents of men's sexual liberation had the satisfaction of hearing the Archbishop of Canterbury himself not just apologise for, but say that the Church had been *guilty of* treating pre-marital, extra-marital and self-indulgent sex too seriously as a sin. The Church ought to be more interested in such issues as global poverty.[10]

For a brief period, too, the social and self-control of fornication did not seem to matter so much because of the reduced threat posed by venereal diseases. Fleming had written his paper about penicillin in 1928. Its clinical potential was discovered by Flory and his team in the 1940s, and was used in controlling venereal disease among servicemen and servicewomen during the war. After 1945 it came into use in the civilian population.

Serious inconvenience resulting from sexual activity was also much reduced for the man by the much greater ease with which the option of abortion could be chosen by the woman. Before 1967 nearly all abortion was illegal. By 1995 20 per cent of all conceptions were being aborted. In Greater London the proportion was 25 per cent. In inner London it was 35 per cent.[11] By August 1996 the medical profession was making it clear, if somewhat inadvertently, that the provisions of Abortion Act 1967 were being applied in the spirit of 'abortion on demand'. A professor of obstetrics, Phillip Bennett, was reported to have performed more abortions than he had delivered live babies. The comprehensiveness of the conquest of the abortion issue by the unconditional pro-choice viewpoint and its dominance of medical and popular culture was highlighted by the fact that the professor's own reported belief was that abortion was morally wrong. Within the context of what was taken for granted about a professor of obstetrics' job in the 1990s this had not prevented him from performing 3,000 abortions in the course of ten years.[12] Professor Bennett's part in the decision to abort a healthy twin because its mother already had one child, and she did not feel she could cope with two new babies at once, was defended by the head of ethics of the British Medical Association. She is quoted as giving as her grounds the fact that 'the legislation is there' which says that 'babies born when the women don't want them are often psychologically harmed' (sic). This formulation, astonishing in several respects whether regarded as an ethical or legal justification for the abortion in question, was perhaps the result of the BMA's senior ethical expert being misreported. The report quotes her as adding that she did not think that there was 'really any difference' between an operation that left no foetus and one which aborted one of two twins; and that 'nature' destroys one twin 'often' anyway. The Department of Health said it was legal to abort the healthy foetus of one of the twins because, on the grounds of the mother's view that she would be able to manage one, but not two, additional babies, the Abortion Act would have allowed any doctor to abort both.[13] The editor of the *Journal of Obstetrics and Gynaecology*, a consultant obstetrician, was reported as saying that 'any woman who has an early pregnancy and wants a termination can get it'.[14]

For a week or so the Bennett interview was discussed widely in the press and other media. Although reporters from the *Daily Express* eventually unearthed the fact that the woman in question was the well-to-do working wife of a company director and not a struggling lone mother, Professor Bennett had described her in the original interview as single and in straitened circumstances.[15] But for as long as Professor Bennett's version that she was an unmarried mother was believed, I came across no statement either in print or on the radio or television that paid the slightest attention to this fact. The effect on the past and future behaviour *of the man* of the destiny of his unborn child being defined as no business of his was rarely if ever mentioned. Abortion was treated exclusively as a women's issue. At the time, the BBC did incidently deal with men and abortion when a panel of selectors approved a list of fifty ideal males. But the panel's choice of the ideal was clearly predicated upon the man's conformity with the view that abortion was not a man's business. Pride of place among 'ideal men' went to those who had given women 'control over their own bodies', most notably (in the panel's opinion) Sir David Steel for his role in the passage of the 1967 Abortion Act.[16]

Yet 'abortion on demand' was a social usage that did not only affect the woman. It had profound effects on what it meant to be a man. A public opinion that approved his agreeing to the abortion of his own child, if that was what the mother desired, had broken the link between his sexual conduct and the potential of his being a father within his family. For the link to be broken it did not require that public opinion should be uniform on that point. All that was necessary was that strong elements of public opinion, and especially of prestigious and influential public-opinion formers like BBC editors and BBC journalists, should deprive the man of all responsibility for, and obliterate all male disgrace and guilt from, sexual practices that resulted in the termination of an extra-family paternity. Nor did it mean that all doctors should be willing to certify in nearly all circumstances that the provisions of the Abortion Act 1967 had been met, or that all gynaecologists should be willing to terminate pregnancies. It only required that the culture of the medical profession generally had shifted decisively in that direction. A contribution that strikingly demonstrated the content of culture of both medicine and the media at the very top came from one person who united the two roles—from the chairman of the BBC, who was simultaneously chairman of Professor Bennett's hospital trust. He said, 'I find nothing in what Professor Bennett has said or done to be worthy of censure'. When the woman's real circumstances were disclosed, the chairman of the Birth Control Trust said, 'A woman can be in a well-paid job, have lots of money and support from her partner, but feel very strongly that having two children is not what she wants. She should have that freedom'.[17]

This is not a discussion of the right and wrongs of abortion in general, or of any abortion in particular. It is solely a discussion of the effects of abortion-on-demand on the sexual and childcare conduct of boys and men and, through that, on their civic conduct. For abortion at the request of the pregnant female has profound effects also on the conduct of the impregnating male. The new system meant a man's chances were greatly improved of enjoying sexual activity without further consequences when the woman chose to control her own body by giving him access to it. Her control of her own body at the stage of sexual intercourse could wilfully, carelessly or through misfortune lead to a conception. The woman's control over her own body at the next stage, that of terminating her pregnancy, did not mean any longer to the same extent that she also controlled specifically his life-time resources as husband and father. (Even though the case under discussion was that of a married couple, the Chairman of the Birth Control Trust said 'partner' and not 'husband'.) The resources she controlled in order that she might 'control her own body' were state resources through the state's provision for abortion purposes of professors of obstetrics, nurses, orderlies, hospital beds, furnaces and so on, a state of affairs in which the biological father's own responsibilities were diluted to that common to all tax payers and national insurance contributors.

In 1996 the Inland Revenue rules governing who could continue to benefit from the pension of a person who had died were clarified to ensure that the man who expressed his sexuality in such a way that he was the economic dependant of another man would qualify. 'An unmarried partner, whether of the same or opposite sex, can qualify for a survivor's pension.' Financial interdependence, not conformity to the system that favoured the procreation and sustenance of children within marriage, 'would be an acceptable criterion'.[18] Questioned on the speech on the family delivered in October 1996, referred to in the Introduction, the Leader of the Labour party, Tony Blair, was non-committal on whether he included in his definition of the family a gay couple raising a child.[19] Such an extension, of course, would have deprived his speech of all practical significance. Translated as 'a Labour government's family policy must be to foster all *varieties* of "family"', it would mean only that he was in favour of the sexual and childrearing status quo of 1996.[20]

Men have been progressively released since the mid-1950s from social pressures and institutional arrangements that required them to channel their sexual energies into reproduction within the family. Public opinion, the law, and the tax structure before the 1960s had favoured the man who had done so. By the mid-1990s this was no longer the case. The average married family was much better off than the average lone-parent family. But the married family on a low income was made much worse off than the lone-parent family with the same income by the benefit and tax system. As Patricia Morgan points out:

taking all benefits, taxes and rents into account, a married couple with two small children earning £150.00 gross will end up with £136.11. A single parent with two small children claiming her £40.00 disregards with a gross wage of £150.00 ends up with £170.62.

The married man's family of four, that is, ended up with having £14 deducted from his £150. The lone-parent household of three ended up by having £21 added its £150. The larger household, because it was a married family, was therefore £45 worse of than the smaller lone-parent household on the same gross earnings. Even on a part-time gross wage of £75 a week the lone-parent household of three received more than the married family of four on a gross wage of £150—over £163.[21] But in 1995 a start was made in reducing the 'premium' (=reward) paid to the lone-parent by the benefit system. The universal one-parent benefit, and the one-parent premium for those on income support, were frozen for *new* lone-parents. They were no longer to be increased in line with inflation. By the autumn of 1996 measures were under discussion to freeze these supplements for all lone parents and, within the lone-parent category, to treat lone parents who were widows or widowers better than never-married lone-parents.[22]

Except for the handful of cases of divorce by Private Act of Parliament, divorce in this country was allowed only from 1857. After 1857 divorce was possible if one of the spouses committed a grave matrimonial offence. This was for long perceived primarily as the offence of throwing the issue of paternity into confusion within marriage—the offence of one man being betrayed, possibly, into the care and maintenance of another man's child.

In the late 1950s about 10,000 men a year, without children as well as with children, were divorcing their wives. When the law was changed under the 1969 Divorce Reform Act the number rapidly rose to nearly 40,000 men a year, with and without children.

By the mid-1990s there were 95,000 divorces a year of married couples *with at least one child*, affecting 176,000 children a year.[23] One hundred years before, by contrast, the average annual divorce rate was about 300 in total, of couples without children as well as those with children. Just as by the mid-1990s the medical profession were operating the 1967 Abortion Act in the spirit of 'abortion on demand', so by the mid-1990s the lawyers were operating the 1969 Divorce Act in the spirit of 'divorce on demand'.

In 1988 a discussion paper from the Law Commission suggested that there was no need for the legal system to support marriage any more than it supported 'any other living arrangement'.[24] The subsequent Green Paper, and the Family Law Bill of 1996 that followed it, in effect announced that *spousehood* in itself was no longer the business of the public.[25] The Foreword to the Green Paper contained the statement that the law can never 'prescribe the expectations' with which people enter marriage 'and so cannot enforce them'. Thus was the sociologically exceptional opinion of Britain's social-affairs élite of the previous thirty years presented to the softened-up public as a universally valid generalization.

Those who expressed the view that the law made no difference, and had made no difference, to the stability of the average marriage based themselves on the implausible proposition that although there were only 32,000 actual divorces in 1961, there were in addition 160,000 couples in that year, and another 160,000 in 1962, another 160,000 in 1963, and so on, who were actually married still, but were only together because the law did not allow them to divorce. They were 'divorce equivalents'. They were 'virtually' divorced couples. According this view, the law did not affect the determination of married people to make theirs a life-long relationship which, if it could not be loving, fruitful or fulfilling, then at least it could be tolerable. Changes in the law, the experts on the family in the legal profession were now saying, had simply made visible what previously existed. According to this proposition, the fact that the law did not enable them to divorce except on the grounds of a serious matrimonial offence (or by them elaborately faking one) had no or little effect on how they related to each other and to other people from day to day.

By the mid-1990s, of course, that *was* the situation. The situation had been brought about by a series of small movements. Seen from the point of view of the population it was a process of drift. From the point of view of most of the senior guardians of the culture in the church, the law, the universities and the responsible media it was the result of their apathy, naïvety or misjudgement. From the point of view of those actively encouraging those changes, it was the population's shunted progress down a 'betrayal funnel'.

By the 1990s, it *was* true that the law could neither prescribe nor enforce something that public opinion would not *by then* accept. But in Britain for centuries the law and public opinion did together most strongly define and effectively enforce through marriage (and the endless array of rewards and penalties that supported marriage) the social obligations of the man for his own children within the household of his children and his children's mother.

When the Family Law Act of 1996 comes into operation, a husband even blatantly at fault will be free to terminate the relationship with much less legal difficulty than the *defaulting* party in almost any commercial situation. Marriage thus became almost unique among relationships in so far as one's own delinquency was sufficient grounds for dissolving it. The amendments proposed in Parliament by MPs who wished to support the institution of marriage, even where they were accepted, did not touch on this basic point. The privatization of marriage had already gone so far that the amendments concerning 'mediation' periods of eighteen or twenty-one months instead of twelve could only be of symbolic significance to any but those professionals and semi-professionals who themselves had a financial stake in mediation.

A principal concern of the BBC's social-affairs editor appointed in 1988 (a highly representative figure of the cultural élite in a key cultural position) had been to 'take the shame out of divorce', and she was one of the first to celebrate the passage of the Bill into law. The Marriage Guidance Council had changed its name to Relate, and its Chief Executive also publicly welcomed the Act's 'no-fault' essence and its 'mediation' auxiliaries. Her *credo* was that individuals should be given the opportunity to 'talk through their feelings' so that the 'relationship is stronger in the end'.[26]

The Lord Chancellor, whose Bill it had been, said that the criterion of the Act's success would be that it 'strengthened marriage'. But these innocent sentiments from the most senior legal official in the land, who was himself an adherent of a strict Scottish Christian sect, were an effective demonstration of how thoroughly the social-affairs élite had been impregnated by anti-family propaganda (where they were not already active disseminators of it). Since *Putting Asunder* in the mid-1960s, first the appeal *to* the churches, and then the case *from* the churches, has been that weaker divorce laws will strengthen the institution of marriage. Senior clerical figures were on hand to make the same claim for the Family Law Bill 1996:

> I hope that opponents of the present Bill will not go on repeating unsubstantiated charges that it will 'undermine the strength of the marriage contract' ... It is far more likely to have the reverse effect.[27]

Why were there so many fewer divorces before the 1960s? It was because the system before the 1960s was a child-centred one. As it takes fifteen or twenty years to raise a child in the home, for all practical purposes the two adults had to settle down from the beginning to make their own relationship a life-long one. If they subjected their children to either marital quarrels or to their parents' separation, then they were the subjects of public censure. However much it would have suited the husband, or the wife, or both of them, to part, they had to find a *modus vivendi* and stay in the same home. That was because it was generally believed (even before research showed the old intuitive public opinion to be probably correct) that on the average children of divorced parents did worse than even the children of quarrelling parents.[28] Parents stuck together, and most of them did their best, even if their own adult situations were unhappy, 'for the sake of the children'.

Spousehood (as distinct from parenthood), from being up to the late 1960s the most binding of contracts, by the mid-1990s has become one of the least binding. By mid-1996, therefore, Dutschke's 'long march through the institutions' had been almost entirely completed so far as the traditional family was concerned.

> Some commentators have argued that the relative proportion of children affected by 'broken marriages' was at least as high in the past as it is today.[29]

> It looks very much as if modern divorce is little more than a functional substitute for death.[30]

Two comments must be made on this very popular and influential view of the matter.

The first is that losing a parent through death is very different in its consequences from losing a resident parent by divorce. Certainly, on today's evidence, being made a widow or widower, or having a widowed mother, are quite different in their effects from having divorced a spouse or having a divorced parent.[31]

The second is that the argument, that families were broken as quickly by death in the past as they are by divorce today, and therefore the man (and the woman) were as free from the bonds of marriage then as they are today—that men's situation has not changed significantly—depends upon an elementary demographic error. It is true that the expectation of life *at birth* was much lower in the past than it is today. In the 1870s the expectation of life for a man at birth was only 41 and for a woman only 45. At the end of the nineteenth century a man's expectation of life at birth was still only 44. It is now 73.[32]

But the relevant figure is not the expectation of life at *birth*. It is the expectation of life at *marriage*. The first reliable figure for the expectation of life *at the age of 20* in this country is that for 1871. A man *aged 20* could expect to live, not until he was 41 (his expectation of life at birth), but until he was 59.[33]

Marriage is increasingly being preceded or replaced by the freer association of cohabitation. Whatever may be the true picture for times for which we have no reliable data, the much more reliable data of the past thirty years show a great expansion in men's freedom to live with a woman without marrying her first. Of those women under 30 years who first married in the years 1965-69, only three per cent had cohabited with their future husband. Among those marrying for the first time 1970-74 the rate had suddenly quadrupled to 12 per cent, and by 1985-89 it had more than quadrupled again to 51 per cent.[34]

A sense of the extreme rapidity of men's liberation from marriage as a condition of living with a woman, and an indication of future trends, is provided by the figures on 16-19 year-olds. Among 16-19 year-old women living in 'unions' in Great Britain in 1980, 13 per cent were cohabiting. This proportion tripled 1980-86 (1986=42 per cent), and increased almost five-fold 1980-89 (1989=62 per cent).[35]

For some time those who attributed the rise in social disorder to low income and a widening gap between those high and low in the income scale propagated the view that cohabitation was marriage without the meaningless piece of civil paper or a meaningless church ritual. But by the mid-1990s the instability of cohabitation was clearly established, and the breakup of cohabiting couples was making its due contribution to the rise in the number of fatherless households.[36]

In 1976 there were 90,000 households in Great Britain with dependent children where the father had not married the mother and was not a member of the household of the mother and child or children. By 1991 there were 430,000. In 1976 290,000 households with dependent children did not have the father as part of the household due to divorce or separation. By 1991 there were 680,000.[37] That was how rapidly and how greatly the cultural position of men in British society had been transformed.

All these trends had mattered to everybody in their capacity as consumers with an interest in a buoyant economy. To most who were not in the category of the low-income lone-parent household, diffusely it was highly beneficial in economic terms. With a stable population and therefore potentially a stagnant size of market for consumer goods, the breakup of the population into ever smaller units came as a Godsend to industry and services.

A never-married mother and her non-cohabiting boyfriend required not one but two dwellings. Even if they were cohabiting, the technicalities of state benefit provisions very often meant that he, as well as the mother, had to have, even if he did not live in, a council house or other accommodation to make sure that they jointly received as much state benefit as was obtainable.

A divorced couple needed a house each, a refrigerator each, their own carpets, curtains and TV. Few of those planning and supporting the Divorce Reform Act 1969 or the Family Law Act 1996 had that in mind. The predominantly stated and no doubt in many cases genuinely meant intention and expected result was to stabilize the institution of marriage, to strengthen and solidify it, by ridding it of several thousand accumulated and a few thousand future failed ones.

But from the *economy's* point of view, the hardships at the bottom of the income scale are a matter of indifference. In the short run the economies of certain cities depend very heavily on incomes from state benefits, state grants, or state salaries of one kind or another, including the benefits generated by lone parenthood.

Similarly, the successive international campaigns for 'children's rights', as currently exemplified by the European Convention, by weakening the control of parents over their children generally, made the child *economically* a more powerful force, as a consumer making claims on its parent's income.[38] The intention was to protect children from slavery and sexual abuse, not to boost the market in Morphin Power Rangers' spin-offs. But that was the desirable macro-economic effect. The advantage to the economy of this attack on the authority of the adult was that it was effective whether the child was at home with both his married parents or in a home without his father being part of the household. It was probably more effective, indeed, in the latter instance than the former, that is, in the fatherless home than in the home with a father.

No capitalist plotted the downfall of the family. But it is very likely that if the economic consequences had been as severely detrimental to the economy as they were in practice beneficial to it, much more attention would have been paid to the adverse effects of the breakdown of the family on children and, through the deterioration of young men's conduct, on civil safety.

Greater attention would have been paid also to the long-term adverse effects on the economy itself. With the erosion of the obligation on men to take responsibility for their children within the context of a permanent common home, the motivation for men to improve their skills and adjust to the requirements of efficiency comes to depend more on themselves as self-regarding individuals, and less on their responsibilities as husbands and fathers for the long-term well-being of their family.

By the mid-1990s this had already made itself quite apparent in the schools. From being about equally successful in O-level days, by 1994 48 per cent of girls achieved five A-C GCSE passes, but only 36 per cent of boys. Boys had clung on in 1994 to a slight lead at A-level overall, but by the mid-1990s male students made worse use than female students of the opportunities of sixth-form colleges and colleges of further education.[39] In 1996, in the ranking of independent and state schools on A-level results, 23 of the top fifty were girls' schools, 19 were boys' schools.[40]

Boys and men had seen the diminution in their future family responsibilities, publicly defined and sanctioned. For obvious biological reasons, girls and women knew quite well that, with or without a husband and permanent father for the child, they would continue to carry the serious consequences of deliberate conception or failed contraception. At the same time, new opportunities had been opened up to them. The result was that where both the family had remained strong, and female opportunities outside the home had been opened up, educational achievements were maximized. The strength of family factors and the weakness of other alleged influences, including racial discrimination, were demonstrated clearly by the fact that, by the mid-1990s, in British schools and colleges the academic results of the children of Indian immigrants were 'consistently in excess' of those of their white counterparts at the same economic level, from the same areas, and in the same schools. The best-behaved pupils were the children of Chinese immigrants.[41]

It was because they had been deprived of the context of firm social expectations directing them to family responsibilities that British boys and youths became much more prone to deal with their frustrations by turning to crime, to riotous destructiveness, and—a problem that could and looked as if it was increasingly likely to overshadow all other economic and social problems—to drugs. In David Popenoe's words, commenting on the American scene, 'the decline in marriage has been a disaster for father-hood', and the attenuation of fatherhood has been a catastrophe for civic safety.[42]

On the morning after the passage of the Family Law Bill through the House of Commons, the reporter giving an account of the proceedings for the BBC said that the opposition to it had been the work of 'right-wing Tory MPs'. In the programme that followed a highly skilful—and, in his consistently unbiased chairmanship, exemplary—BBC presenter, Nick Ross, said that opposition had been the work 'if I can paraphrase it, of the Religious Right'. Marriage as the *private* affair of the couple, on the other hand, had been successfully defined not, of course, as 'Left-wing', but as normal, sensible, pragmatic.

So far as sexual matters were concerned, the procreation and care of children, and the relationship between their parents and other relatives, 'Right' and 'Left' were labels that had been switched round since the 1960s. Until the 1960s what Thorstein Veblen called 'male sexual incontinence' was regarded widely on the Left as the degenerate and unconscionable prerogative of the exploitative upper class.[43] The middle-class family had taken for granted in the early Victorian period that the limitations it placed upon male sexuality in the interests of responsible childrearing ranked it above the barbaric and feckless aristocracy.[44] By late Victorian and Edwardian times the main-stream working-class Left in England shared this view, and looked with disapproval equally on the licence of the very rich man and of his sexually irresponsible counterpart in the segregated 'dissolute or criminal class'. The similarity in the basic psychology and the sexual conduct of the degraded male loafer of the slums and the male of the leisure class at the other end of the social scale was stock Left-wing propaganda until well into the twentieth century.

There has always been in modern times, of course, a meeting of the extreme Left and Right in anarchism and nihilism. In both, each separate individual should do just what he or she wanted to do.

The anarchism of the Left has said that if people do as they like, all acting in accordance with their own unique moral judgements, the result will be harmony, peace, energetic activity and altruism, in sexual and parental relations as elsewhere. That is what true human nature leads us to. The anarchism of the Right has said that if people do as they like, the weakest will go to the wall. But in their case the conclusion is, 'and a good thing too'.[45]

In practice self-styled anarchists, whether in principle altruistic anarchists or in principle egoistic anarchists, often claimed complete freedom for themselves, but demanded strict adherence to rules by others. If they ruined themselves they demanded to be rescued by formally or informally socially-provided welfare measures. 'You must be a stodgy, conformist husband, grandfather, parent, neighbour or citizen, vulnerable to feelings of guilt if you don't behave decently, so that I can be a free spirit. You must do your duty towards me so that I don't have to consider my duty towards anyone.' As the parish priest wrote, 'The egoist does not tolerate egoism'.[46]

But the overwhelmingly most important body of the non-anarchist and non-nihilist Left in this country, the Labour party in this century and its predecessors, envisaged the characteristics of the *well-functioning* family of the permanently married couple and their own children—love, loyalty, duty, and service to the family's common good—should be spread into all other parts of society. In particular, public service and unselfishness on a small scale, as evidenced in the ordinary British working-class families of the time, should replace on the large scale the (supposedly) self-centred mentality of the market economy. The relationships within the voluntary association, the municipality and the state ought to be those simply of a 'larger family'.[47]

The division of labour within the working-class family in the first half of this century was not a matter of principle, but a function of the hard and dangerous demands of work outside the home, and the time-consuming and arduous work within the home. At the time no reasonable person argued—it could hardly occur to him or her—that working-class work outside the home was a privilege retained by men and perversely and selfishly withheld from women. Labour was the party of male and female equality, not least in its demand that as high a standard of fidelity, continence, sobriety and refinement should be required of fathers as was already the ideal and, as compared with men, the practice of working-class mothers.[48]

What was true of the whole forty-year period from the mid-1950s to the mid-1990s of increasing crime, violence and drug abuse was the rapid weakening of the public opinion (in which the weakening of the law played its not inconsiderable role) that had previously required men to get married to, stay married to, and live in the same home as the woman who would be the mother of their children. Over those forty years both upbringing and social control had largely ceased to take seriously even the possibility that it would be the normal experience of the child to have a married mother and father when it was born, and a home with the same mother and father until it reached adulthood. When the child had these things, then it also had a lifelong array of clear and certain grandparents, great-uncles, and great-aunts, uncles, aunts and cousins which was rich in potential providers of unconditional services and sentiments. What had marked the whole period of the rise in crime, riot, drug abuse and the loss of male motivation in education and employment had been the progressive emancipation of the boy from socialization, and the youth and man from social control, that formerly required him to be a father to his children in one home for the duration of his adult life.

As the evidence in this book has shown, the steep rise in the crime rate, the drug-addiction rate and the frequency of riots in the period 1961-79 (to revert to the time period covered by the Rowntree Report 1995) coincided with a long period of *low* unemployment; with the construction of new towns and new housing estates; with *rising* standards of living for working people absolutely; and with *declining* income inequality. Even when the highly selective data on reported income rather than on expenditure were used; even when the significance of the changed composition of the lowest tenth of income receivers was elided; even when the correlation of crime rates and unemployment rates was exaggerated, it was only for its period 1979-92 that the Rowntree Report could muster its rickety case at all.

Clearly the choice of British society by the mid-1990s was heavily skewed in the direction of men's sexual liberation. By and large, adult men, especially young men, reaped self-regarding benefits in improved sexual access to females and others, and in increased freedom from the extremely onerous responsibilities of monogamous spousehood and fatherhood. These moral choices having been made by the beneficiaries, then children, drug addicts, struggling lone mothers on housing estates, directionless young men, crime victims and eventually the economy paid the diverse costs.

The fact that these changes and their consequences might in the course of time prove to be irreversible did not alter the fact that they were *cultural* not monetary changes and their consequences. If they were to be reversed, it would be by cultural changes. They could not be reversed by the reckless repetition, by however so many persons of eminence and good will, of the message that more money would make up the deficits in children's lives due to families without fatherhood, and that more money would restore civic safety by removing the frustrations of fathers without families.

Appendix

Choice and Personal Responsibility

T he Rowntree Foundation's findings on poverty and unemployment, its interpretation of the consequences of poverty and unemployment, and its recommendations for relieving the condition of the poor and solving the problems of crime and disorder, were widely accepted in the 1990s. They were accepted across the political spectrum, and were attractive to people of good will with no interest in politics apart from the immediate interests of their clients. But its findings, as this book has shown, were tendentious. Its theory was patently, even ludicrously, false. Its recommendations were therefore fatally flawed.[1]

'Choice' and 'personal responsibility' today in Britain, as descriptions of the interaction between a person and his circumstances, are words which, where they are not excluded altogether from intelligent discussion, have to appear in the quotation marks of print, or the now common post-modernist two-fingered quotation marks of conversation. Another use of quotation marks is to indicate that the discussant dissociates himself from the concept as at least problematical and at most absurd. The same applies to the quotation marks around similar concepts such as 'voluntary conduct', 'responsibility' and 'self-help'; to many weaker words such as 'rationality', 'prudence' and 'foresight'; and of course to stronger concepts like 'free-will'.

Every individual who has ever lived has come into the world with his unique genetic endowment. That unique endowment has already been acted upon by the environment of the womb and by the circumstances of birth. The interaction of the genetic endowment with each set of circumstances produces each unique person at a given stage of his development. 'Every instant

173

is the cradle of the next.' It is this person, the product of the unceasing interaction of endowment and environment to that moment, upon which a new set of circumstances act. It is this person, as he is at that stage, who reacts to them.

In terms of physique, intelligence and hormonal balance some people come with an endowment that potentially enables them to deal with a given set of circumstances in a wide variety of ways. The endowment of others limits their responses to that identical set of circumstances to a narrow range. In terms of the environments they encounter, some people, well-endowed or poorly endowed, are fortunate in finding themselves with room to manoeuvre from occasion to occasion. Others, perhaps before the start of their lives, find themselves in the environment of the womb which, when they are born, would have hemmed them within tight limits of the number of possible human responses, or leave no room for choice at all.

The human being's reaction to his environment is qualitatively different from that of non-animate matter, and is different at least in degree from even the highest of other mammals. For the human being responds not only to what the environment is. He responds also to the environment as he believes it to be. He acts, that is, in concrete circumstances as mediated by abstract information, his own and that supplied by others. This peculiar human combination of concrete experience and abstract information may supply him with a far better version of reality than that which is available to other species or other human beings. It may also on occasion be a far worse one.

The human being is peculiar in another respect. He responds to the environment not in terms of a few crude criteria of assuaging thirst, satisfying hunger, avoiding pain, bonding with nurturers, finding a place in the hierarchy of the group, and so on. He responds in terms of the *value* he places or does not place upon one response rather than another to his environment as he believes it to be. Even the person who sees himself as an out-and-out individualist, free of all moral codes, has committed himself to the single value of self-centredness. The nihilist, who in principle puts no value on anything about his own conduct or that of anybody else, and regards all outcomes as being of equal worth, probably never even approaches his ideal in the way he actually conducts his own life.

The notion of 'outcome' is crucial in the distinction between human conduct and the behaviour of other species. Like other species, the human being reacts to his environment in terms of the immediate needs of personal survival and the security of the group, and in terms of relatively simple responses like flight and fight. But he is peculiar in the degree to which he responds in terms also of complex and remote states of affairs that he wants to bring about. To a degree not matched by other species, the human being can *imagine* more or less exotic or threatening future circumstances. The *meaning* to him of his present actions is his intention to realize those future circumstance he desires and eliminate or avoid those he fears.

The human person at any point of time, then, will respond to the circumstances in which he finds himself strictly in accordance with his personality at that time. He is the inevitable product of the series of interactions between what he has been as a person at innumerable other stages, and his circumstances at those stages. He has responded to what he believed to be the facts of his circumstances. He responds always in terms of his personal or culturally-inculcated values. His response, however, relates not only to the current situation as he perceived it and evaluated it, but also to a more-or-less deliberately contemplated future.

A distinction must thus be drawn between the person and his circumstances; between what his circumstances actually are and what he believes them to be; between the way the facts are perceived and the person's moral evaluation of them; and between the person's perception and evaluation of his current situation, and his perception and evaluation of features of the future that he fears or desires.

A further distinction must be drawn. The actual and perceived circumstances within which the human person acts are two-fold. He acts, like members of other species, on the basis of his individual experience. But again to a degree not matched by other species he acts in an environment of messages transmitted by others. He lives to a large extent in 'second-hand worlds', constructed for him by people who have access to the channels through which powerful impulses of persuasion can flow.[2]

Some of these messages come only from written records. Some come from the oral and visual symbols of people with whom he is in personal, face-to-face contact. The father transmits directly to his child explicit verbal information about what is factually true and what is morally sound. He reinforces his verbal messages with looks and gestures of approval and disapproval. He presents his child with a model to imitate. The good father transmits useful and constructive messages, and acts as a wholesome role model, the bad father does the opposite. In remoter face-to-face contacts, the careless motorist is insulted and the considerate motorist receives the reward of a wave and a smile.

Some of the messages that form part of a person's environment come through formal organizations devoted wholly or partly to the transmission of the facts as the organization believes them to be, or the transmission of messages about the way in which people should respond morally to what it is believed the facts are, or of both facts and morality: churches and sects, universities, schools, the Scouts, the Mothers' Union, the Royal and Ancient Order of Buffaloes.

In both formal organizations and informal, face-to-face, situations, for the person making choices which are correct in their eyes, the others in the organization or informal group have at their disposal a wide range of material and psychic rewards. For the person who makes the wrong choices, they have a wide range of punishments.

But in modern societies messages are also powerfully transmitted to him from the mass media of entertainment and information. Very few of these messages directly preach a sermon. Oliver Stone's 'Natural Born Killers' teaches no explicit lesson. The mass media nevertheless—frequently all the more effectively —define what is relevant to his concerns; or they undermine what he has hitherto taken for granted is relevant. They tell him what he ought to regard as goals to pursue and what are perils to be shunned. They persuade him that this is good and that is bad; or they tell him that nothing is good, and nothing is bad. They open up possibilities of heroic and self-sacrificing conduct that had seemed beyond human scope. Or they tell him that what he had shunned as perverse, is normal, and what he had embraced as worthy is perverse. But if he does not accept these messages, then the song writers, the music-makers, the journalists, the feature editors, the broadcasters, and the film-makers have no other weapons in their armoury. The only power of the mass media is the message from afar.

One person's choice is part of another person's circumstances. The lifestyle choices of an adult in a family, for instance, inevitably form part of the child's environment. Indeed, a salient part of a person's cultural environment are the choices that other people are making. Some of the choices of others which form such an important part of his environment are the relatively predictable ones made in accordance with the structured normative life of an association or community. Others are the much less predictable choices of self-centred personal preference and whim.

A person's constantly changing but constantly present *cultural* circumstances (as distinct from his *material* circumstances) are composed of these structures and this dense flow of the choices others make, their messages of instruction and information, their verbal and gestural symbols of encouragement, exhortation, warning, threat, promise—a process called in the literature 'the social construction of reality'.

What we observe, then, are innumerable types of personality. They have been created by the interaction between each person as he is at a given moment of time, and with the innumerable material and cultural circumstances he confronts at that time. They are constantly remade by new interactions into new personalities ready for the next interaction in an infinitely fine series. We also observe this infinite variety of personalities being exposed to broad common influences in the material and cultural environment.

Both at the micro- and at the macro-level we see that in the identical material and cultural circumstances some people respond in one way, others respond in another. As a shorthand for these personal responses to unique or common circumstances I use the word 'choices'.

Some choices are described as rational. Purely rational choices—a practical impossibility—would be made in the light of the knowledge of all possible effective means and all consequences. Each purely rational choice is made within circumstances the person had correctly predicted would transpire. Purely irrational choices are made without any consideration at all of anything but the immediate stimulus, and what follows is a chain of consequences initiated by the original choice. Intermediate between purely rational and purely irrational choices are the choices of everyday life. In everyday life ordinary choices are made on the basis of the best information available, and with all the prudence and foresight that can be expected in the normal case. But normal ignorance, normal error, and normal admixtures of irrationality mean that there are, as often as not, unpleasant and unintended consequences which spiral out of control.

At a cosmic level, therefore, none of us is responsible for the choices we make. We are all, all the time, blameless victims or beneficiaries of our genetic endowment and its endless interaction with our environments. We can only react to given circumstances in the way that our own personality directs, our 'readiness to react in our own unique way'. At this *cosmic* level of responsibility, the serial killer is as little to blame for torturing his child-victims to death, as is the member of the lynch mob who tears to pieces an innocent person wrongly thought to have committed the serial killer's crimes. At this cosmic level the mugger is as little to blame as a child with measles.

The issue of 'responsibility for one's personal choices' is located at a much lower level than the cosmic and metaphysical. An essential distinction operates in ordinary life, which several modern strands of thought from Marxism to existentialism tend to obliterate. On the one hand there are those webs of cause and effect in which *culturally inculcated doctrines and socially imposed sanctions* play a significant environmental part. On the other hand there are those webs of cause and effect where they do not. These two pure classes of causes and effects represent extreme theoretical types. In real life there are not two clear-cut categories, one of events and conditions totally under social instruction and cultural control, the other of events and conditions totally insusceptible to social influence. Each event or condition in real life lies somewhere along the continuum between the two extremes.

The events and conditions that lie towards the first extreme have the following three characteristics. They are the results of human activity. They are defined in terms of their desirability or undesirability, by a particular person or a particular set of people, and according to occasion or other context. The undesirable human activity or condition is capable of being limited, and the desirable human activity or condition is capable of being fostered, by the unfavourable or favourable reaction of other people. The events and conditions of the second class, on the contrary, while they are also composed of human activities or conditions conceived as desirable or undesirable, are not capable of being influenced by social training or social control.

People are 'held responsible' for their actions within the first class of events, and are the subjects of guidance, social censure, hostility, punishment and all the other social pressures of instruction and sanction. They are not held responsible for their experiences in the second class of events, to which other people respond not with the reactions appropriate to a person's imputed 'negligence', 'fault' or 'guilt', but with the sympathy and support appropriate to their innocent misfortune.

Successful societies are those in which the first class is made as large as possible and the second class is made as small as possible. They inculcate into their members the notion that it is their personal responsibility to make the most constructive use of their abilities in all circumstances, whatever their abilities and circumstances may be. They inculcate into their members the confidence that they are entitled to demand such personal responsibility from others. Societies that are trying to do this, and are failing, have run into trouble. Societies in which the intellectual élites have abjured the whole notion both of culture and of personal responsibility; whose only goal is personal gratification; whose morals are relativistic; whose only explanation for differences in behaviour is the material environment; and whose panacea is cash from outside, have already produced, as Schumpeter said and predicted, their own grave diggers.[3]

Notes

Chapter 1: Introduction

1 Deans, J., 'Blair's Family Values Crusade', *Daily Mail*, 14 October 1996.

2 'Labour Stakes Claim to be Party of Community Care', *The Independent*, 21 September 1990.

3 'Ends and Means: The Utility of Marriage as a Legal Institution', in Eckelaar, J.M. and Katz, S.N. (ed.), *Marriage and Cohabitation in Contemporary Society*, Toronto, Ontario: Butterworth, 1980.

4 Alderson, A., 'Charles Wants Public Backing for Marriage to Camilla', *The Sunday Times*, 1 September 1996. [Emphasis added.]

5 Keats to Benjamin Bailey, 22 November 1817.

6 'Today', BBC Radio 4, 13 June 1996.

I presume that 'the majority of social scientists in the world' do not accept that people are *not* in poverty if they *do* receive more than half their country's average income. That is clearly not the case in common sense terms in very many of the poorest countries of the world.

On this definition, then, people *are* in poverty if they receive *less* than half, but are not necessarily *out* of poverty if they receive *more* than half.

It is thus a 'poverty line' that in principle—already built into it—can be immediately revised upwards again if ever only a few people fell below that line. For most people in the world this is the actual position. In the richest countries of the world this is the reserve position for poverty theorists.

This proves that it is in no sense a scientific standard, but purely a policy one.

7 Invitation from Information Services Director, 26 April 1996, to the simultaneous 'launch' of Kempson, E., *Life on a Low Income*, York: Joseph Rowntree Foundation, 1996, and a Channel 4 TV series entitled 'Poor Britain'.

8 Income and Wealth Inquiry Group, *Joseph Rowntree Foundation Inquiry into Income and Wealth*, Vol. 1, York: Joseph Rowntree Foundation, 1995.

9 Hills, J., *Joseph Rowntree Foundation Inquiry into Income and Wealth*, Vol. 2, York: Joseph Rowntree Foundation, 1995.

10 Hills, J., *op. cit.*, pp. 6-9.

11 *Ibid.*, pp. 21-23.

12 *Ibid.*, p. 26.

13 *Ibid.*

14 Inquiry Group, *op. cit.*, p. 16. Hills, *op. cit.*, p. 31.

15 *Ibid.*

16 Inquiry Group, *op. cit.*, p. 34.

17 The social-affairs intellectuals are those people whose ideas do effectively enter the public arena. They are the people who make their voices heard as they speak from the positions they hold in the universities, in the media, in the churches, in the metropolitan pressure groups, in politics. Along with their honestly-held or manipulative version of 'the facts of the case', they convey their own overt, insinuated or implied ethical or nihilistic evaluation of them.

18 Seeing the crowds, he went up on a mountain ... and he opened his mouth and taught them, saying ... 'Do not lay up for yourselves treasures on earth, where moth and rust consume and where thieves break in and steal ... do not be anxious about life, what you should eat and what you should drink, nor about your body, what you shall put on.' Matt. 5.1, 6.19, 6.24-25.

19 Dennis, N. and Halsey, A.H., *English Ethical Socialism: Thomas More to R.H. Tawney*, Oxford: Clarendon, 1988, *passim.* Tawney died in 1962.

20 Mills, C.W., *The Power Elite*, Oxford: Oxford University Press, 1956, pp. 164-65.

21 Crosland, C.A.R., *The Future of Socialism*, London: Cape, 1956.

22 'A number of Socialists have latterly launched a regular crusade against what they call the *principle of authority'*, Engels wrote. 'Authority presupposes subordination. Now, since both these words sound bad and the relationship they represent is disagreeable to the subordinated party, the question to ascertain is whether there is any way of dispensing with them. ... The automatic machinery of a big factory is much more despotic than the small capitalists who employ workers ever have been. ... Wanting to abolish authority in large-scale industry is tantamount to wanting to abolish industry itself.' The hours during which a worker has to be if not active then at least present in the workplace must be a matter of strict control. Above the gates of hell is the motto, 'Abandon hope all ye that enter here.' Above the portals of the modern factory, whether in the communist utopia or under capitalism one may write, Engels says, *Lasciate ogni autonomia, voi che entrate!* Abandon your *autonomy* all ye that enter here. Engels, F., 'On Authority' (1872), in Marx, K. and Engels, F., *Selected Works*, Vol. 1, Moscow: Foreign Languages Publishing House, 1958, pp. 636-37. Lenin wrote an article dealing with anarchistic radicalism which he entitled 'Left-wing Communism: An Infantile Disorder'.

23 Inquiry Group, *op. cit.*, p. 3.

24 *King John*, IV, ii.

25 e.g. Lombroso, C., *L'Uomo deliquente*, 1889.

26 Arendt, H., 'On Violence', *Crises of the Republic*, Harmondsworth: Penguin, 1973, p. 97.

27 Finkielkraut, A., *Die Niederlage des Denkens*, Reinbeck bei Hamburg: 1989, p. 143. (Translated from the French by O'Keefe, D., as *The Undoing of Thought*, London: Claridge, 1988.)

Chapter 2: The End of Denial

1   Jenkins, S., 'No More Feel-Smug Factor', *The Times*, 6 July 1996.

2   Adie, M., 'Getting on with the Job', *Teaching Right and Wrong: Have the Churches Failed?*, London: IEA, 1994, p. 26.

3   Dennis, N., *Rising Crime and the Dismembered Family: How Conformist Intellectuals Have Campaigned Against Common Sense*, London: IEA Health and Welfare Unit, 1993, pp. xiii-xiv.

4   Home Office, *Criminal Statistics England and Wales 1993*, Cm 2680, London: HMSO, 1994, p. 38.

5   CSO, *Social Trends 26*, London: HMSO, 1996, p. 160. The comparison is between 1981 and 1994.

6   These were the results of a *Sunday Times* survey of the reported-crime figures of 29 police forces, covering about 70 per cent of the population of England and Wales. Burglaries continued a three-year fall, and were down 1995-96 by an average of a further 13 per cent. Grey, S., 'Wave of Muggings Pushes Crime Figures to New Peak', *The Sunday Times*, 11 August 1996. See also Povey, D., Taylor, P. and Watson, L., *Notifiable Offences England and Wales July 1995 to June 1996*, Home Office Statistical Bulletin 18/36, London: HMSO, September 1996.

7   Mayhew, P., Aye Maung, N. and Mirrlees-Black, C., *The 1992 British Crime Survey*, Home Office Research Study 132, London: HMSO, September 1993, p. 111. The figure for 1995 is from *The 1996 British Crime Survey*, London: Home Office, September 1996.

8   *The 1996 British Crime Survey, op. cit.*, 1996.

9   For example Home Office, *Trends in Crime: Findings of the 1994 British Crime Survey*, London: HMSO, 1995.

10 Jenkins, S., 'No More Feel-Smug Factor', *op. cit.* In attacking what he called a 'fit of morality' by the Archbishop of Canterbury the previous day, Jenkins puts one of the typical 'moral-panic' arguments against him. 'Voltaire would see last week's vacuities as no more than the striving of the powerful after more power': the Archbishop of Canterbury and others had 'a vested interest in talking down the

moral state of the nation'. 'Since the dawn of time ... ' etc.

Even the ex-editor of *The Times* seemed to have been at last affected to some extent by the facts. He wrote that 'perhaps there was a golden age when old and young could be induced into unthinking obedience by a process of terror ...'

But those days, which only *perhaps* existed, *were*, he announced, now 'mercifully over'. The 'abjuration of drugs' by 'children' and getting them to 'honour their fathers and mothers' could not be accomplished through the 'total mish-mash' of the Archbishop of Canterbury's 'spiritual precepts'. In so far as either children's abjuration of drugs or their honouring their fathers and mothers may be desirable from case to case, it would be—if we are to follow Jenkins' advice—through acting, apparently, on his non-mish-mash and non-vacuous *credo*, that 'the roots of moral dilemma lie in personal experience, in which right and wrong are not clear cut and choice is by its nature "relative" ...'

11 Income and Wealth Inquiry Group, *Joseph Rowntree Inquiry into Income and Wealth*, Vol. 1, York: Joseph Rowntree Foundation, 1995, p. 34.

12 *The Independent*, 24 February 1994; *The Times*, 22 March 1994; *Guardian*, 22 March 1994.

13 *The Journal* (Newcastle upon Tyne), 18 March 1994.

14 *Sunderland Echo*, 15 March 1994.

15 Sapsted, D., 'Safety Door Traps 2 in Attack Flat', *The Times*, 13 January 1989.

16 Kempson, E., *Life on Low Income*, York: Joseph Rowntree Foundation, 1996, p. 62.

17 Kempson, *op. cit*, pp. 62-63. Kempson's book was based on 31 separate studies commissioned by the Joseph Rowntree Foundation as part of its social policy and housing programme and completed in 1994 and 1995. The 31 studies covered in total 2,400 informants. The studies upon which Kempson relied for this part of her study were Power, A. and Tunstall, R., *Swimming Against the Tide: Polarization or Progress on 20 Unpopular Council Estates 1980-1995*, York: Joseph Rowntree Foundation, 1995, and Speak, S., Cameron, S., Woods, R. and Gilroy, R., *Young Single Mothers: Barriers to Independent Living*, London: Family Policy Studies Centre, 1995.

18 Storey, C., 'Gulf Divides Haves and Have-nots', *Sunderland Echo*, 13 September 1991.

19 Emphasis added. Automatic entitlement to Income Support for 16-17 year-olds had been removed three and a half years before the Meadow Well riot. Their parent or guardian had to maintain them at home. If their parent or guardian was on benefit then he or she

received benefits for them as dependants. The 16-17 year-olds received their own Income Support thereafter only under tight 'hardship' provisions of a crisis situation, e.g. being thrown out of the house by their parents. The measure was designed to stop 16-17 year-olds leaving home and being maintained at the expense of the public.

20 Elderton, J., 'Anger at the Wrong Target', *Socialist Worker*, 14 September 1991.

21 *Op. cit.*, pp. 34-35.

22 Dominic Kennedy, '"Children in this area lack excitement. This has given them a buzz, like crowd hysteria": Boredom blamed for second night of riots', *The Times*, 8 July 1995.

23 *Guardian*, 8 July 1992.

24 'Violence Mars Fans' Celebrations', *The Journal* (Newcastle), 6 May 1996.

25 *Sunderland Echo*, 28 June 1996.

26 'Demolish Downhill Flats, Say Tenants', *Sunderland Echo*, 27 July 1983.

27 Chittenden, M., 'Inner Cities Get Some Bottle', *The Sunday Times*, 8 February 1987.

28 Reid, J., Taylor, M. and Lee, K., 'They Believe That No One Really Gives a Damn ... and Who Can Blame them?', *Sky*, December 1987.

29 See chapter 4.

30 Coleman, A., *Utopia on Trial*, London: Slipman, 1985. A central notion of the 'geographical' explanation is that housing estates built from the 1960s under the direction of architects and planners under strict public control had not incorporated—or had in principle eliminated— what the old developments by speculative builders had enjoyed from accident or common sense, namely, 'defensible space'.

31 Grove, V., 'Valerie Grove Meets the Scourge of the Planners', *The Sunday Times*, 15 September 1987.

32 *Ibid.*

33 Dennis, N., *People and Planning: The Sociology of Housing in Sunderland*, London: Faber and Faber, 1970. Dennis, N., *Public Participation and Planners' Blight*, London: Faber and Faber, 1972.

Chapter 3: Low Unemployment, Declining Poverty and Rising Crime 1961-1979

1 Income and Wealth Inquiry Group, *Joseph Rowntree Inquiry into Income and Wealth*, York: Joseph Rowntree Foundation, 1995, Vol. 1, pp. 57-59.

2 *Op. cit.*, p. 16. Hills, J., *Joseph Rowntree Foundation Inquiry into Income and Wealth*, York: Joseph Rowntree Foundation, Vol. 2, 1995, p. 31.

3 Said, E.W., *Representations of the Intellectual: The BBC Reith Lectures 1993*, London: Vintage, 1994, Lecture 1.

4 Melanie Phillips uses this as an example of what she describes as a 'pronounced characteristic' of the debate about the family in the period from 1960 to the mid-1990s, 'the routine distortion of evidence about family breakdown'. Phillips, M., *All Must Have Prizes*, London: Little, Brown and Co., 1996, p. 247.

5 'The metamorphoses of criticism into affirmation do not leave the theoretical content untouched, for its truth evaporates.' (*Die Metamorphosen von Kritik in Affirmation lassen auch den theoretischen Gehalt nicht unberührt, seine Wahrheit verflüchtigt sich.*) Radical university students used to like that kind of thing.

6 See, for example, Horkheimer, M. and Adorno, T.W., *Dialectic of Enlightenment*, London: Allen Lane, 1947, p. xii and p. 4.
   Karl Popper dismissed this doctrine as 'intelligence destroying'. Like the false clerics of Milton's day, these philosophers were misleaders of a generation:
   The hungry sheep look up and are not fed.
   But swol'n with wind, and the rank mist they draw,
   Rot inwardly, and foul contagion spread. (*Lycidas.*)
   Popper, K.R., 'Reason or Revolution?' (1970), in Adorno, T.W. and others, *The Positivist Dispute in German Sociology*, London: Heinemann, 1976, p. 289.

7 One of the few exceptions was Patricia Morgan, who was almost alone in making an academic case against the dominant and pervasive theory of 'moral panic'. Morgan, P., *Delinquent Phantasies*, London: Temple Smith, 1978.

8 Hall, S., 'Violence and the Media', in Tutt, N. (ed.), *Violence*, London: DHSS, 1976. [Emphasis added.]

9 Pearson, G., *Hooligan: The History of Respectable Fears*, London: Macmillan, 1983, p. ix. That it was a book that found its way onto many undergraduate-course reading lists, including the Open University, may be inferred from the fact that it was reprinted seven times 1983-1992. Geoffrey Pearson became Wates Professor of Social Work at the University of London.

10 *Ibid.*, p. 208.

11 *Ibid.*, p. 35.

12 Home Office, *Criminal Statistics England and Wales 1928*, London: HMSO, 1930, p. xiv.

13 Taylor, I.R., 'Soccer Consciousness and Soccer Hooliganism', in Cohen, S. (ed.), *Images of Deviance*, Harmondsworth: Penguin, 1971, p. 163.

14 *Ibid.*, p. 157 and p. 159.

15 The Rowntree Report 1995 does not attempt to reconcile the 1961-79 data with the 1979-92 data. But quite recently attempts have been made by at least one researcher at the Department of Applied Economics, University of Cambridge, Dr John Wells, to articulate this reconciliation, upon which the Rowntree Report's statements about poverty and disorder utterly depend. His theory states that crime had *not* increased 1961-79; the 'moral-panic' thesis correctly applied to that period. Crime figures rose, even though crime did not. By 1979, the recorded figures had merely come into closer correspondence with the real figures, the real increases in crime 1979-92 can be plotted and attributed to rising poverty and unemployment in that period.

16 Titmuss, R.M., *Essays on the Welfare State*, London: Allen and Unwin, 1958, p. 111.

17 Dennis, N., Henriques, F. and Slaughter, C., *Coal is our Life*, London: Eyre and Spottiswoode, 1956.

18 In the meantime (mid-1996) I use a University lift. Graffiti: *I love you all! Like a blow job. Bill and Bob not Ted. LFC. Shite! Rape!* I walk down the corridor past notices that pour scorn on what they describe as the 'moral panic' about illicit drugs, and protest at the attempts to stop 'us' consuming them as our inclination takes us.

19 Real changes in GDP at factor cost UK 1990=100. The GDP fell in the mid-seventies (oil-price shock), in the early eighties (recession), and in the early nineties (recession), but always only to the level that had been reached two or three years before. CSO, *Social Trends 25*, London: HMSO, 1995.

20 Income and Wealth Inquiry Group, *op. cit.*, pp. 13-14 and Figure 3 (a) p. 16. In the diagrams the dates are given as 1979-92, in the text the date is sometimes 1977, sometimes 1979. Hills, *op. cit.*, pp. 27-29 and Figure 16, pp. 31-34.

21 Mayhew, P., Aye Maung, N. and Mirrlees-Black, C., *The 1992 British Crime Survey*, Home Office Research Study 132, London: HMSO, September 1993, p. 43. Figures for survey burglaries were derived from the GHS for 1972, 1973, 1979, 1980, 1985 and 1986, and from the BCS for 1981, 1983, 1987 and 1991.

22 Damar, S., 'Wine Alley: The Sociology of a Dreadful Enclosure', *Sociological Review*, 22, 1974.

23 Ministry of Housing and Local Government, *Homes for Today and Tomorrow* (The Parker Morris Report), London: HMSO, 1961.

24 Dennis, N., *People and Planning: The Sociology of Housing in Sunderland*, London: Faber and Faber, 1970. Dennis, N., *Public Participation and Planners' Blight*, London: Faber and Faber, 1972. An example of an article written at the time is, Dennis, N., 'Community Action, Quasi-Community Action and Anti-Community Action', in Leonard, P., *The Sociology of Community Action*, Keele: Sociological Review, 1975.

25 Taylor, P.J., '"Difficult to Let", "Difficult to Live In" and Sometimes "Difficult to Get Out Of"': An Essay on the Provision of Council Housing, with Special Reference to Killingworth', *Environment and Planning*, 11, 1979, p. 1305.

26 *Daily Telegraph*, 16 August 1979, 22 September 1979 and 1 October 1979.

27 *Guardian*, 28 April 1993.

28 Though referred to as a new town Kirkby was not a statutory new town, but a collection of four housing estates administered by the Metropolitan Borough of Knowsley.

29 Road, A., 'Self-Destruction of a New Jerusalem', *Observer*, 11 March 1979. See also the report by Chief Superintendent Norman Chapple on Kirkby, *The Chapple Report*, 1976.

30 *Community Action*, Vol. 42, March-April 1979, p. 10.

31 'Bang Goes Council's Mistake', *Daily Telegraph*, 17 May 1982.

32 Road, A., *op. cit.*

33 In that particular case, the members discovered who the culprit was, and the equipment was returned.

34 Moynahan, B., 'A Spanner in the Works', *The Sunday Times Magazine*, 16 June 1996, p. 25.

35 Coleridge, S.T., *On the Constitution of the Church and State According to the Idea of Each* (1830), London: Dent, 1972, p. 36.

36 Clutterbuck, C., *Britain in Agony: The Growth of Political Violence*, Harmondsworth: Penguin, 1980.

37 Alinsky, S., *Reveille for Radicals*, New York: Vintage Books, 1969. Alinsky, S., *Rules for Radicals*, New York: Vintage Books, 1972. Ovenden, K., *Malcolm X: Socialism and Black Nationalism*, London: Bookmarks, 1992.

Chapter 4: The Evidence from the 1950s and Early 1960s

1 Halsey, A.H., 'Provincials and Professionals: The British Post-War Sociologists', *Archives of European Sociology*, 23, 1982, pp. 150-75.

2 Mitchell, G.D. and Lupton, T., 'The Liverpool Estate', in *Neighbourhood and Community*, Liverpool: Liverpool University Press, 1954.

3 Hodges, M.W. and Smith, C.S., 'The Sheffield Estate', *ibid.*

4 Dennis, N., Henriques, F. and Slaughter, C., *Coal Is Our Life*, London: Eyre and Spottiswoode, 1956.

5 Collison, P.C., *The Cutteslowe Walls: A Study in Social Class*, London: Faber and Faber, 1966.

6 Mogey, J.M., *Family and Neighbourhood*, Oxford: Oxford University Press, 1956.

7 Morris, R.N. and Mogey, J., *The Sociology of Housing: Studies at Berinsfield*, London: Routledge and Kegan Paul, 1965.

8 Bracey, H.E., *Neighbours On New Estates and Subdivisions in England and the USA*, London: Routledge and Kegan Paul, 1964.

9 Klein, J., *Samples from English Cultures*, 2 Vols., London: Routledge and Kegan Paul, 1964.

10 Young, M. and Willmott, P., *Family and Kinship in East London*, London: Routledge and Kegan Paul, 1957.

11 Kerr, M., *The People of Ship Street*, London: Routledge and Kegan Paul, 1958.

12 Smoking among working-class women was rare, and frowned upon in working-class communities. It was very common among men, who enjoyed it for its relaxant effect, but also for the sociability of its rituals, even though it was regarded as a health hazard, an addiction and even by many smokers themselves as a waste of money. But its strongest toxic effects had not at that time been established.

13 See, for example, Bracey, H.E., 'Children and Teenagers', *op. cit.*, pp. 126-46.

14 Kuper, L. and others, 'Blueprint for Living Together', *Living in Towns: Selected Research Papers in Urban Sociology*, London: Cresset Press, 1953.

15 *Ibid.*, p. 82.

16 *Ibid.*, p. 19.

17 *Ibid.*, pp. 14-15.

18 Frankenberg, R., *Communities in Britain: Social Life in Town and Country*, Harmondsworth: Penguin, 1966, pp. 60-62.

19 Mays, J.B., *Growing Up in the City: A Study of Juvenile Delinquency in an Urban Neighbourhood*, Liverpool: Liverpool University Press, 1954, p. 1, p. 148 and p. 158.

20 Smith, C., *Adolescence*, London: Longmans, Green, 1968, pp. 88-103.

21 Spencer, J., Tuxford, J. and Dennis, N., *Stress and Release in an Urban Estate: A Study in Action Research*, London: Tavistock, 1964. (Old Southmead, Bristol.) White, J., *The Worst Street in North London: Campbell Bunk, Islington, Between the Wars*, London: Routledge and Kegan Paul, 1986. (Off Seven Sisters Road, near Finsbury Park underground station.) Howarth, E. and others, *The Canford Families: A Study in Social Casework and Group Work*, Sociological Review Monograph No. 6, Keele: University of Keele, 1962. This study in Hackney says that before the 1939-45 War certain parts of the district had been 'notoriously delinquent'. But even here, Elizabeth Howarth and her team write, 'in the second half of the fifties, although there is still delinquency, it does not seem to leave such a definite imprint on the area'. p. 26.

22 See, Mack, J., 'Crime', in Cunnison, J. and Gilfillan, J.B.S. (eds.), *The Third Statistical Account of Scotland: The City of Glasgow*, Glasgow: Collins, 1958.

23 Osborne, J., *Look Back in Anger*, London: Faber and Faber, 1959.

24 Spencer, Tuxford and Dennis, *op. cit.*

25 Some of the most relevant of these studies to the Bristol Social Project were Shaw, C.R., *Delinquency Areas*, Chicago: 1929; Shaw, C.R. and McKay, H.D., *Juvenile Delinquency and Urban Areas*, Chicago: 1941; Zorbaugh, H.W., *The Gold Coast and the Slum*, Chicago, 1929; and Thrasher, F.M., *The Gang: A Study of 1,313 Gangs in Chicago*, Chicago, 1936. (All Chicago University Press.)

26 For example, Kuenstler, P., *Social Group Work in Great Britain*, London: Faber and Faber, 1955. Tuxford, J., and Dennis, N., 'Research and Social Work', *Social Work*, 15, 1958. Dennis, N., 'Changes in Function and Leadership Renewal: A Study of the

Community Association Movement and Problems of Voluntary Small Groups in the Urban Locality', *Sociological Review*, 9, 1, March 1961.

27 For example, Jacques, E., *The Changing Culture of a Factory*, London: Tavistock, 1951. [Glacier Metals, Acton.] Curle, A., 'Transitional Communities and Social Reconnection', *Human Relations*, 1, 42, 1947. There was also great interest in Talcott Parsons' theories of socialization, and especially his attempts to incorporate Freudian ideas into his general theory of socialization and social control. Parsons, T., *The Social System*, Glencoe, Ill.: Free Press, 1951; Parsons, T. and Bales, R.F., *Family, Socialization and Interaction Process*, London: Routledge and Kegan Paul, 1956.

28 Spencer, Tuxford and Dennis, *op. cit.*, p. 339.

29 'Toffs, Bums and Espressos', *ibid.*, pp. 135-66.

30 See Lassell, M., *Wellington Road*, London: Routledge and Kegan Paul, 1962. This detailed, day-by-day diary kept of life with one of Southmead's problem families and its neighbourhood describes simply pathetic and (to others) harmless chaos. 'Mary Johnson' and the man she was married to—firmly— 'Joe Johnson' were easy people to get on with, and although the boys were often in trouble, there was no viciousness at all in what they did.

31 Holman, B., 'Family man', *New Statesman and Society*, 8 December 1995. Holman, B., *Children and Crime*, Oxford: Lion Publishing, 1995.

32 Durkheim, E., *The Rules of Sociological Method*, (1895), New York: Free Press, 1964, p. 67.

33 *Op. cit.*, p. 69.

34 Southmead was the main estate dealt with in Wilson, R., *Difficult Housing Estates*, Tavistock Pamphlet No. 5, London: Tavistock, 1963.

35 Kempson, E., *Life on a Low Income*, York: Joseph Rowntree Foundation, 1996, p. 163.This is the point about Kempson's work emphasized by the Rowntree Foundation, through its Information Services Director. (Letter of 26 April 1996 announcing the launch on Monday, 3 June 1996 of the Channel 4 television series 'Poor Britain'.)

Chapter 5: Poverty, Unemployment and Social Disorder Between the Two Wars and Earlier

1 Dickinson, D., *Crime and Unemployment*, Department of Applied Economics, University of Cambridge, January 1994.

2   Kinvig, R.H., Smith, J.G. and Wise, M.J. (eds.), *Birmingham and its Regional Setting*, Birmingham: British Association for the Advancement of Science, 1950, pp. 253-4.

3   *Report of an Investigation into Maternal Mortality*, Cd. 5422, London: HMSO, 1937.

4   Pilgrim Trust, *Men Without Work: A Report Made to the Pilgrim Trust*, with an Introduction by the Archbishop of York, Cambridge: Cambridge University Press, 1938.

5   *Ibid.*, p. 89.

6   *Ibid.*, p. 90.

7   The 25-34 year-olds were the youngest age group for which data were supplied in the Pilgrim Trust study. The figure might have been higher in Liverpool than the Pilgrim Trust's data indicated.

8   *Ibid.*, p. 91. [Emphasis added.]

9   *Ibid.*, p. 95.

10 *Ibid.*, p. 95.

11 *Ibid.*, p. 98.

12 *Ibid.*, p. 99.

13 *Ibid.*, p. 75.

14 Himmelfarb, G., *The De-moralization of Society: From Victorian Virtues to Modern Values*, London: IEA Health and Welfare Unit, 1995, p. 41.

15 Marshall, A., *Memorials of Alfred Marshall*, (ed. Pigou, A.C.), London: 1925, p. 106, p. 116.

16 Toynbee, A., *Lectures on the Industrial Revolution in England* (1884), Newton Abbot: 1969, p. 147.

17 Webb, B., *My Apprenticeship* (1926), Harmondsworth: Penguin, 1971, p. 188, p. 309.

18 Home Office, *Criminal Statistics England and Wales*, London: HMSO, annually.

19 Board of Trade, *The Labour Gazette*, monthly from May 1893. Department of Employment, *Employment Gazette*, 99, 6, June 1991.

20 The Unemployment Unit estimated that between 1979 and 1996 the government changed the method of counting the unemployed 33 times. The Unemployment Unit estimated that in 1996 unemployment was one-third higher than the official figure—three million, and not two million. Since 1986 the numbers of people who had lost their jobs and had withdrawn from the labour market—not,

therefore, appearing in the unemployment figures—exceeded the numbers officially recognized as unemployed.

21 Povey, D., Taylor, P. and Watson, L., *Notifiable Offences England and Wales, July 1995 to June 1996*, Home Office Statistical Bulletin 18/96, London: HMSO, September 1996, p. 13.

22 Dangerfield, G., *The Strange Death of Liberal England*(1935), London: MacGibbon and Kee, 1966. From a modern perspective, as in so many of these accounts, the domestic 'problems' outside the quasicolonial system of what became the Irish Republic look very small indeed. It is noticeable that *male* disorder, such as it was and not as it was sometimes threatened (gun boats stood off the Mersey at one point), was generally well organized in the unions in labour disputes, and on the Unionist side in the Orange lodges in the dispute over Home Rule for Ireland. It is also noteworthy that Dangerfield himself rather takes for granted that disorder, which largely took place or was threatened in Wales, Ireland and Liverpool was the work of the Scots, Welsh and Irish (including Celtic Liverpudlians), and 'understandably' hardly appeared among stolid and sensible Englishmen. The newly-violent Suffragettes and Suffragists were, of course, English women.

23 MacIver, R.M., *Society: A Textbook of Sociology*, New York: Rinehart, 1937, p. 216. MacIver was Professor of Sociology at Columbia, and one of the most respected sociologists of his generation. He is remarking on the quite unexpected strength of the culture of the family in the first industrialized country, and using it as a telling example of the independent part played by culture in determining how people conduct themselves.

24 Arnot, R. Page, *The Miners: Years of Struggle*, London: Allen and Unwin, 1953.

25 That faint echo of what was it was assumed English cinema audiences would take for granted in 1929 can be contrasted with these facts:

> The average annual percentage increase 1984-94 in all offences of violence against the person was 7 per cent compound.
>
> The average annual percentage increase 1984-94 in the more serious offences of violence against the person was much higher than this, 11 per cent compound.
>
> There were 311,500 crimes of violence recorded by the police in England and Wales in 1994. By 1995 the number had risen to 316,000.
>
> The biggest single rise in the category of violent crime was in robberies. There were twice as many robberies involving firearms in 1995 (64,000) as there had been in 1985.

Home Office, *Criminal Statistics England and Wales 1994*, Cm 3010, London: HMSO, November 1995.

26 Lowndes, G.A.N., *The Silent Social Revolution: An Account of the Expansion of Public Education in England and Wales 1895-1935*, Oxford: Oxford University Press, p. 44.

27 Cole, G.D.H. and Postgate, R., *The Common People 1746-1946*, London: Methuen, 1946, pp. 604-605.

28 *Ibid.*, p. 564.

29 *Ibid.*, p. 605.

30 For example, Bowley, A.L. and Burnett-Hurst, A.R., *Livelihood and Poverty: A Study in the Economic and Social Conditions of Working-Class Households in Northampton, Warrington, Stanley and Reading*, London: Bell, 1915. Also included was information on Bolton; Mess, H.A., *Industrial Tyneside: A Social Survey*, London: Benn, 1928; London School of Economics, *The New Survey of London Life and Labour: With Special Reference to Changes Since the Publication of Charles Booth's 'Life and Labour in London'*, 9 volumes, London: London School of Economics, 1930-35; M'Gonigle, G.C.M. and Kirby, J., *Poverty and Public Health*, London: Gollancz, 1936.

31 Pearse, I.H. and Crocker, L.H., *The Peckham Experiment: A Study in the Living Structure of Society*, London: Allen and Unwin, 1943. The promiscuity quotation is from p. 234. Due to demand, the book required five print runs 1943-45.

32 Young, T., *Becontree and Dagenham: The Story of the Growth of a Housing Estate*, London: Pilgrim Trust, 1934.

33 Durant, R., *Watling: A Survey of Social Life on a New Housing Estate*, London: King, 1939.

34 For example, Jevons, R. and Madge, J., *Housing Estates*, Bristol: Arrowsmith, 1946; Hutchinson, B., *Willesden and the New Towns*, London: Central Office of Information, 1949; Orlans, H., *Stevenage*, London: Routledge and Kegan Paul, 1952.

Chapter 6: No Stake in Society

1 Income and Wealth Inquiry Group, *Joseph Rowntree Foundation Inquiry into Income and Wealth*, York: Joseph Rowntree Foundation, 1995, p. 35.

2 *Ibid.*, p. 34

3 *Ibid.*, p. 54.

4 Kempson, E., *Life on a Low Income*, York: Joseph Rowntree Foundation, 1996, p. 1.

5 Johnstone, H., 'Tempazepam and Baseball Bats for Modern Macbeth', *The Times*, 22 July 1996. Macbeth is a Temazepam-addicted henchman of Duncan, a local crime godfather on the

Ladywood council estate, Birmingham, surviving through drugs and extortion in a world with no laws.

6   *The Times*, 8 June 1996.

7   Inquiry Group, *op. cit.*, p. 34.

8   Hobbes, T., *De Cive: Philosophical Rudiments Concerning Government and Society* (1642), Oxford: Clarendon, 1983, p. 44 annotation. [Spelling modernized here.]

Chapter 7: The Consumption Levels of the Bottom Tenth of Income Receivers

1   Gittus, E., *Urban Change, Social Income and Life Cycle*, Discussion Paper No. 80, Newcastle upon Tyne: Centre for Urban and Regional Development Studies, November 1986, p. 7. (Paper presented at the British Sociological Association Annual Conference, Loughborough University, March 1986.) [Emphasis added.] Elizabeth Gittus gives a detailed account of the shift in the definition of poverty in *this* direction in her 'Deprived Areas and Social Planning', in Herbert, D.T. and Johnston, R.J. (eds.), *Spatial Perspectives on Problems and Policies*, Vol. 2, Chichester: Wiley, 1976.

2   See, for example, Castells, M., *The Urban Question: A Marxist Approach*, London: Edward Arnold, 1977; Dunleavy, P., *Urban Political Analysis: The Politics of Collective Consumption*, London: 1980.

3   Hills, J., *Joseph Rowntree Foundation Inquiry into Income and Wealth*, Vol. 2, York: Joseph Rowntree Foundation, 1995, p. 111.

4   All the figures in this chapter were standardized in the literature consulted (where the technical term used is 'equivalized'). All expenditures and incomes are weighted according the size and age-composition of the household. The 'equivalized' income or 'equivalized' expenditure is that which would be received or spent by a childless couple. The weights for household size and composition are those of the McClements Equivalence Scale.

5   Rowntree, B.S. and Lavers, G.R., *Poverty and the Welfare State: A Third Social Survey of York Dealing only with Economic Questions*, London: Longmans, 1951, pp. 32-34.

6   Abel-Smith, B. and Townsend, P., *The Poor and the Poorest*, London: Bell, 1965, p. 23.

7   Institute of Social Studies Advisory Service (Issas), *Poverty in Figures: Europe in the Early 1980s*, Luxembourg: Office for Official Publications of the European Communities, 1990, p. 10.

8   Hills, *op. cit.*, p. 107.

9   In relation to their numbers in the general population, the self-employed were over-represented in the bottom tenth of income receivers. They were particularly strongly over-represented among those reporting very low incomes and losses over the year.

In 1992 the full-time self-employed formed 13 per cent of the lowest tenth of receivers of income. *But they formed only four per cent of the lowest tenth of spenders of income.* What is more, the number of households in the Family Expenditure Survey samples reporting negative income after housing costs rose steadily from 26 in 1979 to 133 in 1992.

As Goodman and Webb drily remark, 'This indicates that income may overstate the extent to which the self-employed in particular are poor'.

Goodman, A. and Webb, S., *The Distribution of Household Expenditure 1979-92*, Commentary No. 49, London: Institute of Fiscal Studies, May 1995, pp. 18-20.

For further discussion of poverty statistics see: Pryke, R., *Taking the Measure of Poverty: A Critique of Low-Income Statistics; Alternative Estimates and Policy Implications*, London: IEA, Research Monograph 51, 1995.

10 Between 1979 and 1993 (as distinct from 1979 and 1992) there was an 18 per cent decline in the reported real income of the bottom tenth of income receivers, after their housing costs had been met, as contrasted with a rise of 61 per cent in the real income of the top tenth. Department of Social Security, *Households Below Average Income: A Statistical Analysis 1979 to 1992-93*, London: HMSO, 1995.

11 Goodman and Webb, *op. cit.*, p. 32. Both figures are the sums involved after housing costs have been met. The income left after the deduction of housing costs is the measure used by the Rowntree Report to obtain the worst possible picture of for the bottom tenth's experience 1979-92, i.e. that their absolute standard of living had fallen by 15 or 16 per cent.

12 *Ibid.*, p. 31.

13 *Ibid.*, p. 30.

14 Pahl, R.E., *Divisions of Labour*, Oxford: Blackwell, 1984.

15 Goodman and Webb, *op. cit.*, p. 25.

16 *Ibid.*, p. 23.

17 *Ibid.*, p. 22.

18 *Ibid.*, pp. 23-24.

19 *Ibid.*, pp. 18-19.

20 *Did* this old-fashioned trade-unionist say 'partners'? In these enlightened days no four-letter word is edited out of journalistic copy except 'wife'. With its quite exceptional power to deprave and corrupt, it can appear in print only to compel uncompromising confrontation with the sordid realities of life away from the conventional cocoon of the permissive society, or as a concession to the most compelling and outré artistic integrity.

21 Phillips, A., 'Fleeing the Rut', *Guardian*, 27 October 1990. [Emphasis added.]

Chapter 8: The Young Unemployed in the Bottom Tenth

1 Webb, S., *Poverty Dynamics in Great Britain: Preliminary Analysis from the British Household Panel Survey*, IFS Commentary No. 48, London: Institute of Fiscal Studies, 1995..

2 Lilley, The Rt Hon P., 'Equality, Generosity and Opportunity: Welfare Reform and Christian Values', a speech delivered in Southwark Cathedral, 13 June 1996.

3 Phillips, A., 'Trapped in Hull', *Guardian*, 27 October 1990.

4 Ortega y Gasset, J., *The Revolt of the Masses*, London: Allen and Unwin, 1932.

5 'Once it was the revolt of the masses that was held to threaten ... the civilizing traditions of Western culture. In our time, however, the chief threat seems to come from those at the top of the social hierarchy.' Lasch, C., *The Revolt of the Elites and the Betrayal of Democracy*, New York: Norton, 1994. Juxtaposing Ortega's term 'mass' with élite in this way—as I have also done in the main text—does not in fact do justice to Ortega's concept. For him members of the mass were 'those who demand nothing special of themselves'. In Ortega's sense, therefore, slack and slovenly pseudo-intellectuals among today's cultural élites are mass men and women. Countless working or unemployed poorer people with 'noble disciplined minds' (like, among the miners of Northumberland and Durham, Thomas Burt or Peter Lee, or among the slaves and newly liberated slaves of the American South, Frederick Douglass or Booker T. Washington) are not.

6 Himmelfarb, G., *The De-moralization of Society: From Victorian Virtues to Modern Values*, New York: Knopf, 1995, and London: I.E.A. Health and Welfare Unit, 1995.

Chapter 9: The Fatherless Household in the Bottom Tenth

1 'Children Living in Re-ordered Families', *Social Policy Research Findings 45*, York: Joseph Rowntree Foundation, 1994; Bradshaw, J., *Household Budgets and Living Standards*, York: Joseph Rowntree Foundation, 1993; Burghes, L., *One Parent Families: Policy Options*

for the 1990s, York: Joseph Rowntree Foundation, 1993; Bradshaw, J. and Millar, J., *Lone Parent Families in the UK*, London: HMSO, 1991; Kiernan, K. and Wicks, M., *Family Change and Future Policy*, York: Joseph Rowntree Foundation in association with the Family Policy Studies Centre, 1990; Millar, J., *Poverty and the Lone Parent: The Challenge to Social Policy*, Avebury: 1989; Glendinning, C. and Millar, J. (eds.), *Women and Poverty in Britain*, Wheatsheaf, 1987.

2 Rowntree, B.S., *Poverty and Progress: The Second Social Survey of York.*, London: Longmans, Green, 1941, p. 38 and pp. 88-89.

3 Elliot, D.W., 'The Merchant Navy in Wartime: A Civilian Occupation', *North East Labour History*, Bulletin 28, 1994, p. 55.

4 *Colliery Year Book 1928*, p. 724. In 1921, 1,133,000 people, nearly all men, were employed in the coal mines of England and Wales alone, excluding the Scottish coalfield. In 1931 the number still exceeded one million. CSO, *Annual Abstract of Statistics 88*, London: HMSO, 1952.

5 There were about 9,500 students on the 18,000-student campus in the mid-1990s.

6 *Commonwealth Universities Yearbook 1961*.

7 ONS, *Population Trends 84*, London: HMSO, 1996.

8 Harkness, S., Machin, S. and Waldfogel, J., *Evaluating the Pin Money Hypothesis: The Relationship Between Women's Labour Market Activity, Family Income and Poverty in Britain*, Suntory-Toyota Centre for Economics and Related Disciplines (STICERD) Welfare State Programme Discussion Paper 108, London: LSE, May 1995, p. 4. Schmitt, J. and Wadsworth, J., *Why Are Two Million Men in Britain Not Working?*, Centre for Economic Performance, London: LSE, 1993. (Mimeograph.)

9 Juhn, C., 'Decline of Male Labour Market Participation: The Role of Declining Market Opportunities', *Quarterly Journal of Economics*, Vol. 107, 1992.

10 Machin, S. and Waldvogel, J., *The Decline of the Male Breadwinner: Changing Shares of Husbands' and Wives' Earnings in Family Income*, Suntory-Toyota International Centre for Economics and Related Disciplines (STICERD) Welfare State Discussion Paper 103, London: LSE, 1994.

11 Trotsky, L., *The Death Agony of Capitalism and the Tasks of the Fourth International: The Transitional Programme* (1938), London: World, 1980.

12 Beauvoir, S. de, *The Second Sex*, London: Cape, 1953. When Aristophanes imagined the impossible in his burlesque *Ecclesiazusae* (his *Women of Politics*, 393 B.C.), that women would

rule Athens, how did he come to think that it would be they who would introduce free love as soon as they got the chance?

13 See, Fumaroli, M., 'A Walk in the Desert: The Ghost in the Ruins of the French Literary Tradition', *The Times Literary Supplement*, 14 February 1992.

14 The English working class itself proved a disappointment from a very early date. Marx's bloodthirsty rhetoric to the moribund Chartists in 1856 fell on very deaf ears indeed. 'To revenge the misdeeds of the ruling class, there existed in the middle ages in Germany', he said, 'a secret tribunal called the *Vehmgericht*. If a red cross was seen marked on a house, people knew that its owner was doomed by the *Vehm*. All the houses of Europe are now marked with a red cross. History is the judge: its executioner, the proletariat.' Speech delivered by Marx on 14 April 1856. Published in the Chartist *People's Paper*, 19 April 1856. But because of promising rebellions elsewhere, in France in 1870-71 and in Germany in 1918, for example, it took more than a century thereafter for all Western working classes to prove themselves poor material for revolution.

15 Marcuse, H., *One Dimensional Man: Studies in the Ideology of Advanced Industrial Society*, Boston: Beacon Press, 1964, pp. 256-57.

16 Marcuse, H., *Eros and Civilization: A Philosophical Inquiry in Freud*, London: Routledge and Kegan Paul, 1956; Freud, S., *Civilization and Its Discontents*, London: Institute of Psycho-Analysis, 1930.

17 See, Dennis, N., 'Sociology and the Spirit of Sixty-Eight', *British Journal of Sociology*, Vol. 40, No. 3, September 1989.

18 The claim to be the originator of the phrase is disputed between Rudi Dutschke and Helmut Schelsky.

19 See especially, Working Party of the General Synod Board for Social Responsibility, *Something to Celebrate: Valuing Families in Church and Society*, London: Church House Publishing, 1995. With the striking exception of one chapter, it is not about valuing 'families' in the institutional sense at all. Apart from this single chapter, it is a wholly, even if pale and flaccid, post-modernist account of sexuality and childrearing.

20 Law Commission, *Consent and the Criminal Law*, Law Commission Consultation Paper No. 139, London: HMSO, 1996, para. 10.52.

21 See, as the most important, pervasive and highly influential source of this doctrine, the United Nations Convention on the Rights of the Child.

22 The record of babies being born without their father having married their mother first began to be collected systematically in 1836. From then until the early 1960s the ratio fluctuated only two or three percentage points above and below seven per cent, even in wartime. But by 1984 the rate had risen to 17 per cent. In the mere twelve years from 1984 it had doubled again. Among mothers aged under twenty the ratio was 20 per cent in 1960. By 1996 it was nearly 90 per cent. *Annual Abstract of Statistics*, London: HMSO, various years.

23 Himmelfarb, G., *The De-moralization of Society: From Victorian Virtues to Modern Values*, New York: Alfred Knopf, 1995.

24 Commission of the European Communities, *Employment in Europe*, Luxembourg: CEC, 1993.

25 Morgan, P., *Who Needs Parents? The Effects of Childcare and Early Education on Children in Britain and the USA*, London: IEA Health and Welfare Unit, 1996, p. 4.

26 *Ibid.*, p. 6.

27 Harkness, Machin and Waldfogel, *op. cit.*, p. 5.

28 *Ibid.*, p. 12.

29 *Ibid.*, pp. 22-23.

30 A full analysis of the financial implications of lone parenthood is provided in Morgan, P., *Farewell to the Family? Public Policy and Family breakdown in Britain and the USA*, London: IEA Health and Welfare Unit, 1995.

31 Kempson, E., *Life on Low Income*, York: Joseph Rowntree Foundation, 1996, p. 1.

32 Temple, W., 'Gambling and Ethics', in his *Essays in Christian Politics and Kindred Subjects*, London: Longmans, 1927, p. 125.

33 Yeats, W.B. 'A Prayer to My Daughter'.

34 Oakeshott, M., 'The Tower of Babel', in *Rationalism in Politics and Other Essays*, London: Methuen, 1962, pp. 59-60.

35 Hammond, J.L. and Hammond, B., 'The Defences of the Poor I: The Spirit of Union', *The Town Labourer 1760-1832: The New Civilization*, London: Longmans, Green, 1917, p. 248.

36 The BBC journalist had phoned me on the day before the interview to postpone the arrangements until the afternoon. She had been sidetracked to Teesside overnight.

She recorded from inside the house of a resident on a Teesside housing estate an eye-witness, hour by hour account of that particular night's events as empty houses were being systematically torn to pieces and then set alight by young males. 'Good heavens, there are some as young as 10! ... Now they have a pole and have started to attack the outhouse ... It is now quarter-past-eleven and they've started a fire ... It's quarter to twelve now, O, dear, yes ... I think we'll have to call the fire brigade, it's beginning to threaten this house ...' 'PM', BBC Radio 4, 19 and 22 March 1993, and *Sunderland Echo*, 19 March 1993.

37 'I intend, over time, and without cash losses to individuals, to narrow the gap between benefits that go to lone parents and those who go to couples', *The Times*, 6 June 1996. The writer emphasized that the Social Security Secretary in doing so would be 'defying' (not just not accepting) the recommendations of his 'independent' advisers.

In fact the recommendation of the government's advisory committee was that any future changes in the gap should be 'properly scrutinized and debated in Parliament'. Whether the writer of the report in *The Times* knew that this *was* simply a disingenuous formulation chosen by the committee to make the recommendation that Mr Lilley 'defied', I have no means of verifying.

38 Harkness, Machin and Waldfogel, *op. cit.*

39 The General Household Survey uses the term 'family' to described any household containing a woman and a dependent child. It defines such a 'family' as a couple, or single woman, and any dependent children. Any other adults in the household are excluded. There is thus no reference to marriage, or to the permanency of the relationship between the couple, or to the biological or formal relationship of the adult who is not the mother to the child or children. This fact is in itself a striking index of how far the deinstitutionalization of the family—the long march through the family as an institution—has progressed in Britain.

40 OPCS, *General Household Survey 1993*, HMSO, 1995.

41 Harkness, Machin and Waldvogel, *op. cit.*, pp. 12-13.

42 Hills, J., *op. cit.*, p. 33. [Emphasis added.]

43 Burn, J., 'Children of Broken Homes', *News Digest*, 1, 1996, p. 9.

44 Working Party of the General Synod Board for Social Responsibility, *Something to Celebrate: Valuing Families in Church and Society*, London: Church House Publishing, 1995, pp. 45-46 and p. 160. The *first* step that the Church of England should take, said the report, was to abandon the phrase 'living in sin'. p. 117.

Chapter 10: The Loss of Poverty as a Salient Social Issue

1 Booth, C., *Life and Labour of the People in London*, Vol. 1, London: 1891, pp. 38-9 and p. 131.

2   Webb, B., *My Apprenticeship* (1926), Harmondsworth: Penguin, 1971, p. 171 and pp. 254-55. For Marx and Engels' similarly unflattering view of the ne'er do wells, see Marx, K. and Engels, F., *Selected Works*, Vol. 1, Moscow: Foreign Languages Publishing House, 1958, p. 295 and p. 646. Modern Marxists have been at pains to point out that in this matter Marx was wrong. See, e.g. Bovenkerk, F., 'The Rehabilitation of the Rabble: How and Why Marx and Engels Wrongly Depicted the Lumpenproletariat', *Netherlands Journal of Sociology*, Vol. 20, 1984.

3   Marshall, A., *Memorials of Alfred Marshall*, Pigou, A.C. (ed.), London: 1925, p. 328.

4   Rowntree, B.S., *Poverty: A Study of Town Life*, London: Nelson, 1901.

5   *Ibid.*, p. 11. This meant that some poorly paid non-manual workers like clerks and shop assistants were included, and some working-class people were excluded, like domestic servants, of whom there were over 4,000 in York at that time, and inmates of the Poor Law Institutions—the 'work-houses'—of whom there were about 600.

6   Rowntree, B.S., *The Human Needs of Labour*, London: Longmans, Green, revised edition, 1937.

7   Rowntree, B.S., *Poverty and Progress: The Second Social Survey of York*, London: Longmans, Green, 1936, p. 32.

8   *Ibid.*, pp. 35-36.

9   *Ibid.*, p. 38.

10 *Ibid.*, p. 102.

11 *Ibid.*, pp. 101-102.

12 Scannell, P. and Cardiff, D., *The Social History of British Broadcasting*, Oxford: OUP, 1991.

13 *The People's Year Book National and International 1929*, Manchester: CWS, 1929, p. 299, p. 306.
     A guide to the 'culture' of the time is the people it honours. In a section entitled 'Under the Laurel', wearing the hero's crown, the four people in the world whose birth the Year Book commemorates are Edmund Burke, famous for his defence of English institutions against those introduced by the French Revolution, Lessing, the German poet, Bishop Thomas Percy, famous for his *Reliques*, and William Dodd the Shakespearean scholar.
     The Year Book refers to the growing hopelessness and apathy of the public towards the fate of the miners, but does the opposite to endorsing it.

14 Rowntree, *op. cit.*, p. 101 and pp. 108-109.

15 *Ibid.*, p. v.

16 *Social Trends*, The government expenditure figure includes transfer payments.

17 Income and Wealth Inquiry Group, *Joseph Rowntree Foundation Inquire into Income and Wealth*, Vol.1, York: Joseph Rowntree Foundation, 1995, p. 34.

18 Beveridge, W.H., *Social Insurance and Allied Services*, Cmnd 6404, London: HMSO, 1942, paras. 445-46.

19 London School of Economics, *The New Survey of London Life and Labour: With Special Reference to Changes Since the Publication of Charles Booth's 'Life and Labour in London'*, 9 volumes, London: London School of Economics, 1930-1935. The Director of the survey was Sir Hubert Llewellyn Smith.

20 Beveridge, *op. cit.*, paras. 445-46.

21 Orwell, G., 'Looking Back on the Spanish War' (1943), in his *Homage to Catalonia and Looking Back on the Spanish War*, Harmondsworth: Penguin, 1962, pp. 244-45.

22 Rowntree, B.S. and Lavers, G.R., *Poverty and the Welfare State: A Third Social Survey of York Dealing Only With Economic Questions*, London: Longmans, 1951.

23 *Ibid.*, p. 15.

24 Beveridge, W.H., *Full Employment in a Free Society*, London: Allen and Unwin, 1944.

25 Rowntree and Lavers, *op. cit.*, p. 48.

26 *Ibid.*, p. 49.

27 *Ibid.*, p. 35.

28 *Ibid.*, p. 36.

29 Wedderburn, D.C., 'Poverty in Britain Today: The Evidence', *The Sociological Review*, Vol. 10, No. 3, November 1962, p. 261. [Emphasis added.]
    The author was at the Department of Applied Economics, Cambridge, when the article was written. In the 1990s the Department contained some of the principal exponents of the unemployment=crime school, which stressed that recent crime rates were the creation of recent unemployment trends.
    Dorothy Wedderburn was also known as Dorothy Cole. The study she was referring to was Cole D. and Utting, J.E.G., *The Economic Circumstances of Old People*, Welwyn: Codicote, 1962.

30 *Ibid.*

31 Titmuss, R.M., *Essays on 'The Welfare State'*, London: Allen and Unwin, 1958, pp.35-36.

32 *The Welfare State*, Labour Party Political Discussion Pamphlet, 1952. *One Nation*, Conservative Political Centre, 1950.

33 Titmuss, *op. cit.*, p. 35.

34 Abel-Smith, B. and Townsend, P., *The Poor and the Poorest: A New Analysis of the Ministry of Labour's Family Expenditure Surveys of 1953-54 and 1960*, London: Bell, 1965, p. 9.

Chapter 11: The Search for a Substitute

1 Galbraith, J.K., *The Affluent Society*, London: Hamish Hamilton, 1958 p. 1. On the first page of the text proper, therefore, Galbraith dismisses what ten years after his book appeared was increasingly seized upon as *being* poverty in Western Europe and the USA. By the 1990s this concept had become the unquestioned stock-in-trade of poverty theorists—'relative deprivation'.

2 *Ibid.*, p. 256.

3 *Ibid.*

4 Marshall, A., *Principles of Economics* (1890), 8th edition, London: Macmillan, 1920, pp. 2-4.

5 Galbraith, *op. cit.*, p. 251.

6 *Ibid.*, pp. 2-3.

7 *Ibid.*, p. 251.

8 *Ibid.*, p. 256. [Emphasis added.]

9 *Ibid.*, p. 257.

10 *Ibid.*, p. 97.

11 *Ibid.*, pp. 196-97.

12 *Ibid.*, p. 257. [Emphasis added.]

13 Tawney, R.H., *Equality*, 1931, 4th edition, London: Allen and Unwin, 1952.

14 See, for example, Harvey, D., *Social Justice and the City*, London: Edward Arnold, 1973.

15 Offe, C., in Connerton, P., *Critical Sociology: Selected Readings*, Harmondsworth: Penguin, 1976.

16 Offe, p. 416.

17 Runciman, W.G., *Relative Deprivation and Social Justice: A Study of Attitudes to Social Equality in the Twentieth Century*, London: Routledge and Kegan Paul, 1966, p. 90.

18 Johnson, P., 'A Sense of Outrage', in MacKenzie, N. (ed.), *Conviction*, London: MacGibbon and Kee, 1958, p. 217.

19 *Ibid*, p. 206.

20 *Ibid.*, p. 208. [Emphasis added.]

21 The reference to 'groundnuts' is to a model state scheme of agricultural reform in British East Africa based on their cultivation which failed on a large scale.

22 Johnson, *op. cit.*, p. 210.

23 Marx, K. and Engels, F., 'Manifesto of the Communist Party' (1848), in Marx, K. and Engels, F., *Selected Works*, Vol. 1, Moscow: Foreign Languages Publishing House, 1958, p. 34.

24 Johnson, *op. cit.*, p. 210.

25 *Ibid.*, p. 214. [Emphasis added.]

26 *Ibid.*, pp. 212-13.

27 *Ibid.*, p. 210.

Chapter 12: Unconditional Rights

1   The Royal Commission on the Poor Law was appointed in 1905 and reported in February 1909 with two reports. The Minority Report was largely written by Sidney and Beatrice Webb.

2   Webb, S.J. and Potter, B., *English Poor Law Policy*, London: Longmans,1910, pp. 317-19.

3   Beveridge, W., *Social Insurance and Allied Services* (The Beveridge Report), Cmnd 6404, London: HMSO, 1942, para. 455. [Emphasis added.]

4   Churchill, W.S., 'The War and Future Social Policy', BBC Radio Broadcast, 21 March 1943.

5   Churchill, W.S., *Liberalism and the Social Problem: Speeches and Addresses 1906-1909*, London: Hodder and Stoughton, 1909. The images of the complete ladder and unbroken bridge or causeway were created in a speech at Leicester in 1909.

6   Booth, C., *Pauperism, A Picture: And the Endowment of Old Age, An Argument*, London: Macmillan, 1892, p. 225.

7   Rowntree, B.S., *Poverty and Progress: The Second Social Survey of York*, London: Longmans, Green, 1941.

8   Laski, H.J., *A Grammar of Politics* (1925), London: Allen and Unwin, 4th edition, 1938, pp. 94-95.

9   Lynes, T.A., *National Assistance and National Prosperity*, Welwyn, Herts.: Codicote, 1962, p. 35. Tony Lynes became a prominent figure in the new Child Poverty Action Group (CPAG).

10 Cole, D. and Utting, J.E.G., *The Economic Circumstances of Old People*, Welwyn, Herts: Codicote, 1962, pp. 94-95.

11 *Ibid.*, p. 101.

12 Wedderburn, D.C., 'Poverty in Britain Today: The Evidence', *The Sociological Review*, 10, 3, November 1962, pp. 279-80.

13 Abel-Smith, B. and Townsend, P., *The Poor and the Poorest: A New Analysis of the Ministry of Labour's Family Expenditure Surveys of 1953-54 and 1960*, London: Bell, 1965, p. 60.

14 *Report of the National Assistance Board for 1960*, Cmnd 1410, London: HMSO, 1961, Appendix 10.

15 Abel-Smith and Townsend, *op. cit.*, pp. 61-62 and pp. 62ff.

16 *Ibid.*, p. 65.

17 *Ibid.*, pp. 64-65.

18 The objective situation of working people meant that they could not tolerate slackers. As an ideal, it was inculcated by the English ruling class and made common knowledge by being constantly reiterated in the churches. ('He hath assigned and appointed ... every degree and people in their vocation, calling and office, and hath appointed to them their duty and order.') But from the beginning of the industrial revolution they were vigorously upheld, too, by the principal spokesmen for the English working class. 'What!', Cobbett had roared, 'are you to come crawling, like sneaking Curs, to lick up alms round the rims of a soup kettle!' Cobbett, W., *Political Register*, 30 November 1816.

19 Rowntree, B.S., *Poverty: A Study of Town Life*, London: Nelson, 1901, p. 118 and p. 179.

20 Hagenbuch, W., *Social Economics*, Cambridge: Cambridge University Press, 1958, p. 178.

21 Wedderburn, *op. cit.*, p. 267. By the mid-1990s the national TV Channel 4 was able to screen a programme from Newcastle upon Tyne featuring an able-bodied 'unemployed young man who earns a bit on the side by teaching the guitar' masquerading with a woman who was acting as his 'pregnant girl friend' as a user of money-lenders, and to take it for granted that the viewer will be indignant that the money-lenders should ask for the promised weekly repayments to be made. The rate of interest was extraordinarily high, and anyone would have to be a complete fool to manage their affairs in that way. But there was not the slightest indication that he was

a 'hard case', not the slightest indication of undue pressure on him to borrow the money. Very little pressure was shown on the film being put on him as a defaulter, and there were no allegations of other threats. When bailiffs were mentioned at one point, that was defined by him to the viewer as harassment. The objectionable activities of the money-lenders were to deduct the first week's repayment immediately from the principal, and insure the loan automatically when it ought to have been made clear that it was voluntary. 'Undercover Britain: Bad Debt', Channel 4, 10 June 1996.

One of the 'Poverty Commissioners' for a major series of programmes show by Channel 4 later in 1996 could 'lose her faith' in the trickle-down economy while touring Tesco: she was 'shattered' as she watched the lone mother she was with 'reject a 68p can of fruit juice because it was too expensive'. Kennedy, D., 'Leith Tastes Life on the Breadline', *The Times*, 12 October 1996.

22 Rowntree, B.S., *Poverty and Progress*, London: Longmans, Green, 1941, p. 71. It does not matter here what '10s.' was.

Chapter 13: Relative Poverty

1   Cole, D. and Utting, J.E.G., *The Economic Circumstances of Old People*, Welwyn, Herts: Codicote, 1962. Wedderburn, D.C., 'Poverty in Britain Today: The Evidence', *The Sociological Review*, Vol. 10, No. 3, November 1962, p. 264, p. 264n. and p. 265.

2   For details from the earliest surveys see, *Family Expenditure Survey 1957-1959*, HMSO, 1960, and 'The Family Expenditure Survey: Some Results of the 1960 Survey', *Ministry of Labour Gazette*, December 1961.

3   Wedderburn, *op. cit.*, p. 276.

4   *Ibid.*, p. 257.

5   Runciman, W.G., *Relative Deprivation and Social Justice: A Study of Attitudes to Social Equality in the Twentieth Century*, London: Routledge and Kegan Paul, 1966, p. 90.

6   Bradshaw, J., *Household Budgets and Living Standards*, York: Joseph Rowntree Foundation, 1992.

7   Laurance, J., 'Average Family Now Needs £21,000 a Year for Basics', *The Times*, 11 November 1992.

8   *Ibid.*

9   United Nations, *Human Development Report 1996*, Oxford: Oxford University Press, 1996.

10 Prentice, E.A., *The Times*, 16 July 1996.

Chapter 14: Short-term Changes and Long-term Trends

1 Some poverty lobbyists are aware that this was Marx's view, and are concerned with those lowest in the scale of cash incomes only in connection with their tactics for extending their constituency of the discontented.

2 Marx, K. and Engels, F, 'Manifesto of the Communist Party' (1848), in Marx, K. and Engels, F., *Selected Works*, Vol. 1, Moscow: Foreign Languages Publishing House, 1958, pp. 36-37.

3 Marx, K. and Engels, F., 'Address of the Central Committee to the Communist League' (1850), *ibid.*, p. 116.

4 Sassoon, A.S., 'Let Them Redivide the Cake', *New Times*, 28 October 1995.

5 Trotsky, L., *The Death Agony of Capitalism and the Tasks of the Fourth International* (1938) London: The Other Press, 1979, pp. 10-12.

6 What alterations people are prepared to make to their way of life to take them out of the bottom tenth, or to ensure they do not get into it, is a different matter.

I would like to be richer than I am. Some of the necessary actions to make me richer are beyond my capacities of skill and temperament, and some are within my capacities but the motivation is lacking.

Chapter 15: Fathers Without Families

1 Dennis, N. and Erdos, G., *Families Without Fatherhood*, 2nd edition, London: IEA, 1993; Dennis, N., *Rising Crime and the Dismembered Family*, London: IEA, 1993; Davies, J.G., 'On Duty', in Anderson, D. (ed.), *The Loss of Virtue*, London: Social Affairs Unit, 1993; Davies, J.G., 'Resacralizing Education and Re-criminalizing Childhood', in *Teaching Right from Wrong: Have the Churches Failed?*, London: IEA, 1994.

2 OPCS Monitor 28 June 1995.

3 OPCS, *OPCS Updates*, No. 7, July 1995. The figures are for 1982 and 1992 (England and Wales). In 1992 58 per cent of conceptions outside marriage led to a birth outside marriage, and only eight per cent to a birth within marriage.

Thirty-four per cent of the conceptions outside of marriage led to a legal abortion.

4 Working Party of the General Synod Board for Social Responsibility, *Something to Celebrate: Valuing Families in Church and Society*, London: Church House Publishing, 1995, p. 205.

5 Stone, L., *The Family, Sex and Marriage in England 1500-1800*, London: Weidenfeld and Nicolson, 1977, pp. 612-13.

6 Family Law Reform Act 1987, Section 1.-(1).

7 Cooper, J., 'Births Outside Marriage: Recent Trends and Associated Demographic and Social Changes', *Population Trends 63*, London: HMSO, 1991.

8 Children Act 1989, Sections 2.-(1) and 2.-(2). 'Parental responsibility' means 'all the rights, duties, powers, responsibilities and authority which by law a parent has in relation to the child and his property.' The fact that the father does not have 'responsibility' does not affect any 'obligation' he might have, such as the statutory 'duty' to maintain the child. (Section 3.-(1), (2) and (4).) The Child Support Act 1991 lays upon the absent father his share of both parents' duty of maintenance. The court can grant a father parental responsibility if it approves an application for him, or if it approves a 'parental responsibility agreement' made between the father and mother. (Section 4.-(1.) The rule of law that the father is the natural guardian of his *legitimate* child was abolished under section 2.-4, another considerable liberation from a legal burden.

9 In 1995 many of Newcastle upon Tyne's buses were embellished with the picture of a giant sheath, and the slogan, 'If you want to get it off, get it on', or something to that effect.

10 The Church was 'just as guilty as any other section of the community in thinking sexual sins more significant than other sins'. *The Independent*, 20 March 1992. In 1992 which other section of the community thought any but very few sexual acts were 'sins' at all?

11 ONS, *Population Studies 84*, London: HMSO, 1996.

12 Driscoll, M. and Rogers, L., 'Forced to Face the Real Facts of Life', *The Sunday Times*, 11 August 1996. The interview with Professor Philip Bennett appeared in the *Sunday Express* on 4 August 1996. In that interview he is reported to have said that 'Killing one healthy twin *sounds* unethical. But my colleagues and I concluded this week that it would be better to terminate one pregnancy as soon as possible and leave one alive than to *lose* two babies'. [Emphasis added.] By 'lose' he meant 'abort'. By 'sounds' unethical he presumably meant to convey the meaning that it was nevertheless 'really' ethical to abort one of the two healthy twins—even though, in the abstract for him, abortion was 'morally wrong'.

13 *Ibid.*

14 Driscoll and Rogers, *op. cit.*

15 Kennedy, D., 'Truth About Abortion Mother Increases Pressure for Reform', *The Times*, 16 August 1996.

16 Hellen, N., 'Steel Tops BBC's Politically-Correct Male Pin-Up List', *The Sunday Times*, 11 August 1996. Sir David Steel's reception of this honour and attribution of motives was not noted. The Abortion Act 1967 had been passed with the assurance that it did not legalize 'abortion on demand'. Any suggestions that that was what it might lead to in practice were dismissed as alarmist, unworthy, reactionary and an insult to the moral sense of the medical profession and British women.

17 *The Times*, 16 August 1996.

18 Verity, A., 'Taxman Gives Way to Gays', *The Sunday Times*, 16 June 1996.

19 When interviewed by James Naughtie, 'Today', BBC Radio 4, 21 October 1996.

20 Mr Blair's speech was reported in the *Guardian*, 15 October 1996. He had also said that most lone parents were not in that position by choice, and that a Labour government should support them—on the face of it just another affirmation of the status quo of 1996. The comment from Professor Ruth Lister was: 'But what about those who *are* lone parents out of choice, and homosexual families rearing children? A Labour government's family policy must be aimed at all families' [i.e. at 'supporting' all sexual/childrearing arrangements, whether involving the biological father's committed long-term participation in the household or not]. *Ibid*. Within a few days Labour party spokesmen had veered in Professor Lister's direction. The Shadow Education spokesman, David Blunkett, showed no evasion by 27 October 1996 when asked, 'How do you define a family?' He said it was a 'stable and loving relationship', 'preferably' with 'a father and mother'. Marriage was not mentioned. (BBC Radio 4, 'The World At One', 27 October 1996.)

21 Morgan, P., *Farewell to the Family?: Public Policy and Family Breakdown in Britain and the USA*, London: IEA, 1995, p. 18.

22 Grice, A., 'Lilley Freezes Benefit for Single Parents to Promote Family Values', *The Sunday Times*, 20 October 1996. 'Karen Pappenheim, director of the National Council for One Parent Families, ... denied that the system discriminated in favour of single parents. A lone parent living on income support with one child received £78 a week, while a two-parent family with one child received £99 a week.' But the first figure has to be divided by three, and the second figure by four. As each family received in terms of cash-in-hand £24 a head, plus or minus a few coppers, the system did not discriminate in favour of the two-parent family either.

23 OPCS, *Marriage and Divorce Statistics 1993*, London: HMSO, 1995. In 1993 95,000 couples divorced who had one or more children under 16, the total number of children under 16 being 176,000.

24 *Facing the Future: A Discussion Paper on the Grounds for Divorce*, Law Commission Discussion Paper No. 170, London: HMSO, 1988. Eight years before, one of the Law Commissioners had already written that 'logically we have already reached a point at which ... we should be considering whether the *legal institution of marriage continues to serve any useful purpose*'. [Emphasis added.] See also Introduction, p. 2.

25 Lord Chancellor's Department, *Looking to the Future: Mediation and the Grounds for Divorce*, Cm 2424, London: HMSO, 1993.

26 'Yesterday in Parliament' and 'Call Nick Ross', 18 June 1996.

27 Lord Habgood, former Archbishop of York, *The Times*, 6 April 1996. In a letter to all Labour MPs I remarked at the time, using a figure of speech rather than a figure from any statistics, that 'anti-family publicity has been one per cent self-serving conspiracy and ninety-nine per cent well-intentioned naïvety'.

Lord Habgood must be right that it is unsubstantiated in the sense that the results of the new Act lay in the future. In the nature of things, therefore, they could not be 'substantiated' at the present time.

But the observation that similar measures had hitherto *weakened* the institution of marriage *was* substantiated on the basis of all past experience.

Lord Habgood's claim, then, that the Family Law Bill was '*far more likely*' to strengthen the institution of marriage, was *doubly* unsubstantiated. For like anybody else's claims it can have no 'substantiated' support from the unknown future, and is directly contradicted by the lessons from the known past, which is the only guide to policy that we can ever have.

28 Cockett, M. and Tripp, J., *The Exeter Family Study*, Exeter: University of Exeter Press, 1994. The Cockett and Tripp findings, Melanie Phillips reports, 'enraged the intelligentsia, which launched a whispering campaign against the researchers and threatened their continued funding. From the point of view of such critics, it is essential that evidence such as this should be marginalized because it exposes ... that what they claim to be reality is in fact little other than ideology'. Phillips, M., *All Must Have Prizes*, London: Little, Brown, 1996, p. 248.

29 Giddens, A., *Sociology: A Brief But Critical Introduction* (1982), 2nd edition, London: Macmillan, 1986, p. 128.

30 Stone, L., *The Family, Sex and Marriage in England 1500-1800*, London: Weidenfeld and Nicolson, 1977, p. 56.

31 On divorce in the United States see Wallerstein, J.S. and Blakesee, S., *Second Chances: Men, Women and Children after Divorce*, London: Bantam, 1989.

32 OPCS, *Mortality Statistics General, 1992*, No. 27, London: HMSO, 1994; and OPCS, *Annual Abstract of Statistics 1995*, London: HMSO, 1995.

33 *Statistical Abstract for the UK 1912-26*, London: HMSO, 1928.

34 Bridgwood, A. and Savage, D., *General Household Survey No. 22 1991*, London: HMSO, 1993.

35 Kiernan, K. and Estaugh, V., *Cohabitation, Extramarital Child-bearing and Social Policy*, London: FPSC, 1993.

36 Hoem and Hoem show that in Sweden, for so long the spiritual homeland of anti-family theorists, Swedish cohabitation is far from being as stable as Swedish marriage. Hoem, B. and Hoem, J., 'The Disruption of Marital and Non-Marital Unions in Contemporary Sweden', in Trussel, J. (ed.), *Demographic Applications of Event History Analysis*, Oxford: Clarendon Press, 1992.

37 Figures from the General Household Survey data.

38 Council of Europe, *Draft European Convention on the Exercise of Children's Rights*, Directorate of Legal Affairs: Strasbourg, 18 July 1995.

39 'GCSE and GCSE A-level in England 1994', *Statistics of Education*, London: HMSO, 1995.

40 *The Times*, 23 August 1996.

41 Institute of Education, University of London, *Report on the Education of Ethnic Minorities in Britain*, London: Ofsted, 5 September 1996. In Birmingham, for example, the proportion of Indian GCSE candidates achieving five or more passes at A-C in 1995 was 40 per cent, of white candidates 35 per cent. As Asian families retained much of their cohesion and white families lost more and more of theirs, the gap grew. Between 1991 and 1993 the average GCSE 'points score' for Asian pupils in Brent rose from 30 to 38; the points score for white pupils, from a lower base, rose by fewer points, from 27 to 32.

42 Popenoe, D., *Life Without Father: Compelling New Evidence That Fatherhood and Marriage are Indispensable for the Good of Children and Society*, New York: The Free Press, 1996, p. 25.

43 Veblen, T., *The Theory of the Leisure Class: An Economic Study of Institutions*, London: Allen and Unwin, 1925, p. 326. For an account of male sexual incontinence in the quasi-aristocracy of the United States, and the centrality of the assumption in the early 1960s that such male sexual incontinence, if made public to the family-oriented American working class, would effectively destroy the ambitions of the perpetrator, see Klein, E., *All Too Human: The Love Story of Jack and Jackie Kennedy*, New York: Pocket Books, 1996.

44 Davidoff, L. and Hall, C., *Family Fortunes: Men and Women of the English Middle Class 1780-1850*, London: Hutchinson, 1987, p. 21.

45 Just as it has been a remarkable propaganda coup by individuals and interest groups hostile to the family of life-long monogamy to identify 'the Left', including the Labour party, with anti-monogamous-family sentiment, so was it was a remarkable propaganda coup to identify the Labour party with pro-criminal sentiment.
   In reporting the 'confession' (authentic or not) in the *Melody Maker* of a prominent and successful songwriter to burglary and breaking into cars, *The Times* casually remarks, 'Cue outrage from Tory MPs'—as if *Labour* MPs are supposed to look with sophisticated indifference on residents who come home to find that their houses have been burgled or come back from the shops to find that their cars have been broken into by thieves. *The Times*, 6 April 1996.

46 Roux, J., *Meditations of a Parish Priest: Thoughts by J. Roux*, New York: Crowell, 1886, p. 9.

47 For a typical and everyday statement of this view, see, Reddish, S., 'Annual Report of the Women's Cooperative Guild', *Cooperative Congress Report for 1894*, p. 98. Sarah Reddish was the Guild's organizer at that time.

48 How did it happen that some time around 1970 it became radical chic for first middle-class Labour, and then working-class Labour, to slander these men—in the working-class case, their own fathers, grandfathers and great-grandfathers —and to jeer for the next twenty years, as if he was a barmy Gulliver making up tales about impossible lands, at anyone who cited their indispensable fatherly merits within the realities of their lives at the time? The proletarian male: from universal hero to incestuous and adulterous brute at the flick of a switch!

Appendix: Choice and Personal Responsibility

1 Rowntree's measures, that is, regarded as measures for solving the problems stemming from family breakdown and from the breakdown of the family; as measures for alleviating the problems of children in one-parent families; and as measures for dealing with the problems created by men for whom family-life is no longer the controlling element in their upbringing or ambitions. The *intrinsic* value of educational and training programmes and so forth is not disputed.

2 Mills, C.W., 'The Cultural Apparatus' (1959), in Horowitz, I.L., *Power, Politics and People: The Collected Essays of C. Wright Mills*, Oxford: Oxford University Press, 1963, p. 405.

3 Schumpeter, J.A., *Capitalism, Socialism and Democracy*, London: Allen and Unwin, 1943, pp. 145-46.